YESTERDAY'S FUTURE
CONCEPT CARS of the
1960s

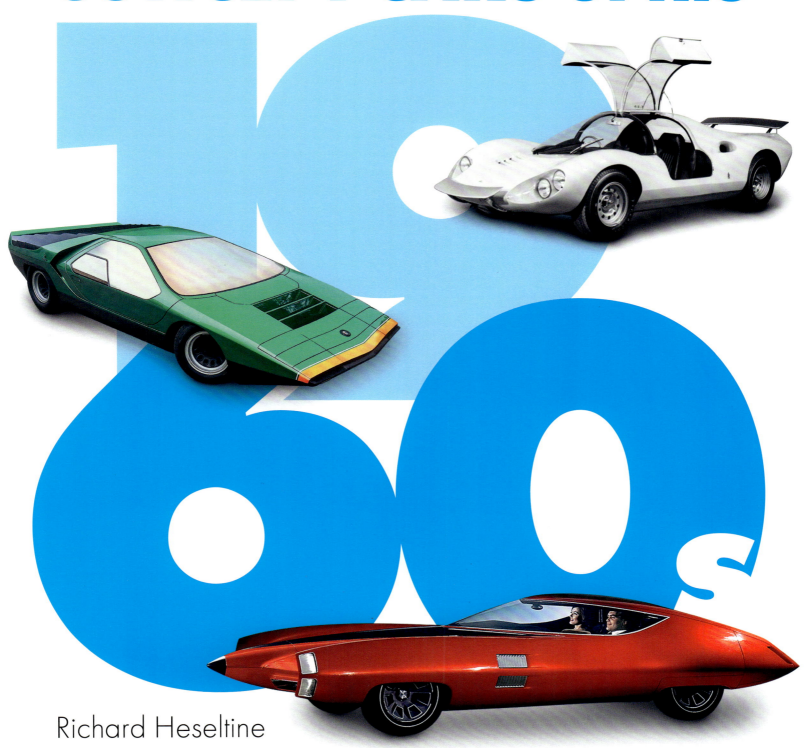

Richard Heseltine

PORTER PRESS INTERNATIONAL

Contents

Introduction 6

1960

Pinin Farina X 16
Alfa Romeo Superflow IV 18
Lancia Loraymo 19
DiDia 150 20
Plymouth XNR 21
Curtiss-Wright Model 2500 'Air-Car' 22
Chevrolet Corvair Coupé Speciale' by Pinin Farina 24
Studebaker Italia 26
Ghia Selene Seconda 27
Chevrolet CERV-I 28
Chevrolet Corvette XP-700 30
Ghia IXG Dragster 31
Stephenson MG 31

1961

Chevrolet Corvair Sebring Spyder 34
Kelly 36
Chrysler Turboflite 37
Pinin Farina Cadillac Jacqueline 38
Pinin Farina Berlinetta Aerodinamica Project Y 39
Aston Martin DB4 GT Jet 39
Ford Gyron 40
Dodge FliteWing 42
McLouth XV'61 42
Ghia Plymouth Asimmetrica/St. Regis 43
Alfa Romeo SS Spider Speciale Aerodinamico 43
Chevrolet Corvette Sting Ray (aka 'Mitchell's Racer') 44

© Porter Press International

All rights reserved. No part of this publication may be reproduced, stored in a retrieval system or transmitted, in any form or by any means, electronic, mechanical, photocopying, recording or otherwise, without prior permission in writing from the publisher.

First published November 2021

978-1-913089-34-4

Published by Porter Press International Ltd
Hilltop Farm, Knighton-on-Teme,
Tenbury Wells, WR15 8LY, UK
Tel: +44 (0)1584 781588
sales@porterpress.co.uk
www.porterpress.co.uk

Edited by Steve Rendle
Design by Martin Port
Printed by Gomer Press Ltd

Copyright

We have made every effort to trace and acknowledge copyright holders and apologise in advance for any unintentional omission. We would be pleased to insert the appropriate acknowledgement in any subsequent edition.

Acknowledgements

Putting together a book – any book – isn't the work of a moment. Nor do you toil away in a vacuum. As such, I would like to heap praise on my brilliant editor, Steve Rendle, who has been a constant source of encouragement. I would also like to thank the team at Porter Press, the book's designer, Martin Port, and Richard Dredge who rode to the rescue more than once. I also need to thank Margaret Heseltine, Bob Hui, Rashed Chowdhury, Chris Rees, and Alessandro Sannia for their assistance and support.

1962

Ford Mustang 1 48

Alfa Romeo 2600 PF Cabriolet Speciale/ Coupé Speciale 51

Pininfarina Fiat 2300 Coupé Speciale 52

Ferrari 400 SA Superfast III/IV 53

Vignale Abarth Record Sperimentale 1000 54

Automobile Year Austin-Healey Firrere 55

Mercury Palomar 55

Chevrolet Monza GT 56

Ferrari 250 GT Bertone Speciale 58

Oldsmobile X-215 59

Chevrolet XP-755 (Mako Shark) 60

Ford Cougar 406 61

Toyota Publica Sports Concept 61

Chevrolet Corvair XP-785 Super Spyder 62

1963

Pininfarina Rondine 66

Pininfarina Lancia Flaminia 3C 2.8 Coupé Speciale 2 Posti 67

Fiat 2300 Cabriolet Speciale Pininfarina 68

Fiat 2300 Coupé Speciale Lausanne 68

Chevrolet Corvair Monza SS 69

Bertone Testudo 70

Prince 1900 Sprint 72

Dodge Charger Concept (aka Charger I) 72

Ford Allegro I & II 73

Ford Mustang II 74

Oldsmobile J-TR 75

Oldsmobile El Torero 76

Michelotti Jaguar D-type 76

Ghia G230 S 77

Chrysler Corporation Turbine Car 78

Vignale New Star Jet 80

Pininfarina Sigma 82

Studebaker Spectre 83

Daihatsu 800 Sport Spider 83

1964

Ghia Ford Falcon Clan 86

Alfa Romeo Canguro (aka Bertone Giulia 1600 Tubolare) 88

Ghia V280 90

Ghia Renault 8 Sports Coupé 90

Mercedes-Benz 230SL Speciale 91

Ford Aurora 92

Fiat 2300 S Coupé Speciale 94

Fiat-Abarth 1000GT Spider Pininfarina 95

Mercer Cobra 96

Lincoln Continental Town Brougham 97

Sibona & Basano Tsé-Tsé 98

Ford Cougar II 98

GM GM-X 99

GM Runabout 100

Chevrolet CERV II 102

Studebaker SS (Excalibur) 103

GM Firebird IV 104

Pontiac Banshee 105

Dodge Charger II 105

Contents continued

1965

Bertone Ford Mustang 108
Ghia Bugatti 101C-X 109
Ghia Cobra GT 110
Pininfarina Alfa Romeo Giulia 1600 Sport 112
Ferrari 206 P Dino Pininfarina Berlinetta Speciale 112
Mako Shark II/Manta Ray 114
Fiat 2300S Coupé Speciale 116
Plymouth XP-VIP 116
Ford 'Bordinat' Cobra 117
Ogle Triplex GTS 118
OSI Ford Mustang 120
NSU Autonova GT 121
OSI Secura 122
Autonova FAM 123
F.A.R.T. Break 123
Saab Catherina 123
Opel Experimental GT 124
Fissore Aruanda 126
Lamborghini 3500GTZ 128

1966

Ferrari 365P 'Tre Posti' 132
AMC 'Rambleseat'/AMX 134
AMC Cavalier 136
AMC AMX II 136
AMC Vixen 137
Cycloac Research Vehicle 138
Lamborghini Flying Star II 139
Vauxhall XVR 140
Fiat 850 Vanessa 141
OSI Alfa Romeo Scarabeo 142
Chevrolet Electrovair II 144
OSI City-Daf 145
Lincoln Continental Coronation Coupe 145
Ford Mustang Mach I 146
Daihatsu Sport 147
Bertone Porsche 911 148

1967

Bertone Lamborghini Marzal
Pininfarina Dino 206 Berlinetta Prototipo Competizione 155
Bertone Pirana 156
Pininfarina BMC 1100/1800 Berlina Aerodinamica 158
Rover 2000 TCZ 158
Chevrolet Astro I (aka Corvair Super GT Low Aerodynamic Coupé) 159
Ford Mach 2 160
Pininfarina Fiat Dino Bodyline Study (aka Special Line Study Coupé) 160
Oldsmobile Thor 161
Gyro-X 162
Ford Bearcat 163
Metzeler Delta 1 163
Lancia Flavia Sport Zagato Exemplar 1 166
AMC Amitron 166
Oldsmobile Mini-Toro 167
OSI Bisiluro 'Silver Fox'
Carter Coaster 168
Rowan Electric 169
Ford Commuta 170
Mazda RX-87 172
AMC AMX III Sports Wagon
Jensen Nova 173

1968

Bertone Alfa Romeo Carabo 176
Bertone Panther (aka Sbarro Tiger) 179
Italdesign Bizzarrini Manta 180
Pininfarina Ferrari 250 P5 Berlinetta Speciale 181
Pininfarina Ferrari P6 182
Pininfarina Alfa Romeo Roadster GS 183
Autobianchi Coupé 184
Pininfarina Fiat Dino Ginevra 186
Ghia Checker Centurion 187
Fiat City Taxi 187
Serenissima Ghia Coupé 188
Maserati Simun 190
Ford Berliner 191
AMC AMX GT 191
Oldsmobile Toronado XP-866 191
Chevrolet Astro II (XP-880) 192
Ford Techna 194
Chevrolet Astro-Vette Concept 195
Rover BS (aka Leyland Eight) 196
GKN Lotus 47D 198
Mercury LeGrand Marquis 200
Cock Cockpit II 200
Ford Thunderbird Saturn 201
Citycar 201

1969

Mercedes-Benz C111 204
Bertone Spicup 208
Pininfarina 512S Berlinetta Speciale 209
Autobianchi A112 Runabout (aka Bertone Runabout) 210
Pininfarina Sigma 212
Chevrolet XP-882 213
Pininfarina Fiat-Abarth 2000 Scorpione (aka Fiat-Abarth 2000 Pininfarina, aka Fiat-Abarth 2000 Coupé Speciale) 214
Pininfarina Alfa Romeo 33/2 Prototipo Speciale 215
De Tomaso Mustella 216
Chevrolet Astro III 217
Ghia Lancia Fulvia HP1600 Competizione 218
AMC AMX/2 219
Austin Zanda 220
Suzuki Punch Buggy 220
Ghia Lancia Marica 220
Zagato Volvo GTZ 222

Opel CD 224
Italdesign Alfa Romeo Iguana 224
Holden Hurricane 226
Buick Century Cruiser 228
Isuzu Bellett MX1600 228
Lincoln Continental Town Sedan 229
Bertone Fiat 128 230
Sessano Mongho 650 231
Abarth 1600GT 232
Giannini 650 Caterinetta (aka 650 Sirio) 232
Ford Thunderbird Saturn II 233
Ford Super Cobra 233
Toyota EX-I 234
Toyota EX-II 234
Toyota EX-III 235
Mitsubishi Commuter 235
General Motors XP-511 Commuter 236
General Motors XP-512 237
General Motors XP-833 237

Index of designers 238

Yesterday's Future
Introduction

Caution equals cowardice. Concept cars, dream cars, teasers – call them what you will – are meant to break moulds and push envelopes; to forecast or establish trends. Designers by their very nature have a propulsive desire to seek out the horizon, to create the kind of artistic tour de force that makes the whole world sit up and take notice. Concept cars afford them the opportunity to let rip; to use their imaginations and envisage the sort of vehicle that we will be driving in years – perhaps decades – to come.

At least that is the theory. The fact is that most concept cars are one-week wonders. By definition, they tend to live ephemeral lives. Some are displayed at an event and never seen again, while others cross continents and become media darlings in the process, only to be placed in storage – or worse – once they are no longer of use. However, a few take on saintly status; somehow escape the scrapman's torch and become icons of the genre. They serve to inspire further generations of car-lovers by trotting along the automotive catwalks decades after they first found fame, promoted by brands with an awareness that heritage is a marketable asset.

Concept cars represent a subspecies of automobile, and one where function does not necessarily follow form. The irony is that, for the most part, they were once frowned upon. Magazine editorials were, in some instances, openly scornful, viewing them as nothing more than frivolous baubles not to be taken seriously. What's more, some marques were loath to join the party because the management took the view that there was no worth in creating and promoting such cars, only cost (be it financial or reputational). The reality is that car design – or rather *styling* – was once frowned upon. Customers got what they were given.

The birth of car design

At the dawn of motoring, there was no such as thing as *styling*. Adopted by the moneyed and the adventurous, the motor car was initially deemed anti-social and perilous by the distrustful majority. Most automobiles of the period resembled carriages, employing the same basic design and construction methodology that had existed for centuries. These days, car designers think in terms of steel, aluminium or carbon-fibre. A century ago it was timber and fabric. What's more, without an outline to copy and paste, inventive types engaged in all manner of ingenious – if occasionally bizarre – conceits: elliptical wheel partners; passengers seated in front of the driver; giro-stabilizers. Nothing was too radical or too daring.

During the 'pioneer era', automobiles were designed and built by engineers. Drivers sat perched atop their horseless carriages and what little bodywork there was served simply to protect the mechanical components from the elements. Driver and passengers alike bore the brunt of whatever the weather threw at them. Wheels, generally constructed with wooden spokes, usually differed in size from front to rear, and typically there was little or no integration between the passenger compartment and the engine. Accordingly, scant artistry was in evidence. However, this was soon to change significantly.

The art of coachbuilding may well have originated in fourteenth-century Hungary, where the first carriage is believed to have been constructed. Crafting horse-drawn vehicles for the aristocracy and landed gentry soon became a respected and profitable business, so the skills of the trade were passed on from one generation to the next. By the advent of the automobile, most towns in Europe boasted at least one such operation. The motor car continued this craft, with innumerable workshops bodying these new 'horseless carriages'. Those that declared them to be a passing fad soon found themselves out of business.

However, as mass-production techniques took hold, manufacturers began to offer a choice of bodies conceived in-house. Nevertheless, at a time when ownership of a car represented a powerful social statement, there was always demand for individuality; for something nobody else had, that was in tune with the fashions of the day. By the 1920s, the car had become a major symbol of the industrialised society and each year the brightest and best coachbuilders would present their 'collections' in much the same way as a fashion designer does today. Over the next decade and beyond, concours d'élégance sprang up throughout Europe. There was a palpable sense of excitement among onlookers as each motorised means of artistic and personal expression was presented.

In many ways, such events became barometers of taste. The more forward-thinking brands realised that 'styling' attracted customers and provided a degree of brand recognition. Far from distancing themselves from the more artistic coachbuilders, they began working hand-in-glove with some of the more respected practitioners. As well as borrowing their ideas, they occasionally offered their creations as officially-sanctioned models if only as a means of generating 'showroom traffic.'

However, as mechanical innovation gathered speed, traditional coachbuilding was in danger of being left behind: new methods of construction had to be learned and perfected. Steel and aluminium had become the materials of choice, spawning panel-beating workshops all over Europe. Bodies became more integrated with chassis by means of 'bushing' between the wooden inner frame and the chassis – a method borrowed from the aviation industry – thus reducing the use of 90° angles demanded by timber construction to ensure torsional rigidity.

Whereas the British coachbuilders were renowned for the strength and quality of their output, and their French counterparts for the rakish sophistication of their designs, the Italian *carrozzerie* soon came to be prized for the sheer elegance of their work. Across the

> *'The more forward-thinking brands realised that "styling" attracted customers'*

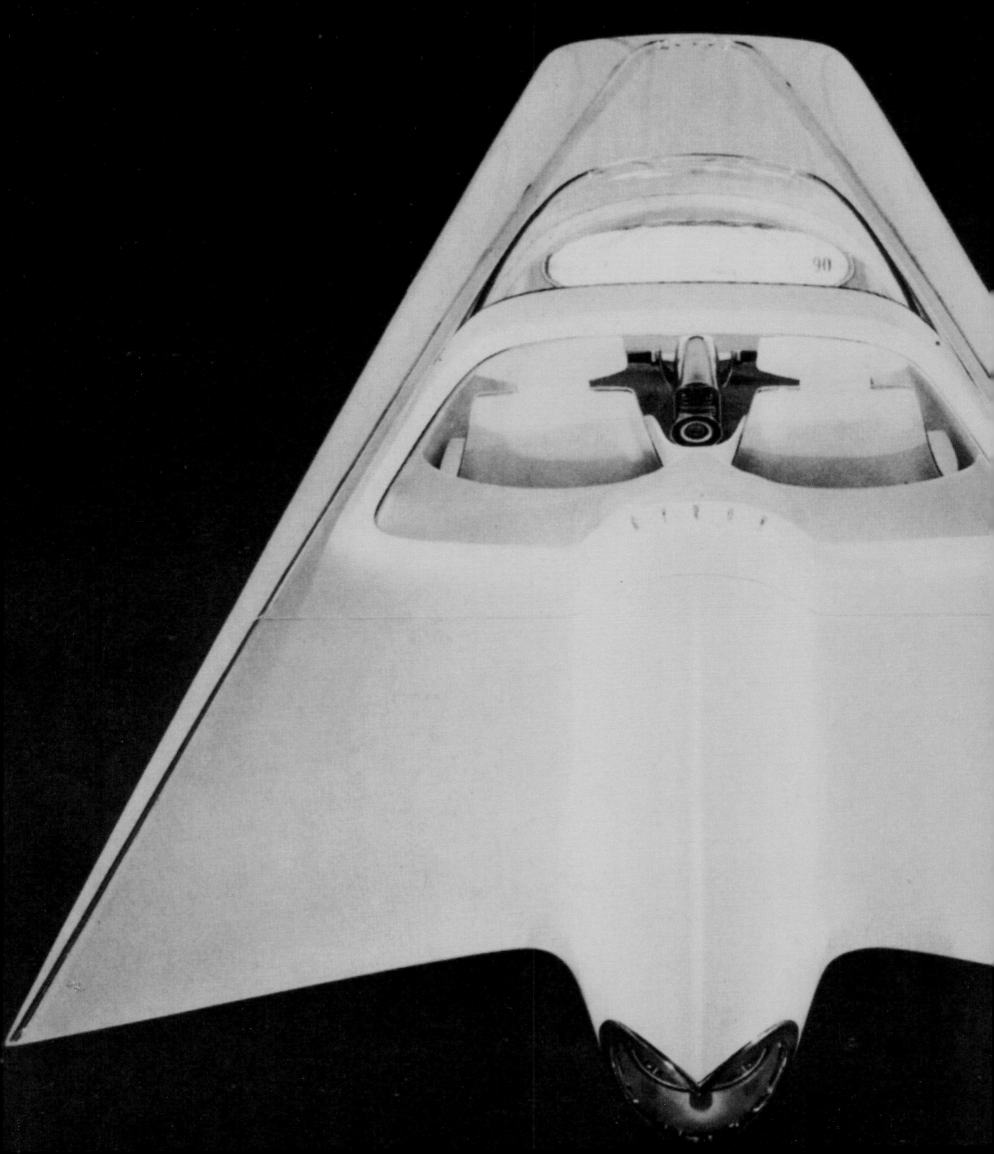

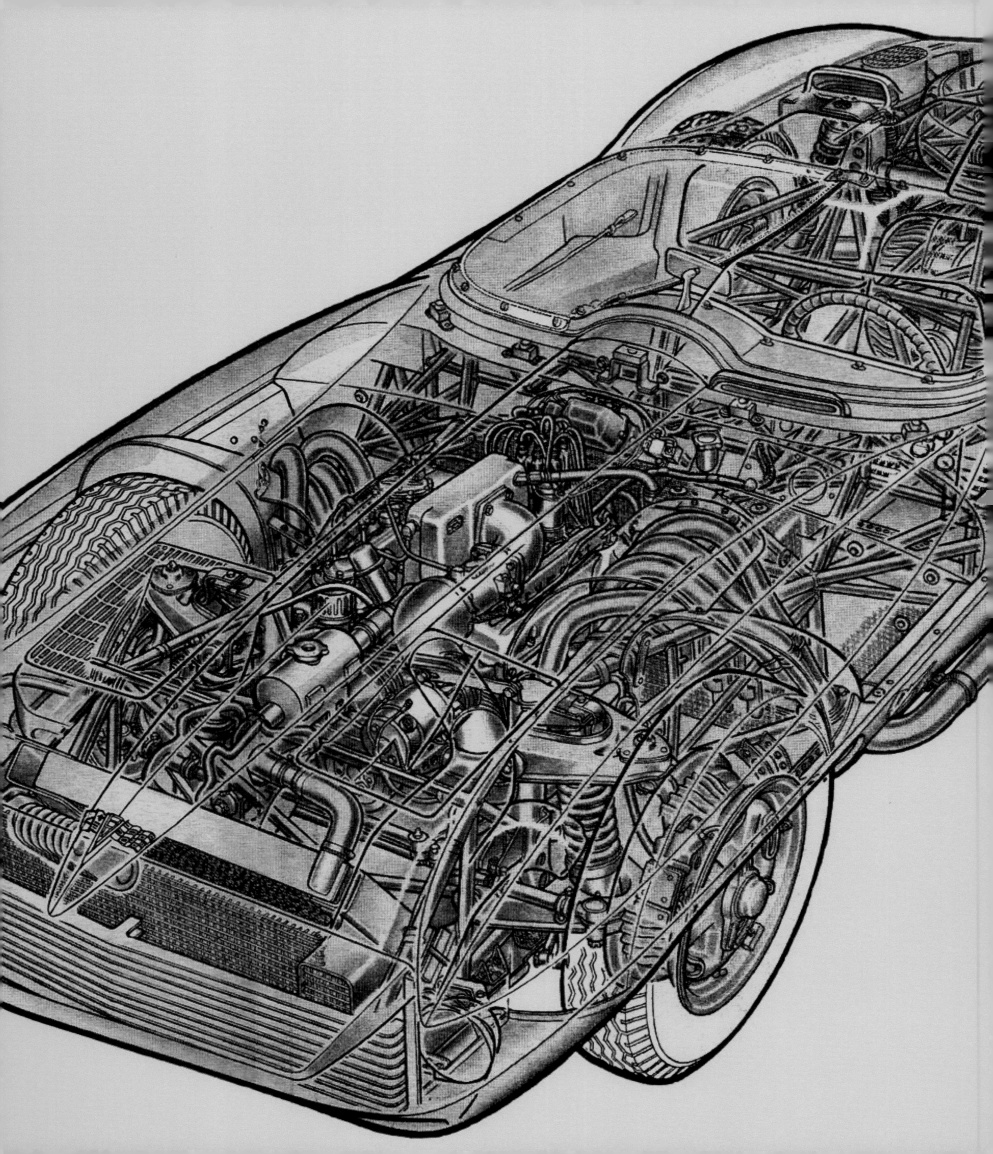

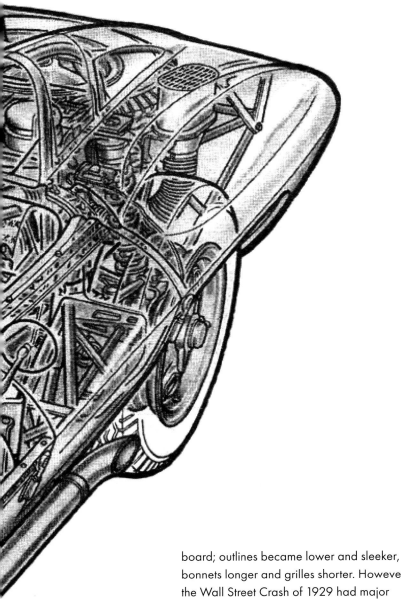

board; outlines became lower and sleeker, bonnets longer and grilles shorter. However, the Wall Street Crash of 1929 had major repercussions for the coachbuilding industry, not least the small matter of there being fewer patrons with the wherewithal to engage them, but car design as a whole would subsequently undergo a major metamorphosis.

The birth of the concept car – the USA leads the way

The 1930s witnessed a major change in the way cars were shaped, if only among the more exotic marques. While mainstream models for the most part continued to appear upright and square-rigged, those adventurous *couturiers* that had survived to fight another day chafed against convention. Bulbous outlines, wheel spats, and chrome accents that bordered on jewellery became evident, with the French and Italian coachbuilders to the fore. However, it wasn't a European designer that ushered in the concept car as we know it. It was a second-generation American coachbuilder.

It is hard not to wax lyrical about Harley Earl's contribution to automotive design, not least because he was arguably the first professional car stylist in the accepted sense. He was unquestionably a pioneering studio head. Prior to the formation of General Motors' Art and Color Section in June 1927, there had never been a styling studio of any description. While not a designer per se, in that he rarely drew anything, Earl was astute enough to realise that style mattered. He and his 'pretty picture boys' were widely mocked within the corridors of GM, but that soon changed.

In addition to employing prototyping methods that would become the norm in styling studios for decades to come, not least the use of clay modelling, Earl and his team saved the Detroit giant a fortune. It did so by the expedient means of using styling to differentiate brands. Rather than tooling up for a range of brand-specific bodyshells, GM instead used the same basic outlines across the various marques in its portfolio. The grille, wings, brightwork, and so on would be changed, but the 'hard points' would be the same. Earl was no longer the boss of the 'beauty parlour,' as his detractors had taken to calling him. He had the ear of those who mattered.

Earl also ushered in the concept car as we know it, via the Buick Y-Job (some historians have latterly taken to claiming that Auburn got there first with the 1929 Cabin Speedster). This was a car built specifically to promote new ideas and foretell styling themes. It was a promotional tool and there was no intention of a production run. Designed in 1938 by George Snyder, and based on a Buick Super platform, the Y-Job boasted power-operated concealed headlights (which were replaced with fixed items, only to revert back to the original set-up), wraparound bumpers and flush-fitting door handles.

Many styling cues were later transposed intact onto post-war production models, the wilfully conspicuous Earl using the car as his personal transport as late as 1951. As for the origins of the odd name, there are two competing theories. Firstly, experimental cars generally boasted an 'X' prefix, so Earl bagged the next letter in the alphabet for this styling study. Alternatively, 'Y' was often used in the aviation industry to denote advanced prototypes, so he merely appropriated this.

Earl's follow up to the Y-Job remains one of the most celebrated concept cars ever made. The story began in 1946 with a brainstorming session between Earl and Buick division head Harold Curtice. Earl came away from the meeting with the brief to construct two new show cars: one, codenamed XP-8, became the one-off Buick XP-300, while the sister XP-9 morphed into the Le Sabre. Both cars were built in tandem.

The Le Sabre represented a mission statement: it prophesied GM's future styling direction. Shaped by Edward Glowacke, its dramatic outline represented an amalgam of Earl's favoured design cues robbed from rockets and jet-fighter aircraft. The prominent grille, for example, mimicked the turbine intake of the transonic North American F-86 Sabre. In reality, it concealed the headlights, below which were a pair of bullet-shaped 'Dagmar' bumpers which would become a genre staple within the Cadillac division.

What's more, General Motors initiated its own events to promote these brave new worlds. The inaugural Transportation Unlimited Autorama event was staged in 1949 at the New York Waldorf Astoria. Rebranded as Motorama in 1953, it became a travelling show which afforded the American public the opportunity to witness the future up close. That same year saw Earl and his group of starry-eyed futurists go for broke with Firebird I.

Again inspired by jet fighter aircraft of the day, and powered by a Whirlfire Turbo Power GT gas turbine, Project XP-21, Shop Order 1921 (in GM speak) was tested at the Indianapolis Motor Speedway by multiple Indy 500 winner Mauri Rose. In true aircraft style, its ailerons were fully-functional and could be used as an air brake. It blurred the line between what was possible and what was permissible in terms of road transport. Firebird I was the very definition of a concept car.

Looking to Europe – the rise of the styling house

The 1950s would witness an epic battle for bragging rights among Detroit's 'Big Three' (GM, Ford and Chrysler). Earl led the way, but Chrysler matched 'The General' in terms of releasing an array of styling studies under

'It's so easy to tie yourself in knots trying to define what constitutes a concept car'

the direction of design czar Virgil Exner. What's more, it looked to Italy for assistance. In period, dozens of *carrozzerie* operated out of workshops large and small, clustered together, most within shouting distance of Fiat's Lingotto factory. Metal-wielding artisans could translate ideas into intricate shapes with consummate skill. That, and speed.

Few Turinese coachbuilders were as daring as Carrozzeria Ghia in its pomp. However, that it saw out the 1940s was nothing short of miraculous, but it was about to embark on a period of further expansion. During this phase, there was considerable cooperation between America and Italy via the Marshall Plan, a flow of information which, in a roundabout way, led to Ghia's Luigi Segre forging a close working relationship with Chrysler vice president, CB Thomas, who handled the Detroit giant's export sales. In 1950, Ghia received a Plymouth chassis, the idea being that it would use it as a calling card. Chrysler was keen to learn more about the 'Italian Line' and how the Italians went about creating one-offs.

The resultant XX-500 prototype was perhaps not overly audacious, but it clearly did the trick. Chrysler had canvassed other coachbuilders, but chose Ghia as its *carrozzeria* of choice. It was keen to impress upon the world that it was a forward-looking manufacturer with a keen eye on design. The XX-500 heralded the first of many official Chrysler 'Idea Cars', the influential K-310. This 1952 super-coupé was styled in its entirety by Exner, with Ghia acting as subcontractor. Nevertheless, construction of this car marked the start of a symbiotic relationship, with ideas continuously flowing between Turin and Detroit.

Other US concerns beat a path to Ghia's door, but also that of Pinin Farina and other now legendary concerns. Italian coachbuilders continued to build one-offs for wealthy, discerning customers, but also acted as subcontractors to mainstream producers, manufacturing small runs of halo products in addition to one-off show cars. However, the 1950s witnessed such firms also morph into styling houses, with British brands in particular commissioning the likes of Alfredo Vignale and his long-time friend and ally Giovanni Michelotti to create outlines for its mass-market wares.

Italy was also quick to embrace the idea of the concept car on the home front, be it the Fiat Turbina, Ghia Gilda, Pinin Farina's Ferrari Superfasts, or Bertone's Berlina Aerodinamica Technica Alfa Romeos. Perhaps more than any other European show cars of the period, this trio of aerodynamic design studies by Bertone's Franco Scaglione wowed the press and public alike. The series kicked off with the Alfa 1900-based BAT 5 which arrived at the 1953 Turin motor show. It was a fully functional prototype that boasted a drag coefficient of a still remarkable 0.23Cd. The follow up arrived a year later, BAT 7 being more aerodynamic still with a drag coefficient of a scarcely believable 0.19Cd. BAT 9 arrived in 1955 and was perhaps the most sober-looking of the trio, all things being relative, with styling cues that were akin to future production Alfas.

For some members of the motoring press, the artful artifice of show cars was too much to stomach. They were mere exercises in titillation and of no real value. The public, however, was rather more receptive, to the point that other manufacturers joined the fray. Scroll forward to the mid-1960s and they were everywhere. This was the decade that began with wraparound windscreens and tailfins and ended with wedge shapes and scissor doors. The concept car had arrived. The concept car was here to stay.

Defining a concept car

It is so easy to tie yourself in knots trying to define what constitutes a concept car. For the purposes of this book, we took the view that we would only include concept cars or prototypes that were displayed publically or that appeared in print. As such, there are cars that never left a styling studio that are not included for obvious reasons, but the likes of the Ford Bearcat are here because they received coverage in period. Similarly, we eschewed including mainstream production offerings that were modified by the likes of George Barris, because in our view they are custom cars as opposed to concept cars. Conversely, however, we have included production cars that were transformed along similar lines internally.

We have also excluded cars that were displayed extensively in period, such as the Duesenberg II and Ikenga. They may have been unique, but they weren't concept cars in the accepted sense, because production runs were announced in the media. On the flipside of that, we have given coverage to the Chrysler Turbine Car even though dozens were made. They were test hacks and most were subsequently destroyed.

Then there is the vexed task of differentiating between a coachbuilt one-off and a concept car. The 1960s witnessed the emergence of countless memorable show-stoppers, but we have deliberately avoided including, say, the Pininfarina Bentley T-series from 1968. It wasn't without influence, but it was built at the behest of James Hanson (later Lord Hanson) as opposed to a manufacturer. Similarly, umpteen Italian coachbuilders exhibited variations of mainstream products, some of which remained unique. If plans to manufacture cars were announced, they haven't made the cut.

However, rather than contemplating what isn't included, let us focus on what is. Herein is a year-by-year rundown of the most memorable concept cars of the 1960s with several obscurities thrown in for good measure. Some have long since earned legendary status, while others fell a long way short. Where applicable, we have attempted to quote magazine reports from the day. We feel they add colour, not least because some cars that are now considered landmark design classics were not received warmly at the time.

This is the opening salvo in what we hope will be a series of books celebrating concept cars. In doing so, we hope to tell stories that have never been told before, and maybe explode a few myths along the way.

Richard Heseltine
Shropshire, November 2021

Car design during the 1960s witnessed seismic shifts in terms of styling trends. Nevertheless, the new decade dawned much as the old one had ended, lashings of chrome and tailfins being prevalent, even if this 'It ain't done 'til it's overdone' approach was starting to wane. The use of such styling tinsel would be toned down appreciably.

For the most part, where Detroit led, the rest of the world followed. However, Italian styling *carrozzerie* had already established themselves as trendsetters, and done so in short order during the second half of the 1950s. They were no longer mere subcontractors building show cars for their North American paymasters. Their influence was beginning to spread – and how.

Also in 1960
John F. Kennedy wins the US presidential election.
100,000 people join the 'ban the bomb' protest rally in London.
TIROS-1, the world's first weather satellite is launched by NASA.
The Soviet Union shoots down an American U-2 spyplane it its airspace, capturing pilot Gary Powers.
A five-piece band from Liverpool perform their first concert using the name 'The Beatles', in Hamburg.

1960

Pinin Farina X

The early 1960s witnessed Pinin Farina at its most prolific. This highly unusual device was something of an anomaly in that it was built by the firm but not designed internally. It was conceived by Professor Alberto Morelli, and championed by Battista 'Pinin' Farina. Morelli, who was a highly-respected expert on aerodynamics at the Politecnico di Torino, had previously created an ultra-low-drag saloon car, the Morelli M100. The X (codenamed Pf-X) was a variation on the theme, only with a significant deviation from the script: it had a rhomboidal wheel pattern.

Powered by a rear-sited 1,089cc Fiat four-cylinder engine, and blessed with a scarcely-believable drag coefficient of just 0.23Cd, it was a fully-functional prototype: the rear wheel was driven, while the front wheel steered. According to its maker, it had a top speed of 90mph (145km/h). The car was unveiled at the 1960 Turin motor show, *Road & Track*'s Gordon H. Jennings commenting: '[This] creation strikes us as good press-agenting but rather bad design: we spent a good thirty minutes staring at it and thinking: what if it gets its centre wheel stuck on a hump? Either the driving or steering wheel would of necessity leave the ground. Or when it turns around a sharp corner, which wheel (or wheels) is scrubbed across the ground? And how would one get it through a carwash?'

Pininfarina displayed the car again at the following year's Brussels Automobile Show, but the 'X' didn't ignite a design revolution, much to the disappointment of its creators.

1960

Alfa Romeo Superflow IV

During the 1950s and much of the 1960s, it wasn't uncommon for show cars to be remodelled between outings. Sometimes, this involved little more than a change of hue, but occasionally it would be something a bit more substantial; revised brightwork or perhaps a new interior. However, of all the many Italian carrozzerie, Pinin Farina wasn't above going one stage further and reconfiguring old concept cars. The Alfa Romeo Superflow was a case in point. In all, there were four different iterations, and that doesn't include the donor vehicle.

The basis for this ever-evolving show-stopper was an Alfa Romeo 3000CM (*Competizione Maggiorate* – 'competition enlarged-displacement'). Six of these 3,495cc straight-six-powered machines were made, with Juan Manuel Fangio and Giulio Sala guiding one to second place on the 1953 Mille Miglia. Chassis 0128 is believed to have been a spare car for that year's Le Mans 24 Hours bid. It subsequently passed to Pinin Farina, where it was reclothed with a new body that incorporated Plexiglas front-wing caps, a wraparound windscreen, vestigial tailfins and gullwing roof panels. Superflow I was displayed at the 1956 Turin motor show, in white with a blue stripe along its beltline.

Six months later, the car was shown again at the Paris motor show as the Super Flow II. The front wings were more conventional-looking than before, with metal having been inserted where there had been none previously, while the tailfins were more pronounced thanks to Plexiglas extensions. Resplendent in red with white stripes, it remained in this form until the end of the decade when it was reformatted a third time ahead of the 1959 Geneva motor show. The Super Spider, as it was now dubbed, was all white and shorn of its roof, windscreen and tailfins, but it retained its *osso di sepia* (cuttlefish-bone) profile.

However, Pinin Farina wasn't finished. A year later, the car was displayed in Switzerland as the Superflow IV (although it is sometimes also referred to as the Alfa Romeo 3500 Supersport, or Coupé Super Sport Speciale). This, its final configuration, represented pure Jet-Set whimsy. There was no denying the sense of theatre here, thanks in no small part to its glazed roof, the central section of which could be slid back to stop the occupants from being broiled alive in hot weather. The scalloped flanks were also a casualty of the makeover. A sharp crease now ran the length of each side of the car.

Superflow IV was displayed at the IAA (Internationale Automobil-Ausstellung) show in Frankfurt later that same year, after which this ruby red GT was sold to an Alfa Romeo distributor from Colorado. It was later displayed in the Rosso Bianco collection in Germany and, more recently, it has been garlanded in the Pebble Beach Concours d'Elegance.

The Superflow in any of its many guises married competition-rooted underpinnings with daring styling flourishes courtesy of Turin's Pinin Farina studio.

Lancia Loraymo

The one-off Loraymo represented one man's dream car and that man was the godfather of industrial design, Raymond Loewy. This former French army captain, who had moved to New York at the end of World War I, lent his genius to all manner of products, from the famous Coca-Cola bottle to locomotives, via fridges and a range of Studebakers. By the late-1950s, he was being courted by manufacturing giants the world over. While he didn't actually design many of the items he is credited with, that didn't really matter. His vision – his mission – was to enhance products through the medium of captivating design. In Nuclear Age America, where the 1950s witnessed a consumer boom, his studio's work could be found just about everywhere.

Always a fan of powerful road cars, Loewy penned several one-offs for his own amusement. Among these was a 1959 Cadillac Series 62 which managed the improbable feat of being even more excessive than the donor car. There was also a Boano-bodied Jaguar XK 140 and a BMW 507-based coupé that in many ways foretold the car described here. Legend has it, perhaps apocryphally, that Loewy considered becoming a small-scale 'boutique' car manufacturer when he conceived the Loraymo. Whatever the truth, his pull was such that Lancia's head of PR, Sandro Fiorio (father of future motorsport legend Cesare Fiorio), offered him a free Flaminia coupé as a basis for his brave new world. If nothing else, the Turin firm would receive plenty of media attention from its association.

Fiorio spoke little English at the time, and Loewy knew only pigeon Italian. Communicating by means of gesticulation, the duo worked closely with artisans at Carrozzeria Motto who were employed to turn his ideas into hand-shaped reality. From most accounts, Loewy was charming and patient, his status ensuring that Motto's men did not proffer opinions. The end result was shown at the 1960 Paris motor show, the Loraymo receiving a lukewarm reception.

The car's front end was particularly strange, the wings ending at headlight level. The massive grille, meanwhile, had its own dampers to absorb energy in the event of a collision. Moving further back, an aerofoil sat just proud of the B-pillars. According to *Mechanix Illustrated*, it was in place to '... act like an airplane wing and is adjustable to improve performance'. However, the rear styling treatment was restrained by comparison with the rest of the car, being clean and unadorned.

The prototype was then shipped to the US, having picked up some Nardi tuning equipment along the way, but no replicas were made. Loewy's team did, however, borrow a few styling cues – primarily the successful hind treatment – for the time-defying Studebaker Avanti that arrived in 1962. Precisely how long Loewy retained the Loraymo is unclear. It was believed long gone prior to being unearthed in California in 1988. The American Lancia Club then gifted the remains to the Vincenzo Lancia Museum which invested three years and an undisclosed amount of lire in restoring this strange confection.

As for the origins of the name, 'Loraymo' was coined by Loewy himself taking three syllables from his first name and surname. A strange car deserves a strange name.

Raymond Loewy was one of the founding fathers of industrial design. Nevertheless, cars created at his behest and in his image, such as the Loraymo, often courted controversy.

1960

DiDia 150

It blurred the line between custom car and concept queen and took seven years to complete. The DiDia 150 was among the wildest of road cars to emerge from Detroit during an era when Motown wasn't exactly renowned for subtlety. The car was the brainchild of a man who was variously a bus driver, machinist and self-styled fashion designer. Andrew Di Dia was a young man in a hurry, keen to leave his mark, and he was already restyling cars for fun when he collaborated with his neighbour, Chrysler designer Edward V. Francoise, on his dream car. That was in 1953.

Scroll forward to 1957, and Di Dia met future superstar Bobby Darin at a concert. The two got to chatting about cars, and Darin made a few suggestions of his own. He declared that should he ever 'make it big', he would buy the car that was already in the throes of creation. While equipped with a Cadillac drivetrain, the rest of the car was largely scratch-built. The body, for example, was hand-formed over wooden bucks and then gas-welded. No filler was used if the press material from the period is to be believed. Each tailfin amounted to 15 weeks' work (the fins sat higher than the roofline). Up front, the retractable headlights were concealed behind thin metal slats, while the front and rear 'floating' bumpers were similarly custom-made.

The paint, a metallic shade of ruby red, was mixed with diamond dust to lend it extra sparkle. The thirty coats were applied over a base coat of gold, and each coat was rubbed down by hand before the next was applied. Inside, there was a rectangular steering wheel (a modified Imperial item) and a record player. The windscreen wipers were apparently rain-sensitive, deploying automatically when moisture was detected on the glass, while the tail-light clusters and indicators purportedly moved in-line with steering inputs, but this may have been promotional flimflam.

Much of the car was built by Ron Clark and Bob Kaiser of the Clarkaiser Custom Shop, the DiDia 150 being finally completed in 1960 at a cost of an eye-watering $93,647. A year later, Darin borrowed the car to drive to the Academy Awards alongside his wife, Sandra Dee. Having made it big, the 20-something bought the car for $150,000. At a stroke it made it into the *Guinness Book of Records* as the most expensive car ever sold to a private individual. The car was subsequently renamed 'The Bobby Darin Dream Car', and retained by the singer/performer until 1970 when it was donated to the Museum of Transportation in Missouri. Intriguingly, the car's designer never penned another vehicle during his lifetime. Andrew Di Dia died in 2014 aged 96.

Many years in the making, the DiDia 150 became the most expensive car ever sold to a private individual after it was acquired by Bobby Darin in 1961.

Plymouth XNR

The words 'Plymouth' and 'sports car' were once mutually exclusive, but the car pictured here could have changed that had it entered production. The late 1950s witnessed Chrysler's resident styling guru Virgil Exner at the height of his creative powers, and 'Ex' (as he preferred to be known) openly campaigned for the smallest of Detroit's Big Three to create a rival for the Chevrolet Corvette. While the board wasn't convinced that making such a car would return a profit, they gave the silver-haired designer carte blanche to create a show queen in 1958–59; one that would promote his ideas and employ the Plymouth nameplate.

Dubbed 'XNR' – a contraction of 'Exner', the prototype was based on a modified 2,705mm (106.5in) Valiant saloon-car platform, complete with 170cu in, straight-six engine that was canted over at a 30° angle and tuned to produce 250bhp. After creating preliminary sketches and a ⅜-scale model in Detroit, responsibility for building the car was handed over to Carrozzeria Ghia which had previously built a raft of one-off and small-series Chryslers.

Bodied in steel, perhaps the oddest feature was the large, offset bonnet scoop which extended all the way into the cabin to form the instrument binnacle. The rear 'stabilising fin', meanwhile, was reputedly inspired by the Le Mans-winning Jaguar D-type. On the passenger side, a folding 'Brooklands-style' fly-screen looked decidedly old-hat by comparison. One feature that has yet to be adopted on a production car was the leather-clad glove compartment lid: it could be removed and used as a camera case.

Barely 1,092mm (43in) high, this two-seater roadster was 4,958mm (195.2in) long and 1,803mm (71in) wide, its wild styling following on from Exner's prior 'Idea Cars'. Its asymmetrical outline confounded as many arbiters of beauty as it bewitched, but *Road & Track*, a magazine known for preferring imports over home-grown fare, put the car on its cover in May 1960. What's more, the XNR was fully-functional and fast with it: initial tests at Chrysler's proving ground in Romeo, Michigan, saw the car attain a top speed of 146mph (235km/h). Aided by a special streamlined nose cone designed by Dick Burke, it later recorded 152mph (245km/h).

However, for all the promotional hype that followed, the XNR never was going to make the leap to production-car reality. Once it had performed in front of the cameras, the car was sent back to Ghia, which in turn sold it to a Swiss enthusiast. Ownership subsequently passed to the Shah of Iran.

The Plymouth XNR was crafted by Carrozzeria Ghia at the behest of Chrysler's styling czar, Virgil Exner. It was later owned by the Shah of Iran.

Curtiss-Wright Model 2500 'Air-Car'

When is a car not a car? When it is a hovercraft. Strictly speaking, this remarkable machine was classed as a 'four-passenger commercial vehicle', which is suitably ambiguous. It may have resembled a biscuit tin, but this was a serious project; one that for a brief period became a media darling in the process. That said, the Air Car – or GEM (Ground Effects Machine) – was conceived in 1958 by the Curtiss-Wright Corporation of Wood Ridge, New Jersey with military applications in mind.

However, the firm's board hoped that in time it would be adopted by the general public. Despite its wacky appearance, it was straightforward beneath the steel skin. The Model 2500 was powered by two 180bhp Lycoming engines: one was mounted up front, the other behind the passenger compartment. Each unit drove, via reduction gears, a single four-bladed fan housed within a plenum chamber. These chambers created a cushion of air up to 381mm (15in) thick. Forward momentum was supplied by air bled from the chambers which was then expelled at low speeds via a row of louvres sited along the car's flanks.

The firm also dabbled with its own take on the Wankel 'rotary' engine theme, and created a bit of history on the quiet, because the Air Car was the first American 'road' vehicle ever equipped with such a powerplant. Curtiss-Wright touted it to Detroit's 'Big Three' manufacturers, with Chrysler and Ford experimenting with this 984cc unit, but ultimately the design found a home with tractor manufacturer, John Deere. In a bid to make the Model 2500 appear more conventional, the vehicle's designers gave it car-like attributes such as dual headlights, rear light clusters, what passed for bumpers, and a convertible roof. Its makers claimed that it could traverse any surface while offering a magic-carpet-like ride. The downside was a top speed of a dizzying 38mph (61km/h).

However, its future depended on the US military adopting the design and, by extension, funding further development. The Army Transportation Research Command concluded that, while highly manoeuvrable, the Air Car wasn't quite the all-terrain vehicle it was purported to be, and gave it the thumbs down. In 1961, the project was quietly dropped, its makers concluding that there was no point continuing without substantial backing.

Claims that the machine could have been adopted as a Studebaker are wide of the mark (Curtiss-Wright was allied to the South Bend, Indiana concern via military contracts, having come to the ailing firm's rescue in the mid-1950s). Curtiss-Wright subsequently turned its attentions to nuclear submarines, which proved an infinitely more lucrative venture.

It may have had the stylistic elan of a biscuit tin, but the Air-Car was a serious project. However, the design wasn't without its drawbacks, which blunted its chances somewhat.

1960

Chevrolet Corvair Coupé Speciale' by Pinin Farina

Anyone who has ever uttered the adage 'There's no such thing as bad publicity' is clearly unfamiliar with *Unsafe at Any Speed* by Ralph Nader. This coruscating 1960s exposé of cars deemed to be unnecessarily dangerous is forever linked with the Chevrolet Corvair. It wasn't singled out for censure, but General Motors' bungled attempts at smearing Nader served only to boost sales of the book. That, and cement the Corvair's status as a widow maker.

It was nothing of the sort unless you couldn't differentiate between braking and steering, but mud sticks. What's more, there were several tuners and coachbuilders that viewed this flat-six-powered saloon as the perfect blank canvas. Pinin Farina was one of the more celebrated styling houses to adopt the rear-engined device, although a degree of confusion surrounds its various attempts at a remodel.

The firm unveiled its initial take on the theme at the 1960 Paris motor show, a year after the donor car was introduced. Based on an unmodified Corvair platform, the 'Corvair Coupé Speciale' did the rounds on the automotive catwalks that year, including an appearance at the Turin motor show, but there was no talk of replicas being made, or of any official sanction from GM. Scroll forward two years and it was a different story. Pininfarina (now one word) unveiled an ostensibly new Corvair-based machine in Paris. According to some sources, General Motors had provided support, if not finance, the thinking being that a sportier model in the range could help boost sales. Quotes attributed to former GM styling chief Chuck Jordan in period stated that it hoped such a car would also appeal to the European market.

Whatever the truth, Italian-domiciled American Tom Tjaarda produced an outline that was well proportioned, even if it wasn't particularly daring. This alleged four-seater (2+2 is more realistic) was exhibited widely in 1962 and also made it onto the cover of *Road & Track* magazine in February 1963, a few months before another variant appeared. Strictly speaking, it was the same car with minor detail revisions and a change of hue from dark green to red.

The Coupé Speciale did not make it into production, although Chevrolet subsequently release the ostensibly similar Monza variant. As for the small matter of how many 'Speciales' were made, it rather depends on whose version of history you believe. According to an auction catalogue description from 2000, Pininfarina retained the final car in its factory museum until it was sold to an American collector in the 1990s. Tjaarda, however, insisted that only one car was ever built. He had simply been tasked with reworking the original 1960 Coupé Speciale for the 1962 show season.

Pinin Farina's original take on the Chevrolet Corvair (opposite) in 1960 was joined by a different variant two years later. However, they may have been the same car, merely reworked.

1960

Studebaker Italia

Unlike the majority of American motor manufacturers, Studebaker did not engage the services of European styling houses during the 1950s and early 1960s. However, Italian marque concessionaire Renato Bornigia wasn't above trying to improve on the regular Lark production model and went so far as to hire the multi-talented Pietro Frua to create his own take on the theme in 1960. The gruff coachbuilding great took a Lark VIII convertible as a basis for a two-door coupé that was revealed at the November 1960 Turin motor show.

The Studebaker Italia was powered by a 259cu in, 4.2-litre V8 and remained standard mechanically, but the body was dramatically different from the production model. If anything, it borrowed styling cues from a near concurrent project for Volkswagen's Swiss importer, not least the quad-headlight arrangement. Sharp creases ran the length of the flanks aft of the front wheelarches, the lower portions of bodywork being concave. Bornigia hedged his bets by also displaying a four-door version. This was similarly a Frua design, but it was built by Carrozzeria Francis Lombardi of Vercelli. While exploring the same styling themes, it emerged that bit more angular and upright. The saloon was subsequently shown at the March 1961 Geneva motor show.

Bornigia, it can be surmised, was interested in producing the Italia in series, and, intriguingly, the four-door variant was displayed on the Italsuisse stand – the Swiss coachbuilder and long-time Frua collaborator. There is no evidence to suggest that the Studebaker Corporation had given its blessing or was even aware of Bornigia's scheme, even if such a scheme existed. Whatever the truth, the four-door Italia was still being shown in late 1961 when it was joined at the Turin motor show by another prototype, this time based on Studebaker Hawk running gear.

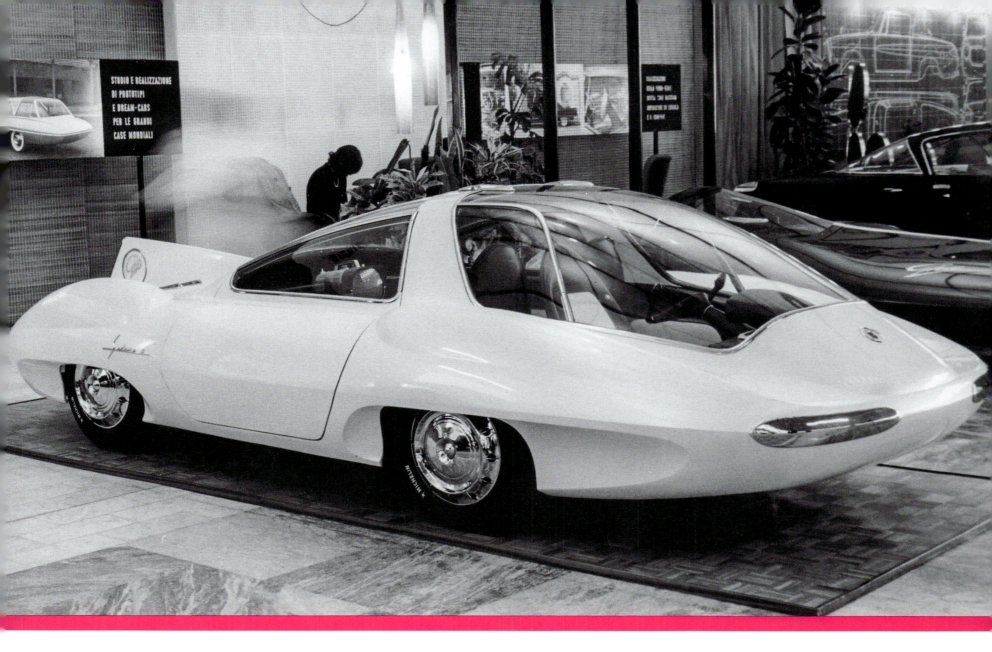

Ghia Selene Seconda

Carrozzeria Ghia and Renault had worked hand in glove on a variety of projects prior to the release of the startling Tom Tjaarda-penned Selene in 1959. This bizarre show car was constructed under the direction of Renault's engineering chief, Fernand Picard, and Yves Georges, who ran the firm's design office. Notionally rear-engined (in reality, it had no powerplant), the driver sat forward of the front wheels, one of its signature features being a steering wheel that could switch from left- to right-hand drive, with two sets of pedals permanently positioned on the floor.

Renault continued to evaluate design themes explored on this first prototype, but ultimately decided that would-be customers would be put off by the unconventional looks and seating arrangement. Ghia, by contrast, decided to push ahead with its own variation on the theme which emerged at the 1960 Geneva motor show. The Selene Seconda (aka Selene II) aped the general layout of its forebear, but was markedly more rounded. The styling has since been attributed to Virgil Exner Jr, this latest strain keeping the 'two-box' profile and cab-forward layout.

As before, there was no means of motive power, although Ghia claimed in a press release that it could accommodate engines of between 1.0-litre and 2.5-litre displacements. It was also promoted under the tagline: 'Already ready for 1970…' This remarkable machine was displayed at the 1961 Geneva motor show before being relegated to life under a dustsheet within Ghia's Turin facility. The Selene Seconda mock-up was sold via auction in 2002 along with dozens of other Ghia show-stoppers. It made $88,000.

The bizarre Ghia Selene Seconda was essentially a mock-up. Unlike so many other concept cars of the period, it wasn't scrapped.

Chevrolet CERV-1

Chevrolet's CERV-1 single-seater served as a mobile test bed. It managed 162mph at the Daytona circuit in 1960 and subsequently received a hike in horsepower.

The end of the 1950s witnessed a seismic shift in racing-car design, with mid-/rear-engined cars taking centre stage. Chevrolet, along with other General Motors divisions, eschewed official involvement in motorsport, but 'Father of the Corvette' Zora Arkus-Duntov was a racer to the core. The Le Mans veteran conceived the Chevrolet Experimental Research Vehicle as a technical exercise; one that would be used to evaluate: '...ride and handling phenomena under the most realistic conditions.'

While outwardly it resembled a stylised version of comparable Formula 1 machinery such as the Cooper T60, it didn't 'make do' with a small four-cylinder unit. Instead, it was equipped with a special lightweight version of the 283cu in Chevrolet V8 engine. That said, lightweight is a relative term because it tipped the scales at 159kg (350.5lb). According to PR material from the period, it boasted a top speed of 172mph (277km/h). First seen publicly at Riverside International Raceway in November 1960, by which time it had been rechristened CERV-I, the car was put through its paces by Stirling Moss and Dan Gurney, who earlier in the year had teamed-up to win the Nürburgring 1,000Kms.

While CERV-1 was never raced, it racked up plenty of miles at high-speed on-track, and at venues such as the Pikes Peak International Hill Climb. It was subsequently armed with an aluminium 377cu in small-block V8 while also receiving aerodynamic tweaks, but it was later restored back to its original configuration. For many years, it was displayed at The Briggs Cunningham Automotive Museum in Florida.

1960
Chevrolet Corvette XP-700

Representing something of a mystery wrapped in an enigma for Corvette fans, this one-off confection was originally built at the behest of GM's newly-installed president of styling, Bill Mitchell. As was typical of the man, the XP-700 was distinctive, if perhaps over-gilded. Based on a standard 1958 Corvette, the front end encompassed a quad-headlight arrangement, scoops, and an oval grille. The rear styling treatment, by contrast, foretold the forthcoming 1961 production model.

Mitchell used his Corvette for a year before it was pressed into service on the show circuit. However, it was at this juncture that Mitchell decided to rework the design. The grille cavity was enlarged, the rear-end augmented and equipped with six individual taillights. The colour was also changed from red to silver. The biggest deviation, however, was the adoption of a 'double bubble-top' roof which was then almost obligatory in Stateside custom-car circles.

The car broke cover in XP-700 prototype form at the April 1960 New York International Automobile Show. Historians cannot agree on what happened next. Anecdotal evidence suggests it was cannibalised and served as a basis for 'XP-755', aka the Mako Shark. Others are of the opinion that it may have survived the chop. Whatever the truth, it has not been seen since the early 1960s.

One part custom car, two parts a regular Chevrolet Corvette, the XP-700 was used by GM styling chief Bill Mitchell for a year before it hit the show circuit.

Ghia IXG Dragster

A communication error blighted the chances of this streamlined flight of fantasy ever turning a wheel in anger. According to most period sources, the 'International Experimental Ghia' was built for record attempts. However, according to its designer, Tom Tjaarda, it was the brainchild of Ghia principal, Luigi Segre. He wanted to build a dragster, and roped-in Tjaarda – as an American – to create a quarter-mile weapon. It's just that, in the words, of Tjaarda: 'Segre didn't know what a dragster was…' Accordingly, he directed the design towards something akin to a typical Italian streamlined record car. He was incensed on learning that the intended engine – a 1.0-litre Innocenti unit – wouldn't fit. The IXG was displayed at the 1961 Turin motor show before being placed in storage. There it remained until 2002, when it sold in an auction of concept cars in Detroit.

Stephenson MG

This distinctive coupé was built for a singular purpose: to springboard its creator to great heights as a designer. C.N. Stephenson graduated from the Central School of Art and Design in 1960, but this reworked MGA Twin-Cam had been in the offing as far back as 1958, when he acquired a rolling chassis from the factory in Abingdon. The body was constructed by FLM Panelcraft of Putney, London, the end product garnering plenty of column inches on its completion in 1960. It appeared on the cover of *Sporting Motorist*, while *The Autocar* and *Road & Track* also dedicated several pages to the newcomer.

The latter reported: '[The interior] is finished in leather and haircord carpet with a washable plastic headliner. The seats are aluminium buckets in foam rubber over elastic straps.' It went on to add: 'Stephenson aspires to the status of consulting designer to small automotive manufacturers. Also, he would like to have his own coachbuilding works for the manufacture of a few special-bodied machines every year.' For all the press attention, which was largely positive, this olive-coloured prototype remained the first and last car styled by Stephenson.

The construction of this distinctive take on the MGA was meant to act as a calling card for designer C.N. Stephenson. It didn't have the desired effect.

This was the year that famously saw jaws slacken in unison as the Jaguar E-type was introduced at the Geneva motor show in March. Arbiters of beauty have been raving about it ever since, this attainable production car appearing unfeasibly slinky and exotic. Intriguingly, the European season-opener saw a raft of new exhibitors, including Russian marques for the first time ever. Nevertheless, many of the bigger brands withheld new models until later in the year.

1961 also saw America continue to lead the way in terms of exhibiting show queens. However, this year also witnessed the emergence of the 'Clap Door' Lincoln Continental that was a literal 'three-box' saloon, albeit on a vast scale. Tailfins were becoming passé, while smaller cars – or compacts in Detroit speak – were increasingly popular.

Also in 1961
Soviet cosmonaut Yuri Gagarin becomes the first human to orbit the Earth.
Construction of the Berlin Wall begins, separating East and West Berlin.
The US-backed Bay of Pigs invasion – an attempt to overthrow Cuban leader Fidel Castro – fails.
***The Avengers* TV series airs for the first time in the UK.**
The Vietnam War officially begins as the first US helicopters and troops arrive in Saigon.

1961

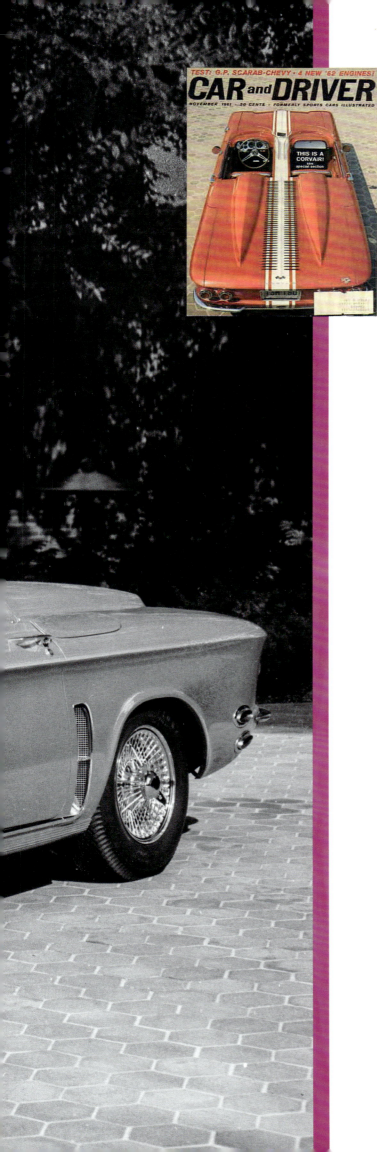

Chevrolet Corvair Sebring Spyder

General Motors' styling czar Bill Mitchell dubbed it: 'A Corvair-Corvette for the smaller sports car market', not that there was ever any likelihood of the Sebring Spyder entering production. This concept car was strictly a one-off, but it was an intriguing one, nevertheless. Breaking cover at the February 1961 Chicago Auto Show, it instilled excitement in onlookers and the media alike, only to disappear into the ether almost as soon as it appeared.

According to *Car & Driver* magazine, the car was conceived with high performance in mind. Writer Dic van der Feen stated: 'Mitchell started with the standard Corvair chassis and reduced the wheelbase by 15 inches, nearly all of it taken from between the back of the stock door and the rear wheel arch. Those doors are the only normal Corvair panels on the Sebring Spyder. All the other body pressings are special steel fabrications. The exception is the rear deck. This quick-lift unit is [made of] glassfibre and covers not only the engine, but the upholstered baggage section behind the seats. The headrest fairings lift right with it. Overall length of the Spyder is 162 inches, against the normal model's 180 inches, but overall width is up from 67 inches to 68.5 inches. The Spyder is strikingly low. It measures just 37 inches off the ground at the top of the headrest fairings.'

The scoops sited just in front of the rear wheel arches weren't for show, either. They were in place to cool the brakes behind the glossy 13in Dayton wire wheels. The regular Corvair suspension was also upgraded. It received a front anti-roll bar, two degrees of negative camber at the rear and special coil-over shock absorbers at either end. Then there was the six-cylinder powerplant to the rear. According to the *Car & Driver* report: 'Bill Mitchell turned the engine over to Zora Arkus-Duntov, the Corvette's godfather, who promptly installed the special cam... It is fully balanced with all the clearances to dead-on engineering specification, and is fitted with – surprise – an awesome Paxton supercharger.' The blower provided a 32bhp increase over the standard car's 98bhp.

'Absolutely nothing was available on power or performance specifications, but we could – and did – sit behind the wheel where we blipped the tacho to the 5,500rpm mark,' the article continued. 'The engine wound up freely so we wondered if the accelerator pedal was connected directly to the needle. The rear area of the tacho is from 5,200 to 5,800rpm, with the higher mark being the danger point... The twin pipes from each side of the familiar opposed "six" run to the opposite side behind the engine but inside the rear body panel before reaching the rudimentary muffler. This gives the necessary length for optimum extraction effect with no abrupt curves in the pipes.'

Inside, the dished wood-rim wheel fronted a raft of instruments which stretched to a 140mph speedometer. Then there were the signature individual aero screens and go-faster stripes which represented pure race-car-inspired whimsy. Sadly, however, despite receiving plenty of positive press in period, GM wasn't sentimental about its show cars. The Sebring Spyder was scrapped in 1966.

According to Bill Mitchell, this supercharged one-off represented a 'Corvair-Corvette for the small sports car market.' Sadly, it was destroyed in the mid-1960s.

1961

Kelly

While not strictly a concept car per se, the Kelly (aka Vignale Kelly) was a show-stopper in period. It was the brainchild of Gordon Kelly who was an employee of legendary industrial designer, Brooks Stevens. Kelly had been mapping out his dream car for several years before he created a 1/8-scale model. He then acquired a C2-series Chevrolet Corvette directly from General Motors and began canvassing the various coachbuilders to help realise his vision.

He did so armed with his scale model, which he carried in a specially-designed holdall, and eventually Kelly arrived at Alfredo Vignale's premises on Strada del Portone, Grugliasco, on the outskirts of Turin. Vignale was responsive, a deal was thrashed out, and the Corvette was dispatched to Italy. Kelly was nothing if not precise, and he had worked everything out in the minutest detail. He travelled to Turin repeatedly to monitor progress, much of the build having been farmed out by Vignale to a much smaller coachbuilder, Sibona & Basano.

Kelly was unaware of this, and was nonplussed on discovering the donor car's glassfibre body had been broken up. He had hoped to sell it in order to recoup part of his investment. Nevertheless, the metal-shapers stuck faithfully to his instructions, right down to the rake of the windscreen, the sharply-creased beltline, and distinctive, rounded tail complete with a hatchback opening that was considered unusual in period. Inside, the car featured much of the regular Corvette's architecture, including the familiar semi-circular speedometer, but with locally-sourced supplementary gauges.

The car – simply dubbed 'Kelly' – broke cover on the Vignale stand at the 1961 Paris motor show, the final build price being around $14,000. *Road & Track*'s event report stated: 'More than before, the joint was crawling with American cars of various shapes and sizes

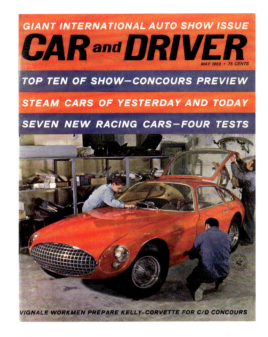

VIGNALE WORKMEN PREPARE KELLY-CORVETTE FOR C/D CONCOURS

which seemed to be drawing more favourable comment than they usually do... I didn't see a Corvette around, but Gordon Kelly made up for this by bringing a Vignale-clad GT coupe of his own design on a standard Corvette chassis... [It] was much better-looking than this sort of thing usually is.' Kelly retained the prototype until his death in 1995.

Chrysler Turboflite

It was a blind alley, but an intriguing one, nonetheless. There was a time – several decades even – when several major marques considered gas turbines to be the propulsion unit of the future. With the possible exception of Rover, few manufacturers invested more in adapting these powerplants for road-going vehicles than Chrysler. The car pictured here was created when the firm's designers and engineers were at their most starry-eyed; when anything seemed possible. It is just that not all was quite as it appeared.

The Turboflite was the last show car created under the direction of design chief, Virgil Exner. However, it was styled by Jack Kenitz within the new Advanced Studio. It looked unlike any other car in the model range. It looked unlike any other car, period. For starters, it featured a green-tinted, aircraft-like canopy, while the rear of this show queen was dominated by a huge rear wing. This was supported by a pair of equally noticeable fins, each housing a stop light with 'day and night' intensity settings. Between the fins was a 'deceleration air-flap' which pivoted up into the airstream when the brakes were applied, creating additional drag and thus lessening the load on the conventional braking set-up.

Up front, the wings were cutaway to expose much of the cast aluminium front wheels. According to PR material of the period, these attractive items featured integral brake drums with wheel spokes acting as centrifugal cooling impellers. The main headlights, meanwhile, were tucked beneath the leading edge of the wings when not in use. Inside, the cabin was designed around four satin-finish, aluminium-framed bucket seats that were lined in blue fabric and green leather. Electro-luminescent door-panel inserts provided a soft blue-green glow to sooth the occupants' mood, while the dashboard featured something equally far-out: a rev-counter that read to 50,000rpm.

This was a significant clue, if it were needed, that powering this monster was something that bit more radical than a pushrod V8. Propulsion was allegedly provided by an experimental 'CR2A' gas-turbine unit that generated 140bhp at 39,000rpm. It was smaller and lighter than a regular V8 and required 80 per cent fewer parts (and did not require a liquid cooling system). Power was transmitted to the rear wheels via a modified TorqueFlite auto 'box.

The Ghia-built Turboflite toured the globe in 1961, and garnered more than a few column inches in the mainstream and specialist press in period. *Motor Trend* was particularly effusive, stating that it: '...offered a glimpse into Chrysler's crystal ball... The gas turbine is sure to come.' There was, however, one small wrinkle: the Turboflite never ran under its own steam. It was a non-functioning 'pushmobile'.

Crafted by Carrozzeria Ghia, the Turboflite was the last Chrysler shaped under Virgil Exner. It hypothetically employed a gas turbine engine that produced 140bhp at 39,000rpm.

1961
Pinin Farina Cadillac Jacqueline

The relationship between the Pininfarina (né Pinin Farina) and General Motors' premium brand stretches back to the early 1930s. The first PF-bodied Cadillac was a one-off V16 Speedster built for the Maharaja of Orchha. It impressed GM head of styling Harley Earl who initiated a meeting with studio chief Battista 'Pinin' Farina with a view to him shaping a series of cars for the La Salle subdivision. This scheme came to naught. The Turin *carrozzeria* would not clothe another Cadillac until 1954, the 'PF200' Cabriolet Speciale being built at the behest of a record producer.

In 1957, Pinin Farina was tasked by GM with shaping a Buick concept car – the Lido V8 – before following through with the Cadillac Four Posti prototype. Based on a Series 62 chassis, this was a GM-funded project, although this open-top show car bore little resemblance to the donor. However, a degree of uncertainty surrounds its fate, or that of a fixed-roof coupe dubbed 'Starlight'. Depending on whose estimates you credit, the latter was either a brand-new car, or the cabriolet reworked with a new Plexiglas roof and given a blow-over in a different colour. The car emerged at the 1959 Turin motor show and was seen again at the following year's Paris motor show.

Pinin Farina was also tasked with building the Eldorado Brougham in limited series, its follow-up Cadillac concept queen being the Jacqueline, which broke cover in 1961. According to some sources, it was built upon an Eldorado Brougham chassis, but others insist it comprised a mock-up body on a skeletal support frame. Just to add to confusion, some claim it was built as a 'driver', but the body was later removed and placed on a 'dolly'. As for why it was created, it has been suggested that Pinin Farina hoped to tempt Cadillac into adopting the Jacqueline for production. Instead, there would not be another PF-styled variant until the Allanté which entered production in 1987.

Pinin Farina Berlinetta Aerodinamica Project Y

Pinin Farina's follow-up to the previous year's Project Y appeared almost conformist by comparison. Based upon Fiat 600D foundations, here the wheels were mounted in conventional fashion, but the silhouette was similarly ovular. However, it did away with the prominent rear stabilising tailfins which were deemed redundant. Vestigial fins were in place initially, but these were removed later. The study in streamlining was unveiled at the 1961 Turin motor show, its makers claiming it had a drag coefficient of just 0.27Cd. Project Y later went on display at the National Automobile Museum (né The Harrah Collection) in Nevada.

Aston Martin DB4 GT Jet

Styled by a youthful Giorgetto Giugiaro, and based on the last-ever short-wheelbase Aston Martin DB4 GT chassis, the Jet was displayed by Bertone at the 1961 Geneva motor show. Remarkably, the car was created in just three months, and it remains the only example of the marque ever bodied in steel (save for a 2/4 model that was reclothed by Spanish coachbuilder, Serra, by which time it was already several years old). Though always intended to be a one-off, some styling cues were subsequently transposed onto a bespoke Ferrari 250GT. The Jet spent its early life in Beirut prior to being exported to the USA. Giugiaro's next Aston Martin-based show car was the Twenty that was displayed at the same event 40 years later. Bertone also revived the Jet tag for the V12 Vanquish-based Jet2 and Rapide-derived Jet 2+2 in 2013.

1961

Ford Gyron

When is a car not a car? When it is a Ford Gyron. Work began on this two-wheeled device in 1959. Designed by former Tucker stylist Alex Tremulis, with input from McKinley Thompson, Bill Daytona, John Najjar, and Syd Mead, this two-wheeled, glassfibre-bodied machine was intended to feature a gyroscope in a bid to make it functional. However, cost considerations came into play, so it featured retractable outrigger wheels instead. Power came from electric motors so, technically, it was drivable (top speed was a giddying 5mph/8km/h). Inside, there was nothing so prosaic as a steering wheel. Instead, there was a dial that controlled driver inputs.

Unveiled at the New York International Auto Show on 1 April 1961, this was a serious project, if only in the minds of its creators. George W. Walker, Ford's vice president of styling, said at the time: 'Despite the fact that tremendous changes and improvement in car styling and design have taken place during this century, one aspect of the automobile has been largely unchanged: it has remained basically a rectangular object with a wheel at each corner. In offering the prospect of adequate stability without being restricted to this four-wheel approach, the Gyron exposes countless possibilities to the imagination of the industry.'

The Gyron was also shown at the 1962 Chicago Auto Show, before it went on display in the futuristic-looking Ford Rotunda in Dearborn. However, a fire in November of that year destroyed the building and the car.

A car with two wheels? The Gyron was shaped for the most part by Alex Tremulis and was intended to employ a gyroscope. It was guided via a dial rather than a conventional steering wheel.

41

1961

Constructed by Carrozzeria Ghia at vast cost, the FliteWing incorporated an unusual mix of gullwing and conventional doors. This arrangement apparently heightened safety for the occupants.

Dodge FliteWing

Crafted by Carrozzeria Ghia, at a cost of around $125,000, the awkwardly-named FliteWing was unveiled before the media in Central Park, New York on 5 December 1961. As with so many concept cars of the period, this 6.3-litre V8-engined one-off incorporated many features; ones that aimed to solve problems that had hitherto not existed. The car's signature 'innovation' comprised flip-up panels in the roof. Essentially, it made for an odd combination of gullwing and conventional doors. According to the PR material of the period, this was an essential safety feature; one that facilitated greater visibility thanks to the lack of B-pillars.

Inside, instrumentation and switchgear were suitably space-age, 'elliptical windows' were provided, rather than a traditional speedometer, displaying the car's speed in increments of 10mph. There were no conventional column stalks for indicators, headlights, and suchlike, either. Instead, there were switches conveniently located in the driver's door card.

McLouth XV'61

One of the most obscure concept cars of the era, the XV'61 (eXperimental Vehicle 1961), was styled by Syd Mead and built at the behest of the McLouth Steel Corporation of Detroit, Michigan. Exhibited at the April 1961 New York International Automobile Show, this rear-engined, cab-forward machine was unique among its contemporaries in that it wasn't really a car at all. According to the firm's press release from the period, it was intended to be used in union with some form of advanced monorail system; one that hadn't yet been created. It stated: 'Transportation engineers and planners believe that future travel will rely heavily on monorail systems for the safe, convenient and rapid transportation of people and goods between distant points.'

Ghia Plymouth Asimmetrica/St. Regis

Derived from the previous year's XNR, Ghia's 1961 follow-up was similarly based on a Plymouth Valiant platform. The Asimmetrica represented a further investigation of styling themes explored on its predecessor but was, if anything, a more conventional offering. By comparison, it was positively practical, thanks in no small part to it having door handles, a full windscreen and a folding roof. Stylistically, developments included a reworked lighting arrangement (lamps were no longer inset in the grille), while inside it was plushly-equipped with leather upholstery and lashings of chrome.

Displayed at the 1961 Turin motor show, the one-off Assimetrica attracted the attention of Georges Simenon. The author of the *Maigret* detective novels was instantly smitten, and acquired the car off the stand for his wife. Some sources insist that more than one Asimmetrica was made, but this claim has yet to be substantiated. Ghia continued to explore the asymmetrical theme, and also produced a coupé variant. The oddly-named St. Regis was exhibited at the 1962 Turin motor show, and there was talk of a limited production run, but the car remained unique.

Alfa Romeo SS Spider Speciale Aerodinamico

The last in a series of show cars that foretold the Alfa Romeo 'Duetto' Spider, the Pininfarina-built SS Spider Speciale Aerodinamico appeared remarkably close to the finished item. The basis for the prototype was a (Bertone-designed) Giulietta Sprint Speciale, the car's striking outline having been retrospectively attributed to Aldo Brovarone. The car was first seen publicly at the November 1961 Turin motor show, *Road & Track* labelling it a '...strained effort on the Alfa Giulietta'.

The prototype's silhouette was subsequently tweaked by Francesco Martinengo, Renzo Carli and Francesco Salamone for the Spider production car. The scalloped sides and rounded tail, which at the time were considered controversial, were retained for the production version, the most significant deviation being the substitution of Perspex-shrouded fixed headlights in place of electrically-retractable items. However, the Spider didn't enter production for a further four years.

1961

Chevrolet Corvette Sting Ray (aka 'Mitchell's Racer')

This famous racer turned concept car only just fits within the scope of this book, but its significance cannot be overestimated. Conceived by Zora Arkus Duntov with motorsport in mind, and initially powered by a 4.7-litre V8, its dramatic outline was styled by Larry Shinoda under Bill Mitchell (but based on preliminary sketches by Peter Brock). The car's two-piece, three-skin glassfibre body (which was supported by balsa wood crossmembers), and styling features, foretold the C2-generation Corvette production car. Underpinning it was an unused chassis from the prior SR-2 programme.

Raced in SCCA (Sports Car Club of America) events by talented semi-pro driver Dr Dick Thompson in 1959–60, it claimed four category wins from nine starts, and a C-modified class title in the latter season against minimal opposition, although it failed to record any outright victories. The car underwent umpteen changes during its competition career, and was subsequently reworked for Mitchell's personal use as a road car, key differences including the addition of a passenger seat and a full-width windscreen.

The Sting Ray, which was known by various monikers including 'Mitchell's Racer' and 'Sting Ray Spider', had been campaigned without any reference to Chevrolet or the Corvette. Mitchell had funded the car's construction and competition bids, but General Motors acquired it ahead of the February 1961 Chicago Auto Show, where it was displayed as an 'experimental racer', complete with Corvette emblems. Nevertheless, Mitchell continued to use the Sting Ray, and at one point it was equipped with a 427cu in big-block V8. The car also appeared in the 1967 Elvis Presley movie, *Clambake*.

The Sting Ray racer was campaigned by SCCA champion Dr Dick Thompson (bottom) and created under Bill Mitchell (in driver's seat, left). The car subsequently appeared in Elvis Presley vehicle, *Clambake* (below).

Manufacturers in North America continued to produce show cars at a dizzying rate, and, like many European brands, explore alternate power sources. Detroit's Big Three also looked to Europe, if only in terms of racing car developments, British constructors having turned Formula 1 on its head at the end of the previous decade by placing the engine behind the driver. At a stroke, it had rendered front-engined machines obsolete. Mid-engined concept cars came in thick and fast, even if such a configuration would not materialise in the mainstream for decades in the USA.

In Europe, Italy continued to dominate in terms of creativity. That, and the sheer speed at which new designs were produced and trends established. Major European brands continued to flock to Italian styling houses, as did the nascent Japanese motor industry.

Also in 1962
The Cuban Missile Crisis takes the US and Soviet Union to the brink of nuclear war.
The Rolling Stones make their debut, at London's Marquee Club.
The first James Bond film, *Dr. No*, premiers in UK cinemas.
Marilyn Monroe is found dead after apparently overdosing on sleeping pills.
The *Sunday Times* becomes the first UK newspaper to print a colour supplement.

1962

Ford Mustang 1

Long before the Ford Mustang ignited the 'Pony Car Wars' in 1964, the name was attached to an altogether different sports car; one that went from preliminary sketch to fully-functional prototype in little more than three months. It was Ford's product planner Don Frey who first petitioned for sportier Fords. That was in 1960. He could see that arch-rival Chevrolet was making hay thanks to its small-block V8, which had usurped the Ford 'flathead' unit as the hot-rodders' engine of choice. It also had the Corvette in its armoury.

Frey voiced his concerns to Henry Ford II, car and truck vice president Robert McNamara, and the firm's vice presidents Gene Bordinat (design) and Herb Misch (engineering). The breakthrough occurred in January 1962, when Bordinat asked competing styling chiefs to come up with concepts for a small sports car. The team of John Najjar, Jim Darden, Ray Smith and Phil Clark, working under senior designer Bob Maguire, conceived the winning proposal.

It was at this juncture that the story moved on apace, as studio engineer Ray Smith suggested the addition of pop-up headlights, a retractable licence plate, fixed seats, adjustable pedals, and a telescopic steering wheel. All of these features were incorporated into the design, but the completed prototype was just a mock-up. It appeared destined to remain that way, until the board decided they wanted to see the car moving under its own steam at the US Grand Prix meeting at Watkins Glen. The deadline was 7 October 1962; the team had just 100 days to build something fit to be driven on a circuit before the global media.

Misch turned to Ford Advanced Vehicles (FAV) manager Roy Lunn to spearhead the project. The expat Briton was the perfect man for the job. He had begun his career as an apprentice toolmaker, aged 14, and went on to become chief engineer for Jowett in 1949. He also devised a special Jowett Le Mans car and, together with Frenchman Marcel Becquant, won the 1952 Monte Carlo Rally for the Bradford marque. Two years later, he jumped ship to Ford of Britain, where he played a major role in the creation of the Anglia 105E, prior to moving Stateside in 1958.

Lunn, together with engineer Bob Negstad, had little time to waste, their first decision being the choice of engine. The in-line four-cylinder unit from the Ford Cortina was considered, but ultimately the Taunus V4 was adopted. That was due in part to packaging requirements, but also because of expected weight-distribution issues: it was theorised that using the British engine would result in a 53/47 forward weight bias. With the German unit, it became 47/53. There was, however, the small matter of cooling the

1962

One of the most celebrated concept cars of the era, the original Ford Mustang was a mid-engined roadster at a time when such a configuration was deemed radical.

engine. Small radiators were placed at either side of the powerplant: the side intakes on the finished prototype weren't there for show.

The car's chassis was essentially a spaceframe affair, complete with an integral roll-bar. All powertrain and suspension mounts were welded directly to the framework. While the underpinnings were being readied in Detroit, the body was shaped and knitted together by Troutman & Barnes in Los Angeles (although California Metal Shaping of Culver City also rolled-out some of the aluminium panels). Ultimately, the body and chassis were united to form what Lunn described as 'semi-unitary construction', with the coachwork being riveted to the spaceframe. The outer skins, cockpit surfaces and undertray formed one seamless whole, while the seat pans, inner wheel arches and headlight nacelles were also bonded to the body. The seats were fixed, while the gearlever, fly-off handbrake and manual choke stood at the forward end of a central floor console.

Lunn's team also added a high-lift camshaft, stronger valve springs, a twin-choke carb, and a freer-flowing exhaust system, while also raising the compression ratio. The regular Taunus unit produced 89bhp at 6,500rpm and 89lb ft of torque at 3,800rpm. The tuned version, however, delivered 109bhp at 6,500rpm and 99lb ft at 5,200rpm. The engine was allied to a four-speed transaxle, while the suspension set-up was formulated following much theoretical work within Ford's nascent computer department. A double-wishbone set-up was devised, while the lowly Ford Consul provided parts such as balljoints and the brakes. The 'Wobbly Web' wheels, meanwhile, originated from a Lotus 23 sports-racer.

The finished article weighed a mere 700kg (1,544lb), Lunn estimating that the addition of a full windscreen (rather than a fly-screen) and bumpers would add 31kg (68lb). However, there was never any intention on Ford's part of putting the car into production, although the Mustang name would go on to become one of the most emotive and instantly recognisable in automotive history. It was coined by Najjar, although it was known, internally at least, as the Mustang Sports Car. It wasn't until the Mustang II concept car was first shown in 1963, that this little two-seater was referred to retrospectively as Mustang I.

Remarkably, Lunn and his team had the completed car out on track for the 1962 Formula 1 season-ending round at Watkins Glen. What's more, it was driven at the Upper State New York venue by Grand Prix winner, Dan Gurney. The Mustang appeared again at Laguna Seca in October of that year and at Daytona International Speedway, where Negstad lapped the banked oval circuit for a promotional film. It continued to be exhibited as late as 1964 across North America and Europe.

However, as is so often the way with concept cars, the car was deemed superfluous once it had served its purpose as a publicity generator. Ford's management ordered the Mustang I be destroyed, but its creators had other ideas. They hid it in a trailer instead. It remained there until 1974, when space was found for the car in the Henry Ford Museum in Dearborn – or rather the storage area.

Alfa Romeo 2600 PF Cabriolet Speciale/ Coupé Speciale

One of the prettiest of Pininfarina's concept cars from the period, this bespoke Alfa Romeo nevertheless remains one of the most enigmatic. Echoing styling themes explored on all manner of other cars created by the Turin design house, it was first seen at the 1962 Turin motor show. Based on an Alfa Romeo 2600 Spider platform, there was little mention of 'prototipo 621' in the Turin firm's press pack, other than a line about its: 'mother-of-pearl paintwork with synthetic leather trim.'

Road & Track correspondent Henry N. Manney III wasn't enthralled, his event report stating: 'Pininfarina always puts on a good show and this time there was no exception... certain members of the production line-up being joined by a hastily finished (judging by the paint) metalescent maroon Alfa 2600 Spider which followed the same general format as those seen at shows since Geneva, '59.' *Quattroruote* was more effusive, gushing over its: '...balanced mass, harmonious curves with design by the hand of the master.'

Style Auto also featured a glittery – if baffling – photo spread, complete with the odd juxtaposition of a woman dressed to the nines with a mink stole, a bunch of people with horse-drawn caravans, and a little girl in a bucket, set against the romantic backdrop of Pininfarina's Grugliasco factory. Following further appearances, and what passed for an 'interim' restyle, the car re-emerged a year on at the Brussels motor show. It appeared suitably different, largely due to the addition of a roof and a change of hue, plus a change of name to Coupé Speciale.

As for the identity of the designer, Aldo Brovarone has retrospectively been credited with shaping the original Cabriolet. His colleague at the time, Tom Tjaarda, claimed in later years that it was more of a collaborative effort within Pininfarina, and that the coupé makeover was done at the last minute because the firm needed a 'stand filler.' The car was found derelict in a scrapyard in Upper State New York in 1987. How it ended up there is another mystery.

1962

Pininfarina Fiat 2300 Coupé Speciale

This bluff-fronted machine was the first in a series of concept cars based on Fiat 2300 foundations. The Coupé Speciale was unveiled at the November 1962 Turin motor show, its standout feature being the unusual roof arrangement: a panel was spring-loaded to hinge upwards by 152.4mm (6in) from the top of the windscreen surround when the doors were opened, which afforded easier access. Pininfarina's *Catalogue Raisonné* states: 'Prototype on Fiat 2300 chassis frame. Dihedral sides, streamlined nose with trapezoidal mudguard heads with twin headlamps.'

Having been a mite sniffy about the Alfa Romeo 2600 PF Cabriolet Speciale, *Road & Track*'s Henry N. Manney III was rather more effusive about its stablemate. He reported: 'An interesting touch, though, was a pearlescent white, all-singing, all-dancing, Fiat 2300 coupé in which the roof moved upward when the door was opened, along with various other accoutrements like special seats. Tricks aside, which undoubtedly sell cars in the luxury bracket, the bodywork was an exercise in clever restraint and looked far smaller than the parent 2300.'

The car was never displayed again publicly, lending some historians to hypothesize that it was reworked to form the following year's Fiat 2300 Cabriolet Speciale.

One of many Fiat 2300 show cars made by Pininfarina, the first boasted a roof panel that was spring-loaded to hinge upwards from the top of the windscreen surround when the doors were opened.

Ferrari 400 SA Superfast III/IV

There was no room for ambiguity regarding the car's name. The first Ferrari christened with the Superfast tag was created by Pinin Farina (then two words) in 1956; a 410 Superamerica (chassis 0483SA) with a dramatic finned outline. It emerged at that year's Paris motor show and caused a furore. A year later, it was followed by the toned-down but still dramatic 410 SA Superfast (chassis 0719SA) that was displayed at the 1957 Paris and Turin motor shows, and subsequently owned by the mysterious businessman/racer, Jan de Vroom.

Scroll forward to 1960, and Pinin Farina unleased the one-off 400 SA Coupé Superfast II (chassis 2207SA), a streamlined GT with retractable headlights, partial rear-wheel spats, and a long, tapered tail. This, in turn, was followed by Superfast III, which was first seen at the 1962 Geneva motor show. It similarly featured retractable headlights and semi-enclosed rear wheels, but had appreciably smaller pillars and lower-sited grille opening. Just to confuse future historians, it may have been based on the prior Superfast II. It was finished in pale metallic-green and, later, silver-grey.

Just to confound enthusiasts even more, that same year saw the emergence of Superfast IV. It was purportedly the same car, just with a more conventional exposed quad-headlight arrangement and fully-exposed rear wheels, plus a change of hue to dark blue.

The dramatic Ferrari Superfast III featured retractable lights and semi-enclosed rear wheels, the Superfast IV (bottom) arriving later in 1962 with a quad-headlamp arrangement.

1962

Vignale Abarth Record Sperimentale 1000

Vignale's study in streamlining is seen here in its ultimate form. Its maker claimed it was built with record attempts in mind, and it boasted a drag coefficient of a mere 0.26Cd.

Purportedly built with speed-record attempts in mind, this wind-cheating concept car was first seen publicly at the November 1962 Turin motor show. This was a period of upheaval for Alfredo Vignale's eponymous *carrozzeria*, not least because his long-time collaborator and foil, Giovanni Michelotti, had struck out on his own. As such, Vignale wanted to create a splash; to make a statement. Alongside relatively prosaic coachbuilt variants of the Fiat 1300 and 2300 saloons was this, the Record Sperimentale 1000 which looked unlike anything else on display.

In many ways, it was a development of the Michelotti-designed, Vignale-crafted Abarth 750 Sperimentale 'Goccia' (Teardrop). A small run of these ovular machines, complete with cab-forward outlines, were made, one of which participated in the 1957 Mille Miglia. This latest variation on the theme was based on a Fiat 600D platform, although the donor car's rear-sited 767cc four-cylinder engine received a displacement hike to one-litre courtesy of Edoardo Zen's tuning firm, ZM (he later co-founded the OTAS marque alongside Franco Giannini).

With its massive wraparound windscreen, glass roof, and cropped Kamm-style tail, the Sperimentale 1000 appeared suitably left-field, and inside it was hardly conventional. Instruments were positioned in a small wooden binnacle sited at the base of the windscreen. Unusually for a record car, there was also a passenger seat, complete with a wraparound headrest (something which didn't feature on the driver's side, curiously). Behind the seats was a spare wheel/tyre.

The Abarth was seen again at the March 1963 Geneva motor show, by which time it was equipped with spats on all four wheels. It was at this juncture that Vignale claimed a drag coefficient of just 0.26Cd. However, despite the intent, and the car's name, there is no evidence to suggest that any record attempts were made.

Automobile Year Austin-Healey Firrere

It was a prototype that has long since been lost to history, but one that spawned all manner of intriguing stories of what might have been. In late 1961, the Swiss title *Automobile Year* organised a car-styling competition to mark its tenth year of publication. It was open to designers professional and amateur, and the victor or victors were to be awarded 10,000 Swiss francs. Not only that, the winning design would be translated into three-dimensional reality by Pininfarina. The brief tasked entrants with creating: 'An automobile which allows at least two people with luggage to make long journeys in all weathers with speed, comfort and safety.'

Henner Werner, Pio Manzù and Michael Conrad, all of whom were students at the Hochschule für Gestaltung (School of Design), in Ulm, West Germany, were announced as the winners at the March 1962 Geneva motor show. They conceived a long-nosed, fixed-head coupé design, their renderings being made tangible using an Austin-Healey 3000 platform as a basis. The resultant prototype was displayed at the British International Motor Show in November of that year, and other major events in Europe in 1963. The Firrere, as it was dubbed, proved a huge hit to the point that the British Motor Corporation (BMC) acquired the rights to the design.

What happened next is murky, at best, but a variation on the theme was trialled with hydrogas suspension, and there was talk of a Bentley-engined (and badged) evolutionary version being constructed, but it remained only a quarter-scale styling model. Drawings exist of a convertible version, which have been attributed to William Towns, but this only heightens the sense of ambiguity: the Midlander was a Rover employee at the time.

Mercury Palomar

Cursed with the longest rear overhang in Christendom, the Mercury Palomar's selling point was what was happening aft of the B-pillars. The rear section of the roof slid forward, in similar fashion to the Brooks Stevens-conceived Studebaker Wagonaire production car. However, the difference here was that the forward-facing third row of seats elevated concurrently, while a boat-like screen popped-up in unison. Appropriately, the car was named after the Mount Palomar Observatory, in California, which was home to the world's largest telescope.

The sole glassfibre-bodied prototype was unveiled at the 1962 Chicago Auto Show. It was then transported to the Ford Rotunda in Dearborn, which was then a major tourist attraction. However, a fire destroyed the building in November of that year. It also did for the Palomar, along with several other concept cars.

(The Chevrolet Monza GT: 92" wheelbase, 165" overall, engine displacement 145 cu. in., 6-cylinder engine featuring dual carburetors, developing 102 SAE BHP at 4400 RPM)

Monza GT sparks the imagination—AC sparks the action

Chevrolet's Monza GT, dream car of tomorrow, is sparked by today's self-cleaning AC Fire-Ring Spark Plugs. Although the car is not for sale, you can buy the spark plugs now and get tomorrow's power today. So, ask for action . . . ask for AC.

AC SPARK PLUG ⚛ THE ELECTRONICS DIVISION OF GENERAL MOTORS

FIRE-RING SPARK PLUGS

Chevrolet Monza GT

One of the most fondly recalled of 1960s concept cars from the USA, the Monza GT was a media sensation following its fleeting appearance during the Road America 500 race meeting in September 1962. According to a General Motors press release, it represented: '...part of Chevrolet's continuous programme of building and evaluating new styling and engineering ideas. While they will not be produced, we will be most interested in show visitors' reactions to them.'

However, this was only issued sometime after the car had done two sedate laps of the circuit prior to being bundled into the back of a lorry and driven away. The media were asked expressly *not* to write about the car, and the same was true when it popped up again a month later during the *Los Angeles Times* Grand Prix at Riverside, and at Watkins Glen for the US Grand Prix. It subsequently appeared at other events in late 1962, not least a spell on display at the Art Center School in California, before it was finally announced officially at the April 1963 New York International Auto Show.

This cat-and-mouse approach between GM's PR team and the global media was clearly a calculated one, and it worked brilliantly. Interest in this exotic-looking machine was white hot by the time it was unveiled in the Big Apple. Styled by Larry Shinoda, Anatole Lapine and Paul Deesen, the Monza GT was based on a Chevrolet Corvair platform that had been shortened by 381mm (15in). The donor car's air-cooled flat-six was turned through 180° and mounted ahead of the transaxle, which made for a mid-engined layout.

Sporting Motorist reported in May 1963: 'The whole car has been designed around an unconventional cockpit, as used on Bertone's special Corvair [the Testudo]... Instead of a fixed roof and two hinged doors, there is one structure comprising the roof, a windscreen which wraps right around the body sides, and the panels of what would normally be doors, and this structure hinges forwards to let passengers enter or leave the car. In the high-sided cockpit, two seats are fixed, the pedals being adjustable, as also is a telescopic, universally-jointed steering column. One can counterbalance this sort of an opening roof, but one could not open it on a wet day without letting in the rain.'

Style Auto, the Italian design title, was untypically cool about the Monza GT. It particularly disliked '...the Venetian blind' rear window, and felt: '[the designers] forgot all the technical and functional inconveniences.' Reporter Paul Sybille concluded: 'A final note about accessibility... I remember that on the car's presentation day, the mechanic on duty was obliged to unscrew and remove the steering wheel, and I am not a giant!'

A distinctive form of concealment was used for the rectangular headlamps, too. Rather than featuring pop-up 'lids', here each lamp boasted a streamlined two-piece cover: one hinged upwards, the other downwards per side as needed. They were, however, sited at an illegally low level for road use, not that there was any chance of the car ever entering even limited production. American kit-car pioneer Bill Devin, who had hitherto sold large numbers of bodyshells cribbed from an Italian Ermini design, announced plans to offer lookalikes from 1964, but they didn't enter series manufacture.

One of the great concept cars of its era, the Monza GT was a cover star the world over. It was also fully functional.

1962

Ferrari 250 GT Bertone Speciale

Sharing some styling themes previously explored on the Aston Martin DB4 GT Jet, this one-off coupé was styled by 20-something prodigy, Giorgetto Giugiaro. It followed a different Bertone Ferrari that was built at the behest of Dr Enrico Wax in 1960. Here, 250 GT SWB (chassis 3269GT) was clothed in a new body that didn't bare even trace elements of the donor car's Pinin Farina-shaped origins. Instead, Giugiaro conjured a much rounder, less bluff-fronted outline, the two 'nostril' intakes that dominated the pointed snout being a nod to the 'Sharknose' Ferrari 156 aboard which Phil Hill claimed the 1961 Formula 1 drivers' title.

First seen in marine blue at the March 1962 Geneva motor show, it went on display at the Carlo Biscaretti di Rufa Museum in Turin a month later, during its seasonal exhibition of coachbuilding. The car subsequently returned to Carrozzeria Bertone, where it was repainted in a subtle shade of silver-grey ahead of its appearance at Turin motor show in November. The car was built for studio chief Nuccio Bertone, but was soon sold. It subsequently spent 25 years as the centrepiece of the Lorenzo Zambrano car collection. Fast-forward to 2015, and it realised $16,500,000 at auction in the USA.

Oldsmobile X-215

Based on an Oldsmobile F-85, the X-215 was built to showcase the all-aluminium 3.5-litre V8 used in General Motors' line of 'compact cars'. The numerical designation signified its engine size in cubic inches, this engine having been announced in 1960 and gone into production a year later to power the Buick Skylark and Pontiac Tempest. The X-215 featured a glassfibre tonneau cover which incorporated an aerofoil/roll bar, the dashboard being designed around two large instruments, but the inclusion of a small pressure gauge acted as a clue to the fact that the car's engine was turbocharged, if only in theory.

1962

Chevrolet XP-755 (Mako Shark)

One of the great American concept cars, the XP-755 was styled by Larry Shinoda under the direction of Bill Mitchell. The outline was, to some extent, inspired by the latter's prior XP-87 racer, and featured elements that foretold the soon-to-be-released C2-series Corvette production car. The rear-end treatment, meanwhile, echoed that of the regular 1961 Corvette. The car was subsequently reworked, and appeared as the Mako Shark at the 1962 International Automobile Show that was staged at the New York Coliseum.

In this form, it lost its 'double-bubble' Lexan roof, while the bonnet and interior was also revised. The revised car's most striking feature was its graduated paintwork. Legend has it, and it's a story that has its debunkers, that the car was resprayed a number of times before Mitchell was satisfied. He had an actual mako shark stuffed and mounted on his office wall, and insisted the colours match it precisely. After several failed attempts, the design team simply repainted the shark to match the car and Mitchell, unaware of what had transpired, was satisfied. Also, some sources insist the car was based on the prior XP-700 concept car.

Unlike many other General Motors concept cars of the period, the Mako Shark (retrospectively referred to as Mako Shark I), wasn't scrapped. However, further changes were made, not least the insertion of a big-block 427cu in V8 in place of the previous small-block unit.

Constructed by legendary customiser Dean Jeffries, the Cougar 406 was unveiled at the January 1962 Chicago Auto Show. It later enjoyed a brief movie career.

Toyota Publica Sports Concept

Ford Cougar 406

Something of a curio among 1960s American styling studies, the Cougar 406 was built by a customiser from scratch, as opposed to within a styling studio. Constructed by Dean Jeffries at Ford's behest, it was an original design, rather than an adapted production car. Unveiled at the January 1962 Chicago Auto Show, this gullwing-doored GT followed on from the first Cougar design study from 1956, which remained only a model. The '406' part of the nomenclature referred to its 406cu in V8 engine.

Strangely, the design appeared dated even by 1962 standards. Nevertheless, it more than earned its keep. In 1963, the original metallic-blue hue made way for a Candy Apple Red makeover ahead of its appearance in the Jack Lemmon movie, *Under the Yum Tree*. In 1964, the car formed part of Ford's Custom Caravan programme, which toured automotive events in a bid to tap the nascent hot rod-influenced youth market.

Derived from the Publica production car, which went on sale in 1961, the Publica Sports Concept was unveiled at the following year's Tokyo Motor Show. The car's most unusual feature was its roof arrangement: the entire upper glasshouse slid rearwards on rails. There were no doors, so occupants were obliged to step over the sides and thread their way into the cockpit. In many ways, the outline foretold the Sports 800 which went on sale in 1965, although the novel roof arrangement didn't make the transition from concept to production reality.

1962

Chevrolet Corvair XP-785 Super Spyder

One of racier concept cars based on the Chevrolet Corvair, the Super Spyder was built on a shortened platform which resulted in an overall length of 4,394mm (173in) and a 2,362mm (93in) wheelbase. The front-end was markedly more aggressive-looking than the Corvair, while the one-piece fly-screen and glassfibre tonneau cover, complete with a sports-racer-style headrest, offered the requisite competition-inspired reference points. *Road & Track's* John R. Bond reported in period: 'The pointed-nose, sculptured effect of the newest show car may be a preview of the 1963 Corvair. I hope not.'

Detroit players led the concept car league tables when it came to churning them out at a dizzying rate. Nevertheless, the Italian styling houses weren't far behind, with Pininfarina in particular being nothing if not prolific. This was also the year that a small start-up operation produced the first mid-engined supercar as we know it, even if the ATS 2500 GT proved a flop. Elsewhere, small concerns René Bonnet and Deep Sanderson also blazed trails by offering mid-engined cars for public consumption.

Curiously, this was the year that saw concept cars from the USA take a turn for the sensible, all things being relative, with concepts often being based on existing production models. Either that, or they released 'teasers' for models that were soon to be introduced.

Also in 1963
President John F. Kennedy is assassinated in Dallas, Texas.
John Profumo resigns from the UK government following an affair with Christine Keeler.
The Great Train Robbery takes place in Buckinghamshire.
Martin Luther King delivers his 'I have a dream' speech.
The first-ever episode of BBC sci-fi series *Doctor Who* is broadcast.

Pininfarina Rondine

It is a car that continues to polarise opinion. The Rondine – pronounced Ron-din-ay – was a design study produced by Pininfarina for the 1963 Paris motor show, which could not have appeared further removed from the car that bore it – a C2-series Chevrolet Corvette. While not conceived with mass manufacture in mind, it eventually spawned a mainstream production car. It is just that it wasn't American.

Who, precisely, envisioned the car is lost in the mists of time, but the man responsible for shaping this bold coupé was Tom Tjaarda. The Michigan-born émigré produced a dramatic outline with a long rear overhang, the roofline initially comprising an inward-slanting rear window with the roof 'chopped' behind the B-pillar. It appeared with this controversial styling treatment when unveiled in Paris, but was subsequently reworked to incorporate a more conventional-looking wraparound rear glasshouse.

As to who actually bodied the car in steel, this too is mired in conflicting reports and conjecture. It is widely assumed that Pininfarina built the car internally, but some company insiders from the period claimed it was shaped by Ferrari's chosen metal-wielder, Sergio Scaglietti. This famous artisan had form when it came to reworking Corvettes, having previously bodied a small run of C1-generation cars at the end of the previous decade for a group of dealer-racers that included Carroll Shelby and Jim Hall.

The Rondine was, for the most part, met with muted praise by the motoring media following its unveiling, and its time on the show circuit proved fleeting. Nevertheless, it impressed Fiat insiders who tasked Pininfarina – and Tjaarda – with reworking Rondine styling themes onto a smaller canvas for what, in time, became the 124 Spider. Tjaarda, however, had departed for his second stint at Ghia by the time the finished item emerged at the 1966 Turin motor show, although he was pleasantly surprised that it remained faithful to his renderings.

Pininfarina Lancia Flaminia 3C 2.8 Coupé Speciale 2 Posti

Styled by Tom Tjaarda, this handsome coupé emerged at the 1963 Turin motor show. The nose featured a large grille flanked by twin headlights per side. The svelte roofline and slender A- and C-pillars, not to mention the lack of B-pillars, afforded it a graceful profile, the rear end boasting

perhaps the most striking element of the design: flush-fitting, trapezoidal tail-lights. Finished in mother-of-pearl white, chrome sill plates provided the finishing touch. Beneath the skin, however, the running gear was standard Flaminia, including the recently-introduced 2.8-litre version of Lancia's enduring narrow-angle V6.

A year later, the car was displayed again in Turin, by which time it had undergone minor upgrades plus a change of hue to 'metallic sand'. Further modifications were made subsequently in a bid to render it road-legal, the most obvious change being the adoption of regular Lancia Flavia rear lamps. The car was then repainted again, this time in silver, before it was pressed into use by studio principal Battista Pininfarina. It replaced the sublime Lancia Florida II which had served him faithfully for seven years. He retained the car until his death in 1966.

1963

Fiat 2300 Cabriolet Speciale Pininfarina

As was typical of the era, this 1963 Geneva motor show star may have been rooted in a prior concept car; in this instance, the previous year's Fiat 2300 Coupé Speciale. The styling has been attributed to Tom Tjaarda, the low-sited quad-headlight arrangement and 'eggcrate' grille being all new, while the roof now incorporated a Targa-style lift-out panel. However, the vestigial rear buttresses and tail-light treatment, not to mention the crease down the flanks, were near identical to the earlier car.

Up-and-coming stylist Pio Manzù critiqued the design for *Style Auto* in period, and labelled it an '...evolution of the coupé presented in Turin'. *Road & Track* considered it to be: '...very coupe-de-ville with a windscreen that moves forward when you get in [sic], this is ideal for taking Bridget Bardot to the movies without messing up her "choucrotte" hairdo or showing her knees...'

Fiat 2300 Coupé Speciale Lausanne

The Tom Tjaarda-styled 'Lausanne' was named in honour of the Swiss Confederation. It is widely held that it was a remodelled version of the Fiat 2300 Cabriolet Speciale Pininfarina, the biggest amendments being a fixed roof in place of the previous Targa-style arrangement. The rear end was also given a makeover, the ovular tail-light clusters being markedly smaller. While created in 1963, the car went on display in the following year's National Exhibition in Lausanne. It was also used during the opening ceremony of the Great St-Bernard Tunnel in March 1964.

Chevrolet Corvair Monza SS

While ostensibly similar to the previous year's well-received Monza GT, the Monza SS was perhaps more conventional beneath the skin. Similarly based on a shortened Chevrolet Corvair platform, here the flat-six engine remained in situ behind the transaxle, rather than sited amidships. As with the GT, the smooth styling has been attributed to Larry Shinoda, the cabin featuring fixed bucket seats with adjustable pedals, the driver peering through a frameless full-width aero screen. It also boasted doors in place of its forebear's one-piece lift-up canopy.

Unveiled at the April 1963 New York International Auto Show, the car was met with praise from most quarters. Even *Road & Track*, a magazine that tended to withhold affection for homegrown fare in period, was highly effusive. However, it disliked the headlight treatment, stating: '[It's a] styling gimmick that looks great when the doors are closed and the lights are hidden from view, but with the doors open, the sleek front-end configuration is relegated to something out of *The Beast From 20,000 Fathoms*.'

While clearly rooted in the prior Monza GT, the open-top Monza SS was more conventional beneath the skin. It also boasted regular doors rather than a canopy.

Bertone Testudo

In many ways, the Testudo was among the most important concept cars to emerge during the early 1960s. Based upon a truncated Chevrolet Corvair platform, complete with a rear-sited 2,372cc, air-cooled six-cylinder engine, it marked the emergence of its chief designer, Giorgetto Giugiaro, as a trendsetter. 'I wanted to give something of myself, from my mind alone; [to prove] that I was no longer following a chain, following other ideas,' he told *Automobile Quarterly*. 'With the Testudo, I proved to myself that I was able to break with the past and begin with something coming from my own imagination. I believe it was a radically new kind of car, a new concept. In my opinion, it seemed to provide a new source for car designs. That was a car with which I felt I contributed to car designing.'

The name, a literal translation meaning 'turtle', was chosen to symbolise the design theme. A sharp crease ran along each flank, dividing the body, with the radically glazed 'bubble roof' being more akin to Stateside custom cars from the likes of Ed Roth or Bill Cushenbery. The canopy hinged forward for access to the cabin with its equally wild rectangular steering 'wheel'. Work began on 3 January 1963 and, just to emphasise the speed with which the Turinese *carrozzeria* could turn out a new car, it was completed in time for March's Geneva motor show. What's more, studio chief Nuccio Bertone drove it to Switzerland.

Reaction to this 1,059mm (41.7in)-high device was largely positive, although *Road & Track* labelled it 'awkward' before railing against its: 'grilled-flounder-eye headlights pointing straight up that would be next to no use.' And while no replicas would be forthcoming, many cues were transposed intact on to the Lamborghini Miura, while Anatole Lapine admitted to being influenced by the car when he shaped the Porsche 928.

As for the sole prototype, it suffered severe rear-end damage during a promotional shoot for Shell. It was subsequently put into storage, where it remained until the early 1990s when newly incumbent chief designer Luciano d'Ambrosio initiated the car's restoration.

In an agreeable twist to the story, Giugiaro had long since wanted to own the Testudo. He had driven the car back from Geneva following its show debut, and later used it as his wedding car. Accordingly, the Testudo had great sentimental value. After leaving Bertone in late 1965, his attempts at acquiring the car had been rebuffed. He finally got his chance during RM Auctions' sale of Bertone concept cars in May 2011. He paid 336,000 euros for the privilege.

Styled by a youthful Giorgetto Giugiaro, the Testudo was driven from Turin to Geneva by studio chief Nuccio Bertone ahead of its public debut in March 1963.

1963

Prince 1900 Sprint

One of the great Italian car designers, Franco Scaglione's talents have perhaps only been fully appreciated in retrospect. The Florentine's resume included a string of jaw-slackening designs for Bertone during the 1950s, not least the trio of Alfa Romeo BAT styling studies. However, the car pictured here is not one of his better-known offerings. Produced for Japan's Prince brand, a firm then best known for its Skyline model line that would latterly wear Nissan badging, this lithe coupé was displayed at the 1963 Tokyo Auto Show.

Scaglione, by now a freelance designer, mapped out a streamlined silhouette for the Skyline platform. Power came from an 1,892cc OHV four-cylinder unit from Prince's larger Gloria saloon that was tuned to develop 63bhp at 4,800rpm. According to Prince, it weighed just 850kg (1,874lb). *Motor* reported in period: 'The maker rather hopefully claimed its top speed to be 112mph, but there seems no possibility of going into production with it.'

Nor was there any intention to. However, it should be stressed that while Scaglione mapped out the car's striking outline, it was left to his former understudy, Takeshi Inoue, to refine the design. Also, distinct from many other prototypes of the period attributed to Italian styling houses and *carrozzerie*, the one-off Sprint was constructed in Japan.

Mapped out by the brilliant Franco Scaglione, whose resume also included the Bertone 'B.A.T.' Alfa Romeo show cars, this shapely one-off was nevertheless completed by Takeshi Inoue.

Dodge Charger Concept (aka Charger I)

Created at the advent of the muscle-car movement, the Charger Concept (retrospectively known as Charger I) was based on a humdrum Dodge Polara production model. It was created to promote the new high-performance 426cu in 'Hemi' V8 engine, the donor car being denuded of unnecessary addenda. The passenger compartment, meanwhile, incorporated a wraparound fly-screen, integral headrest and roll-over bar, plus a central divider. The cabin incorporated well-padded bucket seats, a wood-rim steering wheel and a standard Polara instrument binnacle, but with the addition of a substantially-sized Stewart-Warner revcounter.

Strictly a two-seater, this menacing-looking machine was just 1,219mm (48in) at its highest point, specially-made Halibrand wheels providing the finishing touch. Director of styling Elwood Engel said in period: 'Our design gives this specialty car a youthful, "get-up-and-go", appearance which reflects the Dodge image as an all-out, dependable performer.' While ostensibly a 1964 concept car, it was first seen at the Milwaukee Auto Show in November 1963. Also, despite supposedly being built to plug the new 426cu in V8, none was available when it was constructed, so it had to 'make do' with a regular 383cu in unit.

Ford Allegro I & II

The Allegro I was a product of the Lee Iacocca-instituted Fairlane Committee. In 1960, the Ford Motor Company was keen to promote a more youthful image; to tap into the nascent 'Baby Boomer' market. The Chevrolet Corvair Monza was used as a benchmark, and the advanced design studio run under Bob Maguire was tasked with creating a four-seater fastback based on a Falcon platform. The team toiled away from late 1961 and into mid-1962, the finished article appearing resplendent in a metallic gold hue. It was a hatchback, too, an unusual feature being the rear-facing rear seats. These were later changed to front-facing items.

As to who actually styled the car, that depends on whose estimates you credit. According to Randy Leffingwell's *Mustang: Forty Years*, it was Maguire's work. Other texts credit Gene Bordinat and Don DeLaRossa, the latter being perhaps better known for his work with the Lincoln sister brand. It should also be pointed out that while the car was dubbed Allegro publicly, it had previously gone by the titles 'Avventura' and 'Avanti', if only within Ford.

A press release from 1963 stated: '[The Allegro symbolises] sleekness, motion and, as its name indicates, brisk and lively performance. The Allegro is distinguished by a long hood, compact passenger compartment and fastback roofline with grille wastegates in the fender area.' If anything, the rear styling treatment was closer to contemporary Thunderbirds, while it offered pointers to the first-generation Mustang, albeit via the Mustang II concept car and umpteen studio mock-ups. What's more, a second Allegro coupe – this time a glassfibre 'mule' painted in a fetching shade of ruby red – appeared in a promotional film that accompanied the Mustang's launch in 1964.

That should have been the end of the story. However, in 1967 the original show car was disinterred and reconfigured as the Allegro II. The fastback roof was sliced off, with a wraparound fly-screen connecting with rear buttresses. The rear-end was also heavily reworked. It, too, was painted gold, but this time it also boasted green go-faster stripes and magnesium wheels. It's hard to point out any styling features that subsequently filtered down into other Fords, but the headlight and grille arrangement appeared similar to that found on the '1970½' Chevrolet Camaro.

The Allegro was known by other names, if only internally. The car was reconfigured in 1967, the roof being removed along the way, before it reappeared as the Allegro II.

1963

Ford Mustang II

While very much a show car, the Mustang II was close stylistically to the soon-to-be-released Mustang production model. First seen publicly during the October 1963 US Grand Prix meeting at Watkins Glen, the car was similarly based on a Ford Falcon floorpan, and powered by a 289cu in V8 engine taken from a Ford Fairlane. The prototype – referred to internally as 'Cougar' or by the less-memorable designation 'X 8902-SB-208' – was built by Dearborn Steel Tubing. The car's steel body emerged 127mm (5in) longer and 76mm (3in) lower than the eventual production Mustang, while glassfibre was used for some of the front and rear panels, in addition to the detachable roof.

The firm's vice president Lee Iacocca said at the time of its unveiling: 'Our preliminary studies indicate that a car of this type could be built in this country to sell at a price of under $3000.' When the production model went on sale in April 1964, it caused a furore and became the fastest-selling car in history. Despite its relatively short career on the show circuit, the Mustang II survived the chop by dint of Ford's R&D department requesting it be used as a test mule. It was donated to the Detroit Historical Society in 1975 and remains in its keep.

The Mustang II appeared close stylistically to the soon-to-be-released Mustang production model which caused a furore when it went on sale in 1964. This show car still survives.

Oldsmobile J-TR

Concept cars come and go, with only a few earning legendary status. The example pictured here wasn't among their number, but it wasn't without influence. The narrative stretches back to 1961, when General Motors shuttered its much-hyped Motorama travelling motor shows. This also resulted in far fewer one-off flights of fantasy being made by the biggest of Detroit's 'Big Three'. Greater emphasis would henceforth be placed on presenting cars that foretold what would be appearing in showrooms in a few years' time, rather than in another half-a-century. The Oldsmobile J-TR was one such offering.

While based on a standard F-85 convertible, it received a makeover under the watchful eye of GM's styling czar, Bill Mitchell. Distinct from the production model, the J-TR boasted slender front quarter-bumpers, and a minimalist grille, complete with rectangular headlights (French Cibié items). Simple 'racing' stripes were added to the bonnet and flanks, the sill rocker panels featuring faux louvres and stainless-steel exhaust outlets (non-functioning, naturally). The quarter-bumper theme was echoed at the rear, while the tail-light clusters were recessed. The wheels were elaborately cast alloy items with knockoff hubs, the wheel arches having been widened ever so slightly, while the paint was a striking shade of metallic Firefrost Silver.

Inside, the cabin was even more outré than the exterior, with a specially-made instrument panel which housed four circular gauges in place of the rectangular items of the standard F-85. Then there were brushed-aluminium door cards and leather upholstery, a wood-rim Nardi steering wheel, four bucket seats and a 'full-length floor console'. As for the running gear, therein lies a mystery. The PR material hinted that it had a turbocharged, all-aluminium Jetfire V8, but without explicitly admitting as much. No performance figures were proffered.

The J-TR was unveiled at the February 1963 Chicago Auto Show. Two months later, it was displayed at the New York International Motor Show where it shared the stage at the Coliseum with the reigning Miss America, Jackie Mayer. As to what happened to the J-TR subsequently, unsubstantiated rumours suggest that Mitchell used the car for a spell. This isn't a fanciful hypothesis given that he enjoyed 'borrowing' several GM concept cars. However, it is widely held in marque circles that the J-TR and the other Oldsmobile show queens from 1963 were destroyed once they were of no further use.

Based on a standard Oldsmobile F-85 convertible, the J-TR nevertheless had a distinctive look of its own. It purportedly employed a turbocharged small-displacement V8 engine.

1963

Oldsmobile El Torero

First seen publicly at the February 1963 Chicago Auto Show, the El Torero received significantly less media coverage than the J-TR parked nearby. Based on a seventh-generation Ninety-Eight production model, it was essentially a factory 'custom car', changes over the regular production model comprising little more than a glossy paintjob (several shades of Firefrost Gold that was employed on various iterations of limited-edition Hurst Oldsmobiles from the end of the 1960s), and a retrimmed interior. The name El Torero signified 'Bullfighter' in English, and a Spanish theme was employed throughout, hence the use of gaudy gold-brocade door cards, and red-satin striping used to accentuate the white contoured bucket seats.

Michelotti Jaguar D-type

Giovanni Michelotti was the most prolific car designer of all time, this custom-bodied Jaguar being among his finest-ever work. In 1960, he reclothed this ex-Equipe Los Amigos 'short-nose' Jaguar D-type, which had finished third in the Le Mans 24 Hours three years earlier. Unfortunately, one of its drivers, Jean-Marie Brussin (racing as 'Mary'), crashed fatally during the 1958 running of the endurance classic (he remains the only Jaguar driver ever to perish at Le Mans). The precise backstory behind how the car found its way to Turin remains a source of debate among historians. That, and why the reworked D-type didn't emerge until the 1963 Geneva motor show.

Reaction to the car was overwhelmingly positive, though, with *Road & Track* commenting: 'The celebrated Michelotti, appearing under his own name for a change, brought an extremely interesting coupé on a Jaguar D-type chassis which, of course, would do for the E-type as well. Rather less bulbous than the factory Jag, it resembles more the late-lamented BMW 507 sports with an overbite grille and definite dip at the waistline.' With an air of predictability, this one-of-a-kind Jaguar was robbed of its racing-car componentry during the 1970s.

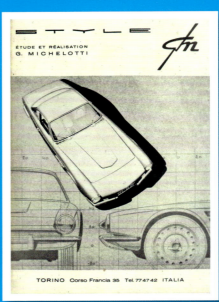

Michelotti's enigmatic – and strikingly attractive – Jaguar coupé was based on a crash damaged D-type. E-type running gear was substituted subsequently.

Ghia G230 S

Arguably the most prolific Italian design house and coachbuilder of the late 1950s and early 1960s, Ghia was also a marque in its own right. The G230 S could, conceivably, have become a production model, too, had fate been kinder. However, in a roundabout way it inspired another that did make the leap from prototype to small-series manufacture. Also, distinct from other, ostensibly, similar cars based on the Fiat 2300 S (itself, a Ghia design), the G230 S represented more than just a rebodying exercise.

Ghia turned to Gioacchino Colombo to create a tubular chassis to accommodate the proprietary running gear. Perhaps better known for acting as a subcontractor to Ferrari and Maserati, and for his pioneering kart racers, Colombo also manufactured chassis frames for the Ghia 1500 GT coupé which was then on sale. The G230 S prototype's engine purportedly employed Abarth tuning gear, and the car was bodied in steel. Reaction following its unveiling at the November 1963 Turin motor show was overwhelmingly positive. American trucking magnate Gene Casaroll – who had previously bankrolled the ultra-exotic Dual Ghia production cars – allegedly attempted to order 200 cars on the spot.

The veracity of this story is open to debate. What is clear is that at least one further coupé was made, the Sergio Sartorelli-penned outline being fine-tuned, a marginally lower roofline being among the changes. Convertible variants were also completed. Neither version made the leap to production-car reality, but the appearance of one of the prototypes on the cover of *Road & Track* in March 1965 led to an unforeseen outcome. American Burt Sugarman was so enamoured, he subsequently charged Ghia with refining the concept and adapting the outline of the convertible version to accommodate Plymouth Barracuda componentry. As many as 57 V8-engined Ghia 450/SS roadsters were made.

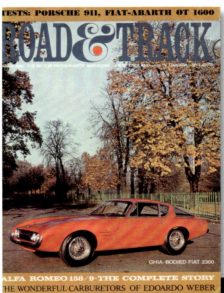

Distinct from other Fiat 2300-based show cars, Ghia's take featured a bespoke chassis. It later inspired the small-series Plymouth-based, V8-engined Ghia 450/SS.

1963

Chrysler Corporation Turbine Car

Born at a time of brave engineering optimism, the snappily-titled Chrysler Corporation Turbine Car was the culmination of more than fifteen years' development work. The firm's gas-turbine programme began during World War II amid much scepticism, and a raft of prototypes followed; some were seen publicly, others were developed in secret. In 1962, Chrysler stunned the global motoring media when it stated that it would build as many as 75 turbine cars that would be loaned to 'typical motorists', who would drive them for three months in return for maintaining detailed records.

It fell to Ghia to produce the monocoque body structures at a rumoured cost of $300,000 apiece, to a design by Elwood Engel. The Turbine Car was announced at the New York International Auto Show on 14 May 1963, and fifty were made. All were painted in Turbine Bronze with a black vinyl roof, although a further five prototypes were made. One of these was painted white with a racy livery for its appearance in the film The Lively Set, and was later used by designer/engineer Giovanni Savonuzzi.

The turbine powerplant featured a fifth as many components as a typical piston engine – 60 rather 300 – and generated 130bhp and an instant 425lb ft of torque at stall speed. This ensured that it was good for 0–60mph in 12sec at an ambient temperature of 85°F. More than 1.1 million test miles were accumulated, but the media wasn't altogether impressed. Autocar's technical editor Harry Mundy described the acceleration as being: '...decidedly inferior to that of a 1.5-litre piston-engined saloon,' and concluded his report by saying: '...there is much yet to be done on the turbine to make it an acceptable power-unit for production cars; as yet it is too expensive, too thirsty, and too bulky with its necessary ancillary equipment.'

Joseph Lowrey, technical contributor to Sporting Motorist, was similarly unimpressed. He wrote: 'To summarise the situation, as a technical tour de force the Chrysler gas turbine is outstanding and thoroughly praiseworthy. But, without taking into account such factors as servicing, maintenance, fuel costs and so forth, it nevertheless seems to have nothing to offer that is not provided in greater measure by a refined piston-engined car.'

Regardless of the reviews, Chrysler planned to build a dedicated turbine car with a dramatic fastback outline penned by – or under the direction of – Engel. Then the plans to commercialise the turbine programme were abruptly cancelled due, in part, to new government emissions regulations which came into force under the Clean Air Act. Aside from anything else, Chrysler needed its brightest and best to get the company's piston engines to comply. That didn't mark the end of Chrysler's experiments with this alternative method of propulsion, but it received markedly less promotion in later years. As to the fate of the Turbine Cars, 45 were scrapped during the winter of 1967.

Unlike most concept queens, the Turbine Car was built in relatively large numbers. However, all were essentially mobile testbeds and the majority were later consigned to the scrapyard.

Vignale New Star Jet

One of the more mysterious concept cars, the New Star Jet emerged at the 1963 Turin motor show. *Auto Italiana* was one of few titles to write about the newcomer, its report stating: '[The] star attraction here is a *monoposto* racing car called the New Star Jet, with a very pointed Perspex snout and a lift-up canopy hood in the same material. The suspension parts have been beautifully machined by Maserati, and the rear section of the car is wide enough to take the transversely-mounted vee-12 1.5-litre engine and integral transmission which the same company has in an advanced state of development.'

Sporting Motorist, by contrast, was less enthusiastic, stating: 'Vignale gave his idea of a modern racing car. The driver is completely enclosed – and how does the poor fellow see where he is going?' The engineless prototype never received the proposed Maserati engine, not least because such a unit never existed, and the New Star Jet was not seen again publicly.

1963

Pininfarina Sigma

Declared '...the safest car in the world' at the 1963 International Traffic Exhibition, the Sigma spread the safety-first mantra across the globe for the next four years. Devised by Italy's *Quattroruote* magazine, and constructed by Pininfarina, it was rapturously received by the mainstream media. The distinctive outline was partially the work of Tom Tjaarda (he claimed it was his fore of the windscreen), *Style Auto* reporting in period: 'The fluid, rounded lines of the Sigma are new but in keeping with the Pininfarina style. The shell of the cockpit is protected by a graduated resistance structure capable of absorbing the crash impact by deforming gradually. One notes on the bodywork the absence of any projections and the wide frontal surface with the rubber-covered bumpers.'

On sliding back the driver's door, the cabin comprised four deep bucket seats plus a padded dashboard and steering wheel. The windscreen and rear windows were also 'ejectable'. Unveiled at the 1963 Turin motor show, the Sigma was labelled 'sensible' by *Road & Track*, which also likened it to 'spinach' in that it was an acquired taste. *Sporting Motorist,* meanwhile, labelled it: '[The] most interesting car of the show.'

Studebaker Spectre

One of the great what-might-have-been stories of the post-war American motor industry, the Spectre was shaped within the Brooks Stevens Studio in Milwaukee, Wisconsin. It was one of several proposals put before the Studebaker board in the spring of 1963, and represented his idea for a replacement model for the Gran Turismo Hawk (another Stevens product). The prototype was constructed by Sibona & Basano, the Turinese minnow charging $16,000 for the privilege. The car's styling was clean and understated in profile, but the front-end represented pure Jet-Set theatre thanks to its 'electric-razor' grille and Sylvania Light Bar system of illumination. However, there was never any serious danger of the outline being adopted for production, even in watered-down form, thanks to Studebaker's parlous financial state.

By way of a footnote, the Raymond Loewy/William Snaith Studio also pitched notchback coupé and fastback iterations of the Studebaker Avanti, with John Ebstein, Bob Andrews and Ron Kellogg producing outlines that were transformed into three-dimensional reality by Pichon-Parat in Paris. Neither model was adopted for production, although both steel-bodied prototypes still exist.

Japan looked to Italy for styling inspiration for much of the 1960s. The 800 Sport was styled by Giovanni Michelotti and Alfredo Zanzellato and built by Carrozzeria Vignale.

Daihatsu 800 Sport Spider

Alfredo Vignale and Giovanni Michelotti collaborated on a raft of design studies for Daihatsu Industry of Osaka, including sports cars, light commercial vehicles, and a four-door saloon which, in time, became the Compagno production car. A coupé and roadster on the same foundations as the Compagno were also built, the Sport Spider being exhibited at the 1963 Turin motor show. Styled by Michelotti, with input from Alfredo Zanzellato, the 797cc, four-cylinder machine was displayed in a standalone exhibit in the main hall, complete with the pagoda roof and doors made of rice paper. Both variants remained unique.

Italian designers and styling houses continued to be in the ascendent, 1964 seeing the release of an array of concept cars. These spanned everything from tiny commuter capsules to elegant GTs with competition-rooted underpinnings. Mainstream manufacturers continued to beat a path to their door, with emerging Japanese brands in particular tapping their expertise as they attempted to find a foothold on the global stage.

This was also the year in which Detroit players continued to produce a raft of show stoppers. These similarly spanned shopping cars to supercars. In addition, independent manufacturers went to the wall while the neo-classic emerged as a sub-species of luxury automobile. This was also the period in which marque revivals entered the lexicon of automotive writers.

Also in 1964
British actors Richard Burton and Elizabeth Taylor marry.
The Queen opens the Forth Road Bridge connecting Edinburgh to Fife.
The final execution under the death penalty takes place in the UK.
The Civil Rights Act of 1964 becomes law in the US, ending legal racial discrimination.
Fights break out at British seaside resorts over Easter and Whitsun between Mods and Rockers.

1964

Ghia Ford Falcon Clan

The 1960s witnessed the emergence of a particular subspecies of Ford, both European and American. Italian designers and coachbuilders were employed to rework mainstream models to suit the home market, with everything from the Anglia and Taunus models being sold with different bodywork to those found in neighbouring countries. The Ford Falcon might have joined their number had fate been kinder, even if the exact story behind the creation of the Clan prototype is clouded in conjecture.

Scroll back to the early-to-mid-1960s, and Carrozzeria Ghia was the coachbuilder of choice for US manufacturers. However, following the sudden death of its entrepreneurial boss Luigi Segre in 1963, commissions from Detroit evaporated amid rumours of 'creative accounting' from the Italian side. It was against this backdrop that the firm found itself newly owned by the son of a reviled Dominican dictator, who had zero interest in Ghia, save for its artistes designing wine labels for his vineyard. The company was scrabbling, and at the 1964 Turin motor show it unveiled the Falcon Clan, ostensibly at the behest of the Italian Ford importer.

This is debatable, however. Ghia's new principal, Gino Rovere, had previously been a highly influential Ford distributor in Italy, so it may just as easily have been a case of him testing the waters in the hope that the Ford concessionaire would bite. Based on an unmodified Falcon Sprint platform, complete with 260cu in (4,261cc) V8, the new outline was styled by Sergio Sartorelli, who also penned the locally-made (by OSI) Ford Anglia 105E-based Torino. Distinct from the car that bore it, the Clan was a fastback/hatchback crossover.

According to *Quattroruote* magazine's show report: '[The Clan] has four seats and a fastback under which the luggage is housed. It is claimed to combine the advantages of a fast sports saloon with the large carrying capacity of an estate car, but the problems of providing good road-holding and handling at the two extremes of load might be formidable with orthodox suspension systems.'

The coachbuilder's press release, complete with random capitalisation, stated not altogether coherently: 'GHIA's duty in this circumstance was to enhance such full performances with their traditional creative hability [sic] in bestowing to the CLAN a perfect equilibrium of lines, harmony and luxurious elegance. In its luminous, unobjectionably finished interior, five passengers can leisurely take place on seats equipped with safety belts and, by reclining the rear seat backs, a large flat compartment is obtained, permitting to carry a lot of additional luggage and miscallenous [sic] sport equipment. By opening its tailgate nearly even with the roof, it offers an extra loading plan on top.'

1964

GENEVA: NEW CARS AT 1965's FIRST SALON

ROAD & TRACK

JUNE 1965 THE MOTOR ENTHUSIASTS' MAGAZINE 3/6 IN ENGLAND 60¢ IN CANADA 50 CENTS

Carrozzeria Bertone – Master of the Italian Style

Alfa Romeo Canguro
(aka Bertone Giulia 1600 Tubolare)

One of the great Alfa Romeo design studies, the Canguro was unveiled at the 1964 Paris motor show and entered into legend immediately. Styled by Giorgetto Giugiaro, and based on an Edo Manzoni-designed TZ (Tubulare Zagato) platform, the car's debut marked the first time that Bertone had exhibited in the French capital. Described in *Road & Track*'s event report as being 'lovely' and 'wildly packaged,' it sadly – and inevitably – remained a one-off.

On the small side of pert, the Canguro (Italian for Kangaroo) was just 1,060mm (41.7in) high, 1,600mm (63in) wide, and 3,900mm (153.5in) long. The glassfibre-bodied GT weighed just 650kg (1,433lb), and was powered by a 1,570cc twin-cam four-cylinder unit from the 105-series Alfa Romeo Giulia Ti. In a subsequent cover feature on the car, *Road & Track* reported: 'The car is obviously an exercise in cleaning up and civilising the concept behind the very spartan, very rapid and successful, Alfa Romeo Zagato GTZ [sic]. The Canguro weighs about the same as the Zagato, is slightly shorter and wider, but is a whole 6in lower... Improving the Tubulare's aerodynamic penetration was one of Bertone's goals here, and it would seem they have accomplished that well.'

Style Auto devoted nine pages to the car in period, and predictably its report was peppered with design speak. 'Bertone's Canguro is a car which derives its harmonious sense of lightness mainly from the general style and continuity of design,' it gushed. 'The stylist's personality emerges in the sleek line combined with the unmistakable impression of power and aggressiveness... The longitudinal rhythm of volumes is sustained by the controlled fluidity of the beltline. The profile, lowered to its limits, visually emphasises the qualities of road-holding and aerodynamic penetration.'

It went on to add: '...one wonders why Bertone has decided not to adopt avant-garde solutions such as a rear engine, which would obviously allow a higher performance.

The sublime Alfa Romeo 'Kangaroo' was styled by Giorgetto Giugiaro while employed by Stile Bertone. Sadly, tragically even, it remained unique.

The reply is equally obvious: the Tubolare must be substantially close, mechanically, to the series Giulia Ti, just to prove to the public how valuable are competition experiments for mass production. The Tubolare takes ninety percent of its mechanical elements from the Ti.... The final detail of Bertone's recent creation is the decorative functional use of the Alfa competition emblem. The four-leaved clover motif has, in fact, been used to characterise an air duct outlet which regulates air exit, and is located on the body side panel in the area between the door and rear windows. This was also a functional necessity (to ventilate the cockpit without opening the windows) that assumes special value on a car born to race.'

However, despite the car's motorsport-rooted foundations, the Canguro was not built with circuit use in mind. However, it did venture trackside at Monza for a promotional film for petroleum giant, Shell. This one-of-a-kind Alfa Romeo collided with the Bertone Testudo at the Parabolica corner and was extensively damaged. The remains were left to fester behind the Bertone factory in Grugliasco, near Turin, although decades later the car was restored ahead of a triumphant appearance at the 2005 Ville d'Este Concours d'Elegance, where it claimed Best of Show honours.

1964

Ghia V280

A degree of confusion surrounds who designed this oddly-proportioned coupé, and the identity of those who commissioned its construction. Chrysler styling czar Virgil Exner has been cited in some quarters as having penned the car, but he had left the firm's employ long before the V280 was seen at the Paris and Turin motor shows in late 1964. Some historians suggest that it was conceived by Ghia's buccaneering boss, Luigi Segre; that he had hoped to entice Chrysler into backing a small run of replicas as 'halo products'. That would make sense but for one thing: Segre died in early 1963.

There is another possibility, though. *Road & Track* wrote an editorial in early 1964 suggesting that Chrysler was keen to manufacture a version of the Valiant attuned to European tastes, possibly in France via Simca. This could, conceivably, have been a toe-in-the-water exercise for such a project. In its Paris show report, the same title described the car as being: '...a somewhat lumpy looking Plymouth Valiant in a depressing shade of plum (why don't they try red?).' The one and only V280 was exported to the USA once its brief show career came to an end.

The Ghia V280 could, conceivably, have inspired a Simca production car, but this is open to conjecture. The lone prototype later headed Stateside.

Ghia Renault 8 Sports Coupé

One of the more obscure concept cars of the mid-1960s, this Ghia offering was the first vehicle designed in its entirety by ex-Michelotti protégé, Fillipo Sapino. Work began on this Renault 8-based two-seater in 1963, although it wasn't seen publicly until the November 1964 Turin motor show. Distinct from most other show cars of the period, stylistically this one-off coupé was anything but starry-eyed. As Henry Manney reported in *Road & Track*: '[It was] the chef d'oeuvre, a blue short-chassis coupe based on the Renault R-8 which is planned to house the Gordini engine. Sophisticated in its contours, the design takes one back most curiously to pre- and immediately post-war Paris shows as it recalled the magnificent Art Nouveau Saoutchik and Figoni bodies on Talbots, Bugattis, Delages et al. Whether Ghia carried it off is up to you, but at least the designers tried something different.'

Mercedes-Benz 230SL Speciale

Pininfarina had successfully reworked Mercedes-Benz production cars as far back as 1955 when it created the 300 Coupé Speciale. That, and the 300B Berlina Speciale 2 Porte and 300S Coupé Speciale, which both emerged a year later. In May 1963, the Turin styling house contacted the Stuttgart firm with a view to producing its own take on the 230SL that had been introduced only two years previously at the Geneva motor show. The German management acquiesced and it fell to Tom Tjaarda to create an Italianate interpretation of the Paul Bracq-styled original.

While the donor car's headlight arrangement was retained, the familiar grille was raked more acutely, while the 'Pagoda roof' was done away with in its entirety. The new roofline, along with the more bulbous wings, lent it a softer, more curvaceous silhouette, the rear-end echoing themes explored on the forthcoming Ferrari 330GT 2+2 (another Tjaarda creation). The results were shown at the Paris and Turin motor show in 1964, with the media being, for the most part, apathetic towards the newcomer.

Style Auto reported: '...the Mercedes 230SL by Pininfarina was received rather coolly by the Italian specialised press... To create a new body from scratch can be easier than to interpret with personal style one already in existence. It is not the first time this great Italian coachbuilder has refused to showily clothe as wealthy clients would like, cars which are famous and traditionally affirmed by virtue of their formal outlines... In the case of the 230SL, the stylist wanted to go to the extent of recreating a typically Italian aspect while leaving intact the fundamental structure of the German coachworks. And, without a doubt, Pininfarina has succeeded in this.'

Once its show career was over, the car was acquired by media mogul, Axel Springer. The car has since been restored to its original splendour and has become a concours d'elegance regular.

1964

Ford Aurora

The whole point of concept cars is that they predict the future; foretell what we will be driving in years to come. Some do so with great aplomb, while others quickly disappear into the ether. Ford's Aurora station wagon concept belongs firmly to the latter camp, but in many ways it accurately anticipated a number of features which we nowadays take for granted.

Unveiled at the 1964 New York World's Fair, it shared stand space with the Allegro II and Cougar show cars. Unusually, this station wagon had three doors: two on the right-hand side and one on the left. While the frontal treatment might have mirrored Ford's then-current 'Bullet Bird' styling themes, the bank of a dozen headlights and six indicators was strikingly new. Then there were the blue-green electroluminescent running lights that ran the full length of the Aurora's flanks.

Ford's marketeers defined the car's name as signifying: 'The beginning or rising of light in the morning.' The luminescent grille treatment, meanwhile, did eventually filter down into the mainstream. This design feature was appropriated by Ford's Mercury division, albeit decades later for the 1986 Sable. Inside, it was even more out there. According to the accompanying press release, the Aurora featured: 'A compartmentalised interior designed for family travel in utmost comfort and convenience.' Up front in the so-called 'Command Centre', there was nothing so ordinary as a steering wheel. Instead, it had an aircraft-like 'steering bar.' Intriguingly, the car's variable-rate steering system foretold the electric set-ups which are nowadays commonplace.

The same is broadly true of the 'Constant Speed Device' which, in latter-day parlance, represented a form of cruise control. There was also a navigational system, complete with rotating maps, which hinted at what we now know as satnav, although General Motors had beaten Ford to the punch with a similar system in its Firebird show stoppers during the 1950s. One aspect that has yet to become mainstream was the windscreen that morphed from opaque to translucent green by merely sliding back a panel in the roof.

Moving further back, the front seats could swivel to face a large sofa, luxuries stretching to beverage holders, a TV set, individual audio controls and a fridge. The sound-insulated hind section – or 'Romper Room' – was partitioned from the rest of the car via a glass divider, while the final bank of seats faced rearwards. Conspicuously absent from the PR material, however, was information regarding the car's running gear. The brochure trumpeted its 3,327mm (131in) wheelbase and 1,397mm (55in) height, but there was no mention of the engine, assuming it ever had one.

Ford's Aurora wonder wagon employed a number of intriguing features, not least what amounted to a navigational system (left) which pre-empted what we nowadays know as satnav.

1964

Fiat 2300 S Coupé Speciale

The fourth in Pininfarina's series of Fiat 2300-based prototypes, if not necessarily the fourth actual *car*, this distinctive coupé emerged at the 1964 Turin motor show. The firm's *Catalogue Raissonné* lends only a few lines to the car, much of which appears to have been lost in translation. It talks of its : '...highly raked front, closed in the mudguards which hide the radiator grill [sic]. Light roof panel which extends towards the luggage boot.' As to the identity of the stylist, Tom Tjaarda's name has been put forward in several texts, but he denied this to the author.

Henry N. Manney III, of *Road & Track*, gave more space to this Pininfarina offering than any other car in his three-page show report. He wrote: 'The Paris Mercedes 230 was also present but the centre stage was occupied by a graceful 2300 Fiat coupé in a deep shade of metalescent blue with [an] airy roof and swallowtail rear fenders reminiscent of the beautiful Flaminia coupé of last year. Pininfarina had craftily placed coloured spots all about which gave the impression of shaded colouring, and we photographers could have prowled around for hours. The interior was also plush, the instruments being in an "ogival" mounting, while [the low] roofline and seats necessitated a proper lie-down to do the driver's work. The 2300 is a much-neglected car, and it is good to see some attention being paid.'

Fiat-Abarth 1000GT Spider Pininfarina

One of the prettiest prototypes of the 1964 show season, Pininfarina's collaboration with Abarth was a styling study, but a fully-functional one, nonetheless. Based on the newly-introduced, rear-engined Fiat 850, the donor car's chassis was lengthened by 27mm (1.06in), while its 843cc pushrod four-cylinder engine was enlarged to 982cc. Power output was boosted from 37bhp at 5,100rpm to 52bhp at 5,200rpm. Weighing just 635kg (1,400lb), it was purportedly capable of reaching 112mph (180km/h) and 0–60mph in around 13sec. Stylistically, the car foretold themes explored on the following year's Dino Berlinetta Speciale, not least the headlight arrangement which was illegal for road use in Europe: headlamps were 599.5mm (23.6in) off the ground, the legal requirement being 609.6mm (24in). In 1965, a coupé variant, complete with a flip-forward canopy, was shown at the Turin motor show. Unsubstantiated rumours suggest it was simply a reworking of the previous year's car.

Pininfarina's pretty Abarth roadster (bottom) may have been later reworked to form the closed variation on the theme (left) which featured a flip-forward canopy.

1964

Mercer Cobra

Following his departure from Chrysler (some might say ousting) in 1962, Virgil Exner became a pen-for-hire, but life as a freelancer wasn't without its headaches. Plans to create an offshoot of the Italian Ghia concern in the USA came to naught, as did hopes of creating an array of parade vehicles and a 14,000-seat amphitheatre for a travelling circus on learning that the project's instigator was suffering from mental health problems. There followed a commission where there was no intention of his designs ever leaving the drawing board – except this one did.

In 1963, Exner was approached by *Esquire* magazine: would he be interested in collaborating on an article forecasting future automotive design trends? 'Ex' was responsive, the brief being expanded to

The wild Mercer Cobra was styled by Virgil Exner and made extensive use of copper, bronze and brass. Predictably, it was a non-runner.

Lincoln Continental Town Brougham

include his vision of how defunct brands might have evolved stylistically had they not been consigned to history. Marque revivals were then practically unheard of, but the 50-something stylist along with his son, Virgil Exner Jr, let rip, and in December 1963 their ideas bearing the Duesenberg, Stutz, Bugatti, Pierce-Arrow, Jordan Playboy and Mercer nameplates generated considerable exposure.

The Mercer offering in particular piqued the interest of George Hartley, president of the Copper Development Association of New York. Hartley wanted to produce a concept car that made extensive use of copper, bronze and brass components, the intention being to make the automotive industry aware of their properties and potential applications. Exner Sr agreed to transform his renderings into a full-scale roadster, and commissioned Sibona & Basano of Turin to create the body on a Shelby Cobra platform (chassis CSX2451) which had been lengthened by 381mm (15in) for this new application.

The finished article took its public bow in December 1964 as the Mercer Cobra. Unique features included swing-out headlights, while the bumpers, grille and wheel covers were treated to a copper coating. Then there were the copper disc brakes, brake lines, radiator tank, instrument bezels and all manner of brass ancillaries on and around the 260cu in Ford V8 engine. The Mercer then went on tour, circling the globe for more than a decade despite never moving under its own steam for obvious reasons.

The Copper Development Association undoubtedly received the publicity it desired and more, although whether the Mercer and the company's other show queens led to greater acceptance of the firm's products is a moot point. In June 1979, the Mercer was sold to General William Lyon for $165,000.

Built originally in 1961, and presented to the White House for the use of Jacqueline Kennedy, the Town Brougham was returned to Dearborn almost immediately. 'Jackie-O' didn't like – or want – the car. The Lincoln sat in storage until it was dusted down ahead of the 1964 show season. While 203mm (8in) longer than a regular 1961 model (and 127mm/5in longer than the ostensibly similar 1964 Continental production car), the Town Brougham's signature feature was its open chauffeur compartment and limousine-style glass central divider.

While the body trim, the lights and suchlike were brought up to date in-line with the forthcoming 1965 Continental, inside it was awash with walnut, leather, and all the accoutrements befitting the moneyed elite. That said, this was a show car, so the radio in the rear was non-functional, nor was there any rear side glazing.

This distinctive Lincoln featured an exposed chauffeur compartment which acted as a nod to coachbuilt American fare from the pre-war era. The car was originally built for Jackie Kennedy.

1964

Sibona & Basano Tsé-Tsé

Carrozzeria Sibona & Basano introduced the Tsé-Tsé at the 1964 Turin motor show. Distinct from most other Italian prototypes of the period, this tiny city car featured a glassfibre body (the Turin concern also moulded bus bodies and commercial roofing from this composite material). Named after a mosquito, this oddly-shaped device was strictly a two-seater, a flip-forward canopy affording access to the minimalist cabin.

Road & Track was one of the few English-language titles to mention the car in event reports, Henry Manney III labelling it: '... an odd fibreglass egg in Paris green....' Power was provided by a rear-sited 250cc 'twin', but this was notional at best given that the prototype was displayed without a powerplant. There was speculation in period that the Fiat 500 unit could be accommodated, but this was academic, as the Tsé-Tsé was never displayed again. Sibona & Basano continued to act as a subcontractor to other design houses, in addition to marques such as Abarth and Bizzarrini, to 1966.

Ford Cougar II

Another of Ford's 'Styling X-Cars', along with the Allegro and Mustang II, a degree of mystery surrounded this rakish coupé for more than half a century, not least the origins of the donor car (assuming there was one). *Road & Track* opined in period: 'The Cougar II follows the 2-place personal car format and, although, not expressly stated by Ford's representatives, the chassis specifications bear a remarkable resemblance to Shelby's AC-Ford Cobra: 90-in wheelbase, track 50.5-in front and 52-in rear, with an overall length of 66.6in... Power is supplied by a 260cu in Fairlane V8, which drives through a 4-speed all-synchromesh gearbox to the independently sprung rear wheels.'

The Cougar II, was displayed in the Ford Pavilion that formed part of the 1964 New York World's Fair, but it made only fleeting appearances thereafter before disappearing from view. It was later discovered in a storage unit in Detroit alongside the Bordinat Cobra. On closer inspection, this Cherry Apple Red GT bore two chassis numbers: Shelby American's CSX2008, and Ford's own XGX035091. Confusingly, some sources suggest it was constructed by Alfredo Vignale's eponymous *carrozzeria*, but, given that the body was made of glassfibre, this is improbable.

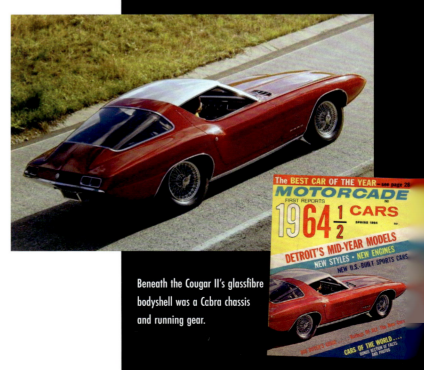

Beneath the Cougar II's glassfibre bodyshell was a Cobra chassis and running gear.

GM GM-X

Another 1964 New York World's Fair exhibit, the GM-X represented General Motors' take on the high-performance sports car of the future. It had a 2,812mm (110.7in) wheelbase, was 5,410mm (213in) long, 1,961mm (77.2in) wide and 1,133mm (44.6in) high, the outline being dominated by its rocket-like nose. Distinctive features included a full-length under-car belly-pan for aerodynamic purposes, and partially-skirted wheels. Flush-fitting flaps towards the rear would pop out to act as a form of air-brake during an emergency stop, while inside there was a dizzying array of 31 lights and 29 toggle switches. Unlike so many other mocked-up concept cars of the period, the GM-X wasn't immediately destroyed following its World's Fair appearance. It was placed in storage, and later reworked before reappearing as the Pontiac Cirrus in 1969.

The GM-X wasn't lacking for instrumentation or switchgear (right). The car reappeared at the end of the decade as the Pontiac Cirrus.

1964

GM Runabout

American car buyers have never taken three-wheelers to heart, which may explain why this intriguing curio is nowadays forgotten. The Runabout was one of three General Motors show cars built for the 1964 New York World's Fair which was held in Flushing Meadows, the others being the GM-X and Firebird IV. It was intended to showcase design innovation, and this sleek trike wasn't without interesting features.

While GM would not get away with such things in today's more enlightened times, the Runabout was trumpeted as being a car for housewives. It was a 'grocery getter', one that was known internally as 'The Shopper'. It was conceived as a four-seater car with a front-mounted engine although what, precisely, powered the Runabout was never divulged. It could, conceivably, have encompassed anything from two- and four-stroke units to a bank of batteries.

The car's unusual three-wheeled layout ensured that it was never going to be conventionally styled. The front end featured a full-width, wraparound headlight/indicator arrangement. Three louvres were positioned directly below, ostensibly for engine cooling. Further louvres were sited just ahead of the windscreen. As with its fellow show stopper, the GM-X, the Runabout didn't feature conventional doors. The windscreen formed part of a canopy that lifted up and forward, allowing passengers access to the cabin. The only 'door', if you can call it that, was the rear hatch. Even then, the only promotional image that showed occupants in the car was of a little girl sitting in the back seat. No adults were ever pictured getting in or out, let alone seated.

Inside, there was a console fore of the driver, incorporated into which were a pair of rotating dials with two buttons sited between them. What function they served was never disclosed. The lower rear section of the outer body incorporated a shopping trolley. Upon arrival at the supermarket, you merely separated it – *somehow* – and small wheels would then pop out. You then did your shopping, pushed the cart back into the rear of the car and the wheels would retract. Once home, the trolley could then be detached from the Runabout, complete with your shopping, and you simply pushed it inside your house and set about putting everything away.

1964

Chevrolet CERV II

Blurring the lines between concept car and competition tool, CERV II was substantially different to its CERV I forerunner. The car was similarly dreamed up in 1962 by Zora Arkus Duntov, and emerged in 1964, but it wasn't an open-wheel single-seater. It represented his take on a sports-prototype that could take the fight to the forthcoming Ford GT40. However, given that General Motors had a strict policy of no official involvement in motorsport, you surmise that privateer teams would have acted as cover for any works bid.

Whatever the truth, emphasis soon shifted to using CERV II as a test bed. The car's composite body was shaped by Larry Shinoda and Anatole Lapine, while power was supplied by an all-alloy 377cu in V8 with Hillborn fuel-injection. Unusually, for a car designed with motor racing in mind, if only theoretically, it encompassed four-wheel drive, which was still some years away from appearing in IndyCar and Formula 1 (where such a set-up served only to add heft and complexity). It also boasted a two-speed automatic gearbox at either end, plus dual torque converters, with the front-to-rear power split being varied depending on the vehicle's speed.

The car was put through its paces at the Milford test facility in March 1964 before specially-selected members of the motoring media. Jim Hall, Roger Penske and Bob Clift took it in turn running laps, CERV II allegedly being capable of reaching 200mph (322km/h). It was still acting as a rolling laboratory to the end of the decade, and was equipped with a 427cu in ZL-1 big-block V8 when *Motor Trend* magazine tested the car in November 1970. Hall, meanwhile, worked hand in glove with GM's 'skunkworks' on his highly-advanced Chaparral racing cars in sports-prototype and Can-Am categories. CERV II was later displayed at the Briggs Cunningham Automotive Museum in Naples, Florida. It subsequently passed through different owners, and was sold via auction in 2013 for $1.1m.

Studebaker SS (Excalibur)

Among the most celebrated of Brooks Stevens' automotive designs was the masterful 1961 Studebaker Gran Turismo Hawk. He followed through with the Wagonaire station wagon, but the Indiana marque's days were clearly numbered. By 1964, the slide into oblivion appeared irreversible. Nonetheless, Stevens continued to produce concepts including the wild Sceptre prototype saloon car, and also a subcompact with interchangeable glassfibre panels.

The game was up, but from the ashes of the Studebaker Corporation emerged a new marque out of an improbable concept car. Studebaker held the US concession for Mercedes-Benz, and Stevens conceived a loose replica of a pre-war Mercedes SS based on a Studebaker Lark Daytona chassis, to be shown at the 1964 New York International Auto Show. However, the Studebaker board got cold feet and decided not to feature the 'Mercebaker' on its stand.

Unbowed, Stevens arranged for it to be shown as a standalone exhibit, and reaction was such that Stevens the designer became Stevens the reluctant motor mogul. And thus, the Excalibur marque was born, with the likes of Dean Martin, Steve McQueen and Jackie Gleason among early adopters.

Brooks Stevens' 'Mercebaker' (right) was commissioned by Studebaker but the ailing Indiana firm got cold feet before it was unveiled. Excalibur the marque ushered in the 'neo-classic' as we know it.

1964

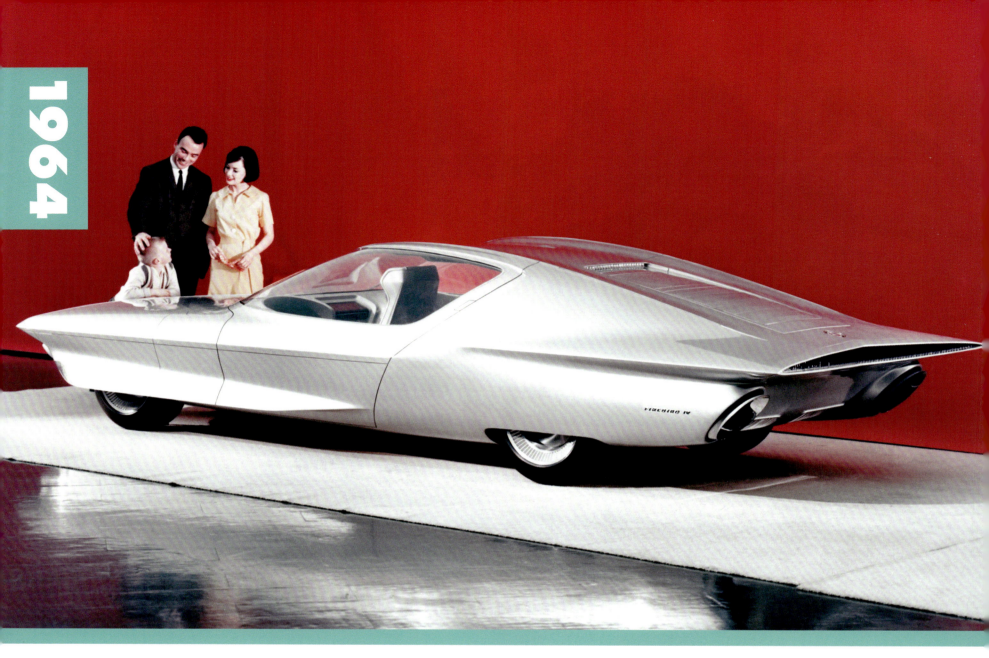

GM Firebird IV

The last – and least-known – of the assorted GM Firebird concept cars, the fourth iteration was yet another 1964 New York World's Fair exhibit. Like its predecessors, it promised gas-turbine power and was similarly imbued with aircraft styling cues. Unlike its forerunners, the Firebird IV was not a functional vehicle. Riding on a 3,022.6mm (119in) wheelbase, it was 5,842mm (230in) long, 1,971mm (77.6in) wide, and 1,143mm (45in) high, the body being a deceptively intricate melange of curves and angles, and dominated by large rear horizontal fins and chrome-capped exhaust ports for the intended gas-turbine powerplant. Inside, it employed joystick controls and an early form of head-up instrumentation display.

The fourth and final GM Firebird turbine car forecast the family saloon of the future. However, unlike its forerunners, it was strictly a non-driveable mock-up.

Pontiac Banshee

He was either a fame-chasing huckster or a product planning genius. Whichever side of the debate you cleaved to, John DeLorean was on a roll during the early-to-mid-1960s. The former Packard man was busy making waves at General Motors, not least by ushering in the muscle-car movement via the Pontiac GTO in 1963. He wanted to further heighten the brand's high-performance image though, not least to help topple arch-rival Ford and its strong-selling Mustang. And thus, the Banshee – or XP-883 in GM-speak – was born.

Plans originally called for a 2,286mm (90in) wheelbase and big-block V8 power. However, a degree of hostility was brewing towards DeLorean and his brainchild. There was a stumbling block, and it came in the form of the Chevrolet Corvette. Fearing a productionised version of the Banshee might steal sales, GM management took a hardline stance. Even with the technical specification watered down, and a straight-six unit that produced a relatively puny 165bhp in place of the proposed big-block eight-cylinder unit, the Banshee was met with a wall of antipathy. Two six-cylinder 'runners' were made, before the axe fell.

However, DeLorean was nothing if not persistent. A further variation on the theme with the internal moniker 'XP-798' was also completed. It purportedly featured a 421cu in V8 and independent rear suspension, plus a strange set-up whereby part of the roof flipped up in unison with a door being opened. However, GM's executive vice-president Ed Cole got wind that the car was to be displayed at the 1966 Detroit Auto Show and had it pulled ahead of the event.

Dodge Charger II

While widely touted as being a 1965 concept car, the Dodge Charger II was first seen publicly at the November 1964 Los Angeles Auto Show. It foretold the 1966 Charger production model, the fastback styling having retrospectively been attributed to Elwood Engel. *Motorcade* reported in March 1965: 'Dubbed the Charger II in view of last year's show car, Charger I, the new fastback is very much unlike its predecessor. Number 1 was purely a customised competition roadster built around an existing car.'

It went on to add: 'In a quick contradiction, the Charger II can be described as being a new design from the ground up, but still with enough of today's basic design to make it a car that could be tooled and built in quantity with a minimum of cost.' While the foundations for the car remained unrecorded, it was dimensionally similar to the Dodge Coronet production car (they shared the same 2,972mm/117in wheelbase). Power came from a 318cu in small-block V8, unusual features for the period including rear seats that folded completely flat, allowing space for skis and suchlike.

105

Concept cars were becomingly almost ubiquitous, with even some of the more risk-averse marques producing wild flights of fantasy. 1965 also saw designers, styling houses and manufacturers create cars that were rooted in the real world, that hinted at the near future rather than decades down the line. In some quarters, a car's user-friendliness and packaging trumped styling. While perhaps not guaranteed to garnish covers of magazines, they weren't without influence where it mattered.

The mid-1960s also saw publishing houses and design firms collaborate on projects with varying degrees of success. This would become a common theme to the end of the decade, with Italian titles to the fore. Among these, *Quattroruote* began pushing its safety agenda, and thus a period of ugly but worthy safety-orientated concept cars was ushered in.

Also in 1965
Great Train Robber Ronnie Biggs escapes from Wandsworth prison and flees to Brazil.
A 70mph speed limit is introduced for UK roads.
Bob Dylan invites controversy by 'going electric' at the Newport Folk Festival in the US.
Corgi Toys introduce the all-time best-selling model of the James Bond Aston Martin DB5.
The first episode of Gerry Anderson's *Thunderbirds* TV series airs in the UK.

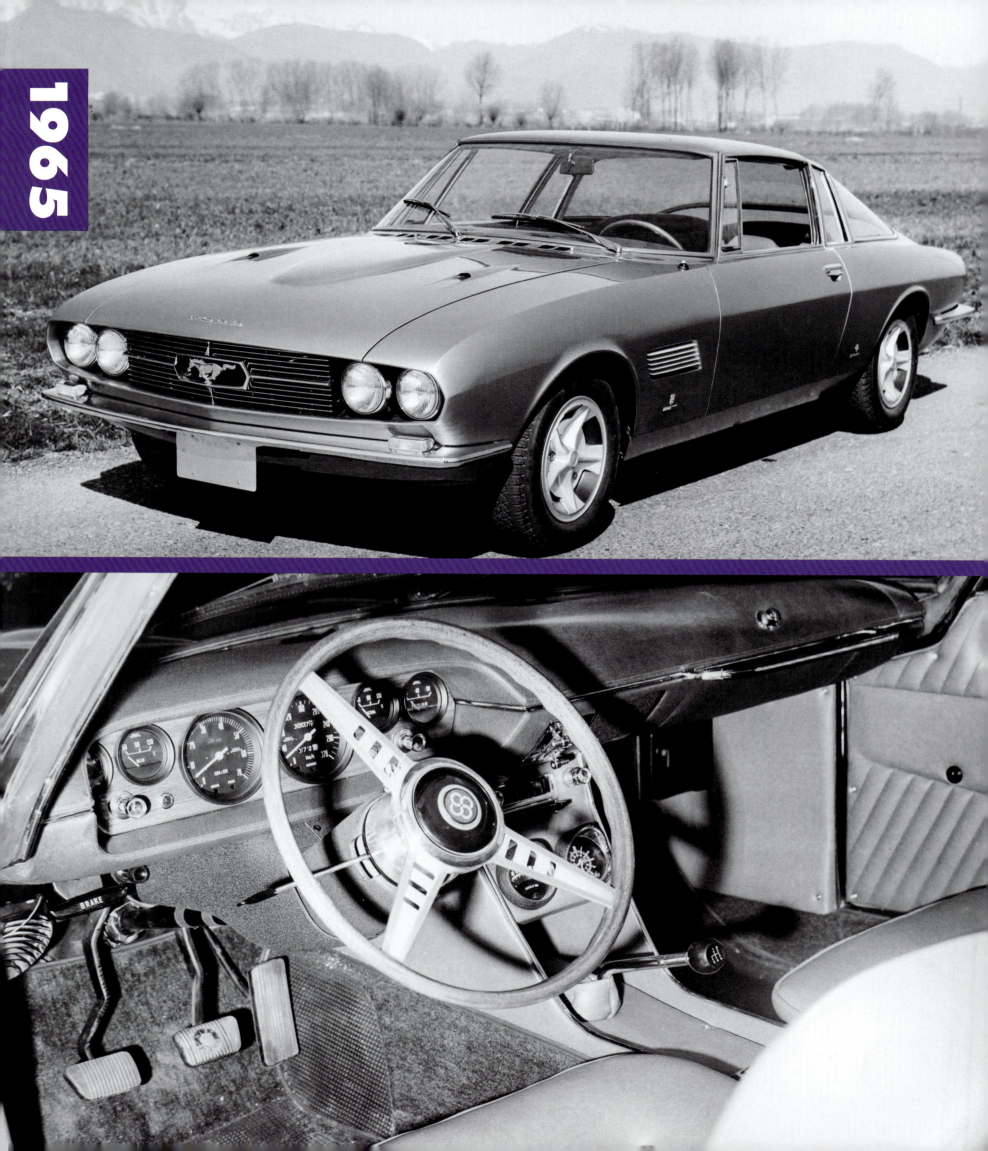

Bertone Ford Mustang

This handsome reworking of Ford's 'Pony Car' was dreamed up by L. Scott Bailey. This multi-faceted American founded *Automobile Quarterly* (AQ) in 1962, the hardback publication raising the bar for the presentation of motoring titles. It encompassed exhaustive features on historic machinery juxtaposed against critiques of the latest design trends. Bailey conceived an AQ project car following a visit to the 1964 Paris motor show where he met studio principal Nuccio Bertone and his chief designer, Giorgetto Giugiaro.

The trio mapped out the Italo-American GT ideal and, following a further meeting in Turin to finalise the design, a bright red Mustang fastback, complete with a 4.7-litre, 289cu in V8, was procured to act as a donor vehicle. This was transported to Italy by Alitalia Airlines which became a partial sponsor of the project. The car was subsequently stripped to its foundations ahead of a substantial makeover.

Giugiaro produced an exotic outline that employed an expansive glasshouse and spindly pillars. The front end, by contrast, was rather more Detroit in outlook: it comprised a full-width grille with retracting headlight covers. The only body parts carried over were the grille mascot and filler cap. The interior, meanwhile, was trimmed in tobacco-coloured vinyl. Mechanically, however, the car was standard save for the radiator which was canted slightly due to the lower bonnet line. Painted in a striking shade of metallic turquoise, the finishing touch was a set of Giugiaro-designed, Campagnolo-made, magnesium-alloy wheels shod in Pirelli rubber.

The Bertone Mustang was met with much hoopla when unveiled at the April 1965 New York International Auto Show, *Automobile Quarterly* basking in the reflective glow of positive media attention. The car was advertised by Bertone shortly thereafter for $10,000, which its makers claimed represented a third of the build cost. The intriguing part, however, is what happened next. Giugiaro claimed to the author in 2001 that it was acquired by a Greek shipping magnate, but admitted that he wasn't certain. Other sources insist the car was stolen from a Monaco dealership in the late 1960s.

Ghia Bugatti 101 C-X

By the early 1960s, design legend Virgil Exner had been shuffled out of Chrysler and was effectively a pen for hire. The car pictured here was a passion project, one that would in a roundabout way lead to a raft of increasingly wild designs that were translated into three-dimensional reality. Basis for this wild roadster was the last-ever Bugatti chassis (produced by the original Molsheim concern). Type 101 chassis 101506 was manufactured in the early 1950s and featured a supercharged 3.3-litre straight-eight engine, but it was never clothed. It was acquired from the Bugatti family estate in 1961 by American Allen Henderson who, in turn, sold it to Exner in January 1965 for $2,500.

Ghia, meanwhile, was still reeling from the death of entrepreneurial boss Luigi 'Gigi' Segre in 1963. Ghia was flatlining under its subsequent owner. It also owed Exner around $27,000 in unpaid design consultancy fees. Both parties reached an agreement whereby Ghia would shape the Bugatti for free, and the bare chassis – now minus 457mm (18in) to make for a 2,845mm (112in) wheelbase – was shipped over to Turin along with a styling model. Ghia had much work to do, not least to shorten the propshaft, before it set about creating the dramatic outline from aluminium.

The results were nothing if not flamboyant, the Italian artisans tweaking Exner's brief somewhat, not least by installing a two-piece, vee-shaped windscreen instead of the intended one-piece item. The lights, meanwhile, were integrated into the wings (unlike those on the scale model) and the exposed exhaust pipes were replaced by underslung items. The 101 C-X was shown at the 1965 Turin motor show, where it was not warmly received. *Sporting Motorist's* succinct verdict was perhaps the most polite. It stated: 'Every show has its cuckoo…' Exner retained the car until 1969.

Ghia Cobra GT

It is a car that appeared out of nowhere and vanished from sight almost as quickly. Who, precisely, commissioned the construction of this Ghia-bodied AC/Shelby Cobra remains open to conjecture, as does the identity of the man who shaped it. The Cobra famously formed a cornerstone of Ford's Total Performance Programme; the one initiated prior to Enzo Ferrari famously rebuffing the advances of Henry Ford II at the eleventh hour. Ford was set to acquire the Ferrari marque, only for *Il Commendatore* to get cold feet.

Carroll Shelby, former Le Mans winner and motorsport's answer to P.T. Barnum, initiated the Ford-backed, AC Ace-based Cobra which, for all its on-track success, never was a big seller. What's more, there was a certain 'not invented here' enmity on Ford's part. Which is where this car purportedly came in. There had been prior internal attempts at clothing the Cobra chassis with contemporary styling, but this was something else entirely.

At some point in 1965, a Cobra 427, complete with big-block V8 engine, was dispatched to Carrozzeria Ghia, the story being that the empire-building Alessandro de Tomaso sniffed an opportunity to build a second-generation Cobra in series. According to some sources, the Ghia principal hoped to impress Shelby and the Ford management. However, de Tomaso didn't assume control of Ghia until 1967, but that wouldn't necessarily have stopped him from using the once-revered coachbuilder as a subcontractor.

Style Auto ran an exclusive feature on the car in period, and referred to it as the Cobra GT. It reported, in typically leftfield fashion: 'The sides sport a hint of dihedron below which, between the front wheel and door, there is a slit for engine compartment air exit. The door handle is replaced by a recessed pushbutton, thus the complete side surface results perfectly smooth. The moderately wrap around windscreen could perhaps do with more rake. Very successful, too, is the tail in typical Ghia style, lightened by the bumper which cuts it exactly in the middle, dividing the large round taillights according to their function.'

Finished in dark blue, with orange/brown leather upholstery, the all-new dashboard appeared to be something of an afterthought. Giorgetto Giugiaro had been credited with styling the car, but *Il Maestro* doesn't list it on his massive resume. The design has also been attributed to Filippo Sapino. A second Ghia Cobra was also purportedly made, an assumption based entirely on photos showing a car with round rather rectangular headlights behind Perspex lenses. Following the unveiling in Turin, all went quiet. There was no clamour for the design's adoption by Shelby or Ford.

1965

Pininfarina Alfa Romeo Giulia 1600 Sport

While perhaps not as well remembered as Giorgetto Giugiaro's sublime Canguro, Pininfarina's take on the competition Alfa Romeo theme wasn't without influence. Based on a TZ2 platform (chassis #750114), and styled by Aldo Brovarone, it didn't feature even trace elements of the car that bore it stylistically. Instead, it featured pronounced overhangs and a ridge that ran aft of the Alfa Romeo crest above the grille.

The car was unveiled at the 1965 Turin Motor Show, *Road & Track*'s Henry Manney enthusing about the 'kinky Giulia coupe.' He wrote: 'This had a very sinuous line reminiscent of the Bertone SS, but as it had a lower silhouette, carried the whole thing off better. It didn't look much like an Alfa, with the tiny rectangular grille, but the fancy cut-out seats were pleated to extinction, the handbrake stuck out horizontally from between driver and passenger (that will have to go!), and the polished holes made it a very sexy package indeed.'

It went on to add: 'Many individuals were seen drooling over it, but as with the ill-fated Bertone Kangaroo on the same chassis (for sale chez Bertone, incidentally), I rather doubt whether it will ever fall into the hands of intended customers. Still, we can but hope can't we?' The sole prototype was displaying sparingly thereafter. After many years of inactivity, it made a triumphant return to the spotlight during the 2010 Concorso d'Eleganza Ville d'Este where it was reunited with Brovarone.

Ferrari 206 P Dino Pininfarina Berlinetta Speciale

One of the most celebrated concept cars ever to wear the *Cavallino Rampante* logo, this design by Aldo Brovarone proved highly influential. Based on a chassis that previously underpinned a Ferrari Dino 206 P sports-prototype, the car was constructed over a six-month period prior to being unveiled at the 1966 Paris motor show.

The curvaceous outline boasted many styling themes that would become design staples of future Dino and Ferrari products, not least the conical side air intakes (devised by Tom Tjaarda for the 365 California), the curved rear glass, and cropped tail. The most daring feature was the quad-headlight arrangement that was housed behind a Perspex cover. *Road & Track* labelled it: '...a very tasty little item in bright red (of course).'

Following further appearances that year at the Turin motor show and elsewhere, the car was bequeathed to Musée des 24 Heures du Mans. There it remained until 2017 when it was sold – minus engine internals – at auction in Paris. It realised 4.4 million euros including premiums.

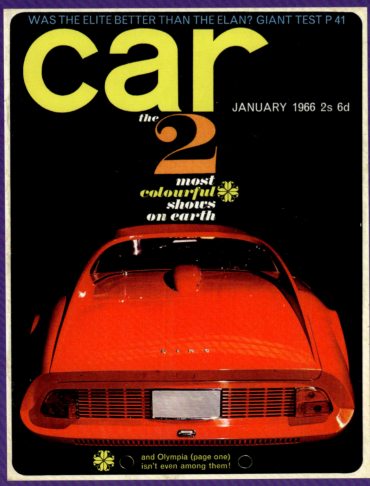

This Aldo Brovarone-styled, Pininfarina-crafted concept car was based on a Ferrari Dino 206 P sports-prototype platform. It inspired what in time became the Dino 206 GT road car.

1965

Mako Shark II / Manta Ray

Unveiled to great acclaim at the April 1965 New York International Auto Show, Chevrolet's newest concept car fully embraced the maxim 'It ain't done 'till it's overdone'. The Mako Shark II, or 'XP-830' in less romantic General Motors' internal speak, was a stylistic tour de force, and a harbinger of the Corvette's future design direction. It also represented pure show-car whimsy, as was to be expected from the firm's styling czar Bill Mitchell in his pomp.

Even *Road & Track*, a magazine that had been a mite sniffy about Corvette production cars in period, was blown away. It reported: 'Chevrolet's "Mako Shark" Corvette – a non-working display model, created a great stir among the performance-minded (which included most of the show patrons) as a potential "coming Corvette".' This mock-up was subsequently scrapped, although a running car – complete with a 427cu in V8 – was completed in early October of that year ahead of a tour of Europe: it was displayed at major international shows in Paris, London, Turin, Brussels and Geneva, prior to making a repeat visit to the Big Apple in April 1966.

Following its showing at Earls Court in the British capital, *Motor* reported: 'General Motors' experimental exercise in styling, safety and electronics, is based on a Corvette Sting Ray chassis, [and has a] 7-litre V8 and a three-speed automatic transmission. It is polychromatic dark blue on top, feathering to pearl grey on its belly (just like a shark), and the car has a strikingly mean look, but Warren Olsen, GM's project manager who is demonstrating it around Europe, revealed that it was more than just a pipedream.'

It went on to add: 'A central console houses so many switches you need to be an organist to play them all. They operate, among other things, concealed wipers which emerge from behind a shutter on the scuttle top, a tail spoiler that protrudes into the airstream at high-speed to give downward thrust at the back (the car will top 150mph), bumpers that extend rearwards when reverse gear is engaged, a "venetian blind" rear window for ventilation (you can't see out of it when it is shut), and a roof panel that lifts 60deg into the air for easy access. A digital computer – once the size of a suitcase, now as big as a briefcase, and soon to be housed in a box that won't hold two cigarette packets, works the speedometer and shows figures on a small screen on the facia.'

Many of the styling cues were subsequently incorporated into the C3-generation Corvette that entered production in 1968. That wasn't quite the end of the story, though. The Mako Shark II was later transformed into a different concept car, the Manta Ray, that emerged in 1969. While ostensibly similar, the front-end now had a pronounced chin spoiler plus a bank of rectangular headlights shrouded in Perspex. The roof and rear-quarters were also revised, the tail now tapering to a point. It also received an all-aluminium 427cu in ZL-1 V8.

Many Mako Shark II styling cues were subsequently incorporated into the C3-generation Corvette that entered production in 1968. This prototype later morphed into the Manta Ray.

1965

Fiat 2300S Coupé Speciale

The fifth and final in Pininfarina's take on the Fiat 2300S theme may – or may not – have been a remodel of the previous year's show car. In profile, it was near identical save for the addition of quarterlights, but here the nose featured a low-sited quad-headlamp arrangement, with the indicators positioned above them on the leading edge of the wings. To the rear, there were prominent bumper over-guards and a vestigial spoiler.

Unveiled at the 1965 Turin motor show, the car was to some extent overshadowed by its stablemates on the Pininfarina stand (which included the newly-introduced Alfa Romeo 'Duetto' Spider). *Motor* reported: 'The Fiat does not look quite as chunky and aggressive as Ghia's production car and bears the unmistakable hallmark of Farina – it also has extractor slots above the rear window.' *Road & Track*, meanwhile, dismissed it as being: '...a light-green, flat-sterned Fiat 2300' in its report. No Pininfarina Fiat 2300-based concept car is known to survive.

Plymouth XP-VIP

While perhaps not the most graceful of concept cars, the Plymouth XP-VIP was awash with novel features. Styled under Elwood Engel, the man who shaped the 1961 'Clap Door' Lincoln, this two-door coupe boasted a two-piece glass roof with a longitudinal dividing strip. The glazing appeared tinted thanks to a photochemical process, darkening or lightening depending on exposure to light. The roof could also be retracted into the boot area in its entirety or merely the left- or right-hand side could be retracted. The cabin, meanwhile, was awash with luxury items befitting a Very Important Person, including more than one television (strictly speaking, the dashboard-sited item was a 'rear-vision scope'), a reel-to-reel tape recorder for dictating letters, a telephone, and controls for a stereophonic system.

First seen publicly at the February 1965 Chicago Auto Show, and billed as '...an exercise in preparation for the future', the XP-VIP was essentially a teaser; one built to gauge interest in a 'personal-luxury coupe'. A year later, Plymouth re-used the VIP tag, but it was merely a more luxuriously equipped variant of the Fury production model. As an aside, the XP-VIP was never displayed with the glass roof sections in place.

Styled under Elwood Engel, the Plymouth XP-VIP boasted a two-piece glass roof with a longitudinal dividing strip. The roof panels were retractable.

Ford 'Bordinat' Cobra

The history of the automobile is littered with 'what if?' stories, the car pictured here being among the most tantalising. It could have been Ford's answer to Chevrolet's C2 Corvette Sting Ray, had the Blue Oval chosen to put it into production. Instead, this achingly handsome machine created column inches in the specialist press before disappearing.

Inspired by GM's Bill Mitchell, who routinely racked up the miles aboard show cars, Ford's vice president of styling, Eugene 'Gene' Bordinat, set about creating a roadster variant of the Cougar II, ostensibly for his own personal use. That was in early 1965. Basis for this one-off was the first coil-sprung 427 Cobra chassis, albeit one equipped with a 289cu in HiPo engine mated to a C4 automatic transmission. Stylistically, it aped the lines of the Cougar II but, if anything, it was prettier still. Unusually, it even looked good with the convertible roof in place.

Distinct from its forerunner, which made do with a glassfibre 'shell that was inches thick in places, this latest strain was the first – possibly last-ever – car to feature a body made of Royalex. According to a period press release, this '...synthetic material, with exceptional impact resistance and low tooling costs, is essentially a one-piece "skin". The doors and bonnet were formed as part of the bodyshell and, after the structural members had been added and bonded to the spaceframe [ladderframe would be closer...], were cut out of the 'shell. Retractable synchronised headlights can be operated through a 180-degree vertical arc'.

Known variously as the Bordinat Cobra and XD Cobra, it was finished in iridescent honey gold and touted around shows in 1965. The car even made it to a trade show at Olympia as late as 1967, when it appeared on the Uniroyal stand. And then... nothing. It remains unrecorded as to how often Bordinat actually drove the car, but it seemingly vanished later that decade. The same was true of the Cougar II. It later transpired that both cars had been in storage in a Detroit warehouse and were largely complete save for a few missing engine parts. They were shown together for the first time ever at the 2012 Amelia Island Concours d'Elegance.

The 'Bordinat' Cobra could conceivably have been a serious rival to the Chevrolet Corvette had the theme been explored. However, the design wasn't adopted but the prototype still survives.

1965

Ogle Triplex GTS

While based on a production car, the construction of this 'shooting brake' was infinitely more involved than the grafting on of a large glasshouse aft of the B-pillars. This striking one-off also had a profound effect on the future of car design, even if its contribution isn't immediately obvious. Commissioned by Triplex, which was by far the biggest glazing supplier to the British motor industry, the GTS was created to showcase the adhesive bonding of glass to a car's body.

Almost every car made today employs bonded-in glass. In the mid-1960s, it was commonplace to use rubber gaskets. By doing away with them completely, it allowed for a smooth screen/body joint. It also had huge ramifications in terms of aerodynamics. On the flipside, the increase in glass also had the detrimental effect of not only passing light, but also heat, which was then trapped. Triplex had created Sundym, a heat-absorbing glass with a trace element that increased the absorption of ultra-violet light. That, and infra-red rays which enormously reduced transmitted radiant heat.

In early 1964, the firm's head of marketing, Tony Cleminson, approached Ogle Design to conjure a concept car that would showcase its wares to the motor industry and wider world. It fell to Tom Karen and Carl Olsen to oversee the project. Three vehicles were mapped out: a three-wheeler with an all-glass canopy, a small taxi with an expansive glasshouse, and a fastback GT with a glass roof. In January 1965, Triplex gave the go-ahead for Ogle to create a concept car in time for the British International Motor Show that would be held in October of that year. However, the cost of building something entirely new from scratch proved prohibitive, so the decision was made to create a car based on the Reliant Scimitar GT.

However, while clearly related to the Scimitar, which itself was an Ogle design rooted in the prior Daimler SX250 (a design by David Ogle that was refined by Karen), it was all new from the waist up. The idea of a four-seater GT-cum-sporting estate was relatively rare at the time, and it fell to Triplex's Holly Grange laboratory to create double-curvature panels and detailed glazing sections that afforded minimal pillar widths. It also carried out the adhesive bonding process. The GTS (Glazing Test Special) was registered on 1 October 1965 and shown to the media on 15 October prior to going under the lights at Earls Court.

The Ogle stand was swamped with the rich and famous, including the likes of Lord Snowdon and Nubar Gulbenkian, many of whom attempted to buy the car. Their offers were rebuffed. After the show, the GTS was entrusted to Basil Cardew of the *Daily Express* and Tommy Wisdom of the *Daily Herald*. These eminent motoring correspondents drove the car to Italy ahead of the Turin motor show. This 'mobile laboratory,' as it was dubbed by the media, then became a roving ambassador for Triplex within the motor industry, until The Duke of Edinburgh dropped less than subtle hints that he too was enamoured of the car.

His Royal Highness succeeded where others had failed, and enjoyed sole use of the car between 1966 and 1968, which afforded massive publicity for Triplex, Ogle, and Reliant. However, contrary to many contemporary reports, His Royal Highness never owned the car. After it was returned to Triplex, the GTS was rarely seen publicly. In 1972, it was loaned to the National Motor Museum in Beaulieu, and there it remained until 1987 when it passed into private ownership. The GTS had around 42,000 miles (67,500km) on the clock, which is among the highest mileages ever recorded by a concept car.

Prince Philip, Duke Of Edinburgh, borrowed the 'Glazing Test Special' which boosted the profile of Ogle, Reliant and Triplex, partners behind this one-off shooting brake.

1965

OSI Ford Mustang

The first-generation Ford Mustang was famously a runway hit for the Blue Oval when launched midway through 1964. Nevertheless, that didn't stop others from trying to improve on perfection, with Italian styling houses being to the fore. All manner of *carrozzerie* had a stab at redesigning the original Pony Car with varying degrees of success, OSI's 1965 offering being perhaps the most radical.

Formed by Arrigo Olivetti (of typewriter fame) and Luigi Segre, then president of Ghia, the romantically-named Officine Stampaggi Industriali was born in 1960 and financed by the FERGAT road-wheel and metal-stamping concern. The intention was to produce prototypes, but also manufacture Ghia designs in small series, much as arch-rivals Bertone and Pininfarina did. A raft of designs followed, some of which made the leap into volume production, all things being relative.

OSI enjoyed a strong relationship with Italy's Ford concessionaire which spawned the Anglia 105-based Torino. This, in turn, led to the Ford of Cologne-sponsored 20M TS coupé which foretold the Capri and sold in reasonably large numbers. Who, precisely, conceived the OSI Mustang is lost to history, but it was clearly more than a mere re-bodying exercise. What's more, it received factory blessing according to *Style Auto* magazine.

While retaining the donor car's 271bhp V8, the wheelbase was shortened from 2,473mm (97.4in) to 2,400mm (94.5in). It also featured a marginally narrower track, front and rear. Much of the platform was cutaway and replaced with a tubular semi-spaceframe structure and, unlike a regular Mustang, OSI's offering featured an independent rear-suspension arrangement, complete with a self-locking ZF differential, plus all-round disc brakes.

The big news, however, was the outline. OSI's offering didn't share even a token resemblance to the car that bore it, save for the badges. Riding on Borrani wire wheels, secured by knock-offs, and bodied in glassfibre, the car's signature feature was the fold-flat headlight arrangement which foretold the Porsche 928. Inside, there was the obligatory mahogany dash, alloy-spoked steering wheel and a mixture of burgundy leather and plaid trim.

Making its public debut at the November 1965 Turin motor show, the OSI Mustang was met with muted praise by the motoring media. Sergio Rogna of *Style Auto* was perhaps the most effusive, reporting not altogether lucidly: 'Although from the styling standpoint some discordance has been noted in details, it is not difficult to foresee that it will appeal to the public to whom it is directed.' Some doubt lingers over whether or not OSI ever intended producing replicas, or whether it was simply a show car. As it stands, only one OSI Mustang is believed to have been made and its whereabouts remains a mystery.

While nominally based on a Ford Mustang, OSI's take on the Pony Car borrowed relatively little, to the point that it largely boasted a tubular frame and had independent rear suspension.

NSU Autonova GT

Influential in its own way, this distinctive sports car-cum-GT was conceived by *Der Spiegel* journalist Fritz B. Busch who teamed up with Michael Conrad and Pio Manzù to form the Autonova design consultancy. In early 1965, the trio set about creating a styling study armed with 60,000 Deutsche Marks provided by NSU. It also supplied a Prinz 1000TT platform. The prototype, known simply as GT, was built in just four months and emerged to considerable acclaim at the 1965 Frankfurt motor show.

With its unusual headlight arrangement and body-integrated plastic bumpers, the GT's striking profile looked unlike any production car then on the market. It may well have entered production, too, had show-goers had their way. The NSU stand handed out ballots requesting visitors to state whether or not they would be prepared to pay around 8,000 Deutsche Marks for such a car. The response was an overwhelming 'yes', and even the President of the Federal Republic of Germany, Heinrich Lübke, was among their number.

However, the project never went any further. NSU was committed to bringing the RO80 saloon to market (it was unveiled in Frankfurt in October 1967). Developing a further model, and a niche one at that, would have represented an unnecessary distraction. In a roundabout way, the GT did eventually inspire production cars: the prototype was displayed in the Porsche studio while the 924 and 928 models were being mapped out.

1965

OSI Secura

There is a rich history of magazines and styling houses collaborating on projects, the Alfa Romeo Gran Sport *Quattroruote* Zagato being perhaps the most famous. However, while that car was a pastiche of a pre-war classic, the follow up was anything but. Unveiled at the 1965 Turin motor show, the *Quattroruote* Secura was not an attractive car but it was a robust one. If you were going to crash, this was the car to do it in, its makers claimed.

The Secura was conceived in 1965 by *Quattroruote*, with OSI being responsible for its construction. While there was never the suggestion of a production run, the Secura was a serious project; one that *Quattroruote* and OSI hoped would prove influential. The brochure trumpeted: 'Developed as a public service, the Secura is the second and latest design study offered by *Quattroruote*, the motor magazine. Unlike other publicised designs, the Secura is a fully operative car utilising a Fiat 1500 engine and running gear. It incorporates features that may well become standard equipment on cars of tomorrow.'

It went on to add: 'To increase safety, the car has a rigid passenger compartment protected by front and back structures designed to offer multi-stage resistance to collision. Part of the protective body sections extend beyond or overhang the frame. These reinforced extended sections absorb considerable shock energy, then the impact force meets the additional resistance of the frame and body section. The use of a separate chassis frame, which has a wide perimeter-type centre section, provides added protection from side impact. Also, sliding doors bridge the frame sides to the reinforced roof.'

Resplendent in a vivid shade of lobster red over ivory, the car featured reinforced bulkheads front and rear and a windscreen designed to pop-out on impact. That, and a mercury switch that automatically turned off the 83bhp four-cylinder unit in the event of a collision. Inside, there were four heavily-bolstered seats, with just about every square inch of the cabin featuring thick padding. The steering column was deformable.

The Secura was not met with hoopla, *Road & Track*'s review being perhaps the haughtiest. Henry N. Manney derided it for being: '...one of *those*, an extremely ugly safety car brought forth in company with some Italian magazine. I am almost as tired of safety cars with sliding doors as I am with titchy little Buck Rogers town cars.' *Sporting Motorist* described it as: '...already looking like an accident casualty.'

The OSI-built Secura was intended to offer high levels of crashworthiness, but was not well-liked by the motoring media in period.

Autonova FAM

One of the great concept cars of the 1960s, albeit perhaps the least exotic-looking, the FAM was another product of Pio Manzù, Fritz B. Busch, and Michael Conrad. With backing from the likes of Glas (which supplied running gear from the 1304 production car), Veith-Pirelli, Recaro, VDO, and BASF, two prototypes were constructed by Sibona & Bisano in Turin to an exacting brief. Displayed at the 1965 Frankfurt motor show, the FAM (a contraction of 'Familiare') was a one-box concept that foretold the modern MPV/Minivan, seating five despite a relatively small footprint. Overall, the FAM was 3,500mm (137.8in) long, 1,600mm (63in) wide, and 1,600mm (63in) high.

Inside, the rear seats could be folded and adapted to suit different requirements, while the raised driving position also predicted more recent trends. The car was also equipped with automatic electro-hydraulic suspension and progressive-rate steering. Though widely lauded in the specialist press, the FAM was soon consigned to history.

Constructed by Sibona & Basano in Turin, and employing Glas running gear, the FAM was a masterwork of packaging. However, the design was not adopted for all its undoubted influence.

F.A.R.T. Break

Cursed with a name guaranteed to reduce English speakers to a fit of giggles, the F.A.R.T. (Fabbrica Autoveicoli e Rimorchi Torino) was the brainchild of Carlo Ferrari (no relation to Il Commendatore). First seen at the 1965 Turin motor show, this skimpy off-roader employed Fiat 600-derived running gear and a 499cc Fiat 500 twin-cylinder engine. Just to heap on the ignominy, the model name chosen by Ferrari was 'Break'. Two prototypes were made, although the ostensibly similar Ferves Ranger – which was unveiled in Turin a year later – sold in reasonable numbers, with Radbourne Racing acting as the UK concessionaire.

An acronym too far? The F.A.R.T. Break may have had a comical name but it was a serious project that proved adept off-road. Power came from a half-litre Fiat 'twin'.

Saab Catherina

Designed by Sixten Sason, and constructed at the Aktiebolaget Svenska Järnvägsverkstäderna (ASJ – the Swedish Railroad Works) in Katrineholm, Sweden, this sports car concept was based on running gear from the Saab 96. Its most distinctive feature was its roof, which incorporated a lift-off panel that could be stowed in the boot. This arrangement predated that of the Porsche 911 Targa that popularised it. A full-size model was completed in late 1964, and the finalised version was completed and presented to the Saab management in February of the following year. It passed on the project, and instead opted to manufacture the Sonett II.

1965

Opel's Experimental GT was largely built in secret so as not to spook the risk-averse management. The design was later tweaked to create the strong-selling Opel GT production car.

Opel Experimental GT

One of the biggest surprises of the 1965 Frankfurt motor show was the emergence of a small GT car from Opel. General Motors' German arm had hitherto manufactured products that were, for the most part, designed in Detroit. However, the creation of a standalone styling studio in 1962 led to locals penning cars to suit local tastes. The Experimental GT was the first prototype created internally to be displayed externally. That said, young designer Erhard Schnell and his team went about their business quietly, concerned that the risk-averse GM management might axe the project before it reached fruition.

They need not have worried. Reaction to the show car was overwhelmingly positive. While in retrospect, the styling has been likened to the C3-series Chevrolet Corvette, the American sports car did not reach the market until 1968. The Mako Shark II that foretold it was first seen in 1965, but Schnell has insisted that it had no bearing on the Experimental GT. He claimed he was inspired by Italian exotica. Powered by a 1.9-litre four-cylinder unit from the recently introduced

Rekord B, the show car was fully-functional, too, with select journalists being invited to test the car following its debut.

Such was the response from the press and public alike, Opel was practically forced to put a variation on the theme into production. The visually similar GT was introduced in September 1968 and remained on sale to 1973.

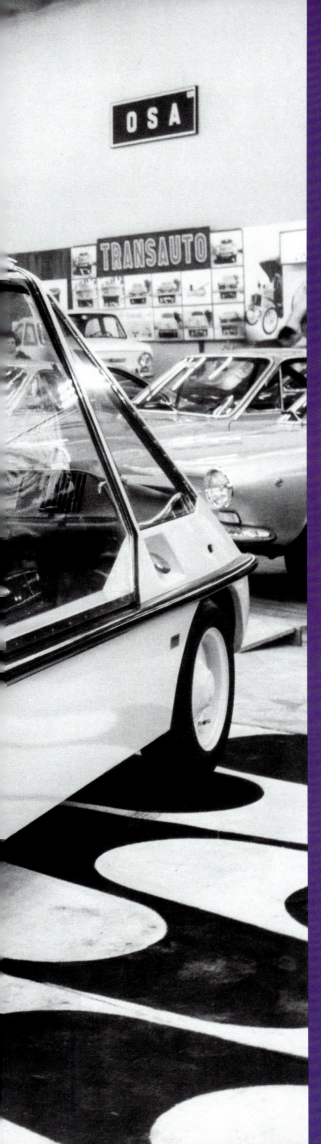

Fissore Aruanda

The 1960s witnessed its fair share of car design competitions, many promising to transform the winner's rendering into a fully-functional, three-dimensional reality. The Aruanda was the end result of one such contest. The Aruanda was designed by Brazilian architecture student Ari de Rocha in 1963, and built by Carrozzeria Fissore in 1964, but it wasn't seen publicly for another year.

De Rocha had entered a competition sponsored by *Luccio Meira*, the brief being to conceive a car specifically tailored for urban use. The São Paulista devised a 'one-box' machine that was notionally powered by either a petrol engine or a raft of batteries. How, precisely, Fissore came to be involved is lost to history, but it was possibly due to its prior work with Brazilian firm, DKW-Vemag, and other South American concerns. The Savigliano-based coachbuilder faithfully reproduced de Rocha's original renderings to 1:1 scale. Basis for the car was a Fiat 500 Giardinetta, which was stripped and shortened, but the rear-sited 499cc 'twin' was retained.

The Aruanda's outline may have appeared angular – even the steering wheel was rectangular, but there were some subtle compound curves. It was well-received on its unveiling at the 1965 Turin motor show, too. Finished in an eye-watering shade of yellow, it was certainly noticeable. *Autocar* reporting:

'The Aruanda is a real solution to the town car problem, one which looks right and, within the limitations of the Fiat layout, seems to satisfy all the engineering requirements. Its Fiat-based unit [chassis], has been shortened so there are only two seats. Wheel arch clearance is restricted, but a lot of wheel work is not required for town use.' *Design Journal*, meanwhile, stated that: '...the Aruanda has plenty of interior space as well as exceptional visibility.'

It also reported that one particularly intrigued visitor to the Fissore stand was five-time Formula 1 World Champion, Juan Manuel Fangio, but it's hard to believe the Argentinian superstar was in the market for a city car. That said, several firms did show an interest in at least evaluating the prototype, Fiat and MV Agusta among them, but there were one or two issues that ultimately hobbled the Aruanda's chances.

Firstly, the high beltline ensured that there was no easy or graceful means of entry. Also, with the sliding glass 'doors' and roof in situ, it got very warm very quickly. Hopes of attracting a Brazilian backer to develop the concept further also came to naught and the project was dropped. As for de Rocha, he never designed another car, while the fate of the one and only Aruanda remains unrecorded.

1965

Lamborghini 3500GTZ

The legend behind how Ferruccio Lamborghini became a motor mogul makes for great reading but is perhaps a mite fanciful. The tractor manufacturer wasn't happy with his Ferrari and decided to inform *Il Commendatore* in Maranello of his feelings, only to be left kicking his heels while he waited for an audience. Thus began a 50-year feud between the two marques. The truth of the matter is probably more prosaic: there was greater kudos in having your name attached to an exotic GT car than there was to a mud-plugging farm implement.

Whatever the truth, Lamborghini's first production model – the 350 GT – was a daring machine, and one of the best-handling cars of its type produced in period. It's just that its Franco Scaglione-penned outline had been tweaked by Carrozzeria Touring to the point that it was a mite compromised. The media made some rather cutting comments about its looks, and Lamborghini responded by delivering two chassis (0310 and 0322) to Zagato in Milan; what could this Milan styling house do with them? What happened next has been mired in mystery and conjecture ever since.

The first 3500GTZ, as it was dubbed, made a low-key debut at the 1965 London Motor Show at Earls Court, sandwiched between an Alfa Romeo Gran Sport *Quattroruote* and a Lancia Flaminia 3C 2800 Supersport Zagato on the British Zagato Ltd stand. The car obviously failed to make much of an impression given that it was barely mentioned in the British motoring weeklies. Styled by Ercole Spada, and some 100mm (3.9in) shorter overall than its donor car, the 3500GT's lines were, if anything, just as challenging as the regular 350 GT. That would explain why the project was aborted almost immediately, but then Lamborghini was embroiled in turning the motoring world on its head with the mould-breaking Miura, so it was perhaps just a distraction.

The London show car, 0310, was subsequently acquired by Lamborghini's Milan agent and sometime racing driver, Gerino Gerini. The real mystery surrounds the sister car. No photos of it were ever published in period. What is known is that it was painted silver and used as everyday transport by Lamborghini engineer Paolo Stanzani until a crash ended play when the car was just eight months old. What, precisely, happened next depends on whose story you believe: it was either repaired and sold to someone in the USA before ending up in Japan, or it was broken for parts at the Lamborghini factory following the crash in 1966.

Zagato's youthful stylist Ercole Spada created the outline for the Lamborghini 3500GTZ that was typically leftfield. Two cars were made, the fate of one remaining a mystery.

This was the year in which a production car outshone many a concept car. The arrival of the Lamborghini Miura P400 in completed form at the 1966 Geneva motor show caused a furore. The upstart start-up operation from Sant'Agata had stolen a march on the exotica establishment and created the first true supercar in the accepted sense, the term having been coined by the British title, *CAR*. It didn't matter that it was unproven – that it was a long way from being perfected, it appeared wildly innovative.

It also prompted something of an arms race among rivals firms, with the mainstream also adopting the supercar, if only in concept form. Low-slung, mid-engined machines became almost obligatory. Even so, there remained some designers who were evangelical about conceiving cars for the many rather than the few.

Also in 1966
The first episode of the groundbreaking science fiction series *Star Trek* premieres on US television channel NBC.
England defeats Germany to win the football World Cup at Wembley Stadium.
China's Cultural Revolution begins under Chairman Mao, as intellectuals are purged.
US troop numbers in Vietnam pass 500,000 as the war escalates.
The Action Man toy figure is first launched in the UK.

1966

Ferrari 365P 'Tre Posti'

A degree of confusion surrounds the genesis of the 365P 'Tre Posti'. What is beyond doubt is that it wasn't conceived by Ferrari. It was the brainchild of Sergio Pininfarina. Legend has it that it was a personal project, and that he styled it himself. The veracity of this is shaky, at best, not least because most Pininfarina insiders from the time insist it was shaped by Aldo Brovarone. It borrowed heavily from his Dino Berlinetta Speciale concept car that was first seen at the 1965 Paris motor show. The 365P was effectively an upscaled version, albeit with additional styling cues that pointed to the forthcoming Dino 206GT production car.

However, to dismiss this as just an enlarged Dino is wide of the mark. Basis for the 365P was a 'Type 557A' tubular-steel chassis. Suspension was independent front and rear, with all-round disc brakes. Powering the car was a 4.4-litre V12 with a single cam per bank. According to period figures, it produced 380bhp at 7,300rpm. The all-alloy unit was allied to a five-speed ZF transaxle. The standout feature, however, was the three-abreast seating arrangement. According to its creator, this wasn't a gimmick. It was meant to make the car more practical (the middle seat was mounted on runners and had a rotating base so the driver could get in and out easily, all things being relative).

Construction of the car was overseen by Leonardo Fioravanti who would subsequently rework Brovarone's efforts into the Dino production car as we know it. He was also responsible for shaking down the prototype, often on the Turin-Ivrea autostrada towards Mont Blanc. With a degree of predictability, it was the unusual seating arrangement that garnered the most comment when the 365P broke cover at the 1966 October Paris motor show. It was the only car on the large Pininfarina stand. *Autocar* commented: 'It is possibly the best solution to the problem of housing the occupants of this type of car comfortably. Even two people would find the restricted foot room disagreeable with side by side seating.'

Road & Track, meanwhile, reported: 'The rear engine and control layout almost oblige the driver to be in the centre... The whole thing

shows restraint. They weren't trying to build the lowest car in town.' Later that month, the prototype was displayed at the International Motor Show at Earls Court, London, and it is at this juncture that the story gets a little muddy. According to some sources, the 365P displayed in Paris and London was a mock up (inspect period images and it is clearly lacking an exhaust system, and ventilation slats have not yet been sunk into the rear decklid). The functional prototype was still in the throes of creation.

This tallies with paperwork from the period, an invoice from Pininfarina to first owner, three-time Le Mans winner Luigi Chinetti, suggesting the body cost $7,690 to fashion. A separate invoice from Ferrari for a P2 chassis and engine amounted to $6,350. An outwardly similar car was also built for Giovanni Agnelli, which was displayed at the 1966 Turin motor show. Agnelli's Ferrari – chassis 8851 – was, however, significantly different in that it reputedly featured a 250LM-derived platform. It was originally painted silver with a blue stripe (it was later repainted black and then red).

Due to a weakened left leg, Agnelli had an electro-mechanical clutch installed, creating in effect a semi-automatic set up. Sometime later, however, the car was returned to Pininfarina after its owner complained that it was a mite unstable around its alleged top speed of 186mph (299km/h). This story is perhaps apocryphal, but the car subsequently gained a large rear aluminium spoiler which sullied its good looks. The Agnelli car is now believed to be somewhere in South East Asia.

Chassis 8971 arrived Stateside in 1967 and was shown at that year's Imported Car Show. It was acquired by Marvin Carton, who traded the car in a year later. It then passed to sometime racer Jan de Vroom, an American-domiciled Dutch-Indonesian who had helped support Chinetti's NART (North American Racing Team) equipe. De Vroom found the car unsuited to New York traffic, so traded it in with Chinetti in 1969, only to die in mysterious circumstances four years later. The car has remained in the Chinetti family ever since.

The 'Tre Posti' foretold the Dino 206 GT road car but also the McLaren F1 with its central driving position, passengers being offset either side. Two cars were made, but they differed significantly.

1966

AMC 'Rambleseat'/AMX

American Motor Corporation was looking for an image overhaul during the mid-1960s. With the arrival of a non-running, glassfibre-bodied concept car at the February 1966 Chicago Auto Show, it got that and more. This fastback coupe hinted at a new breed of Pony Car, even if some of its design features were a little off the wall. Dubbed 'Rambleseat' due to its 'rumble seat' that substituted for a boot, it did enough to convince the management in Kenosha to press ahead with the construction of a second prototype.

Though keen to continue investigating the use of glassfibre for any potential production run, AMC's subcontractor, Alfredo Vignale, was unfamiliar with composites, so his employees produced a hand-finished, steel-bodied car instead. Based on a modified 1966 Rambler chassis, complete with 290cu in V8, it was delivered on the eve of the 1966 New York International Auto Show. It formed part of AMC's Project IV programme, a concept car quartet that toured events throughout the US and also included the two-door AMX II sports car, the four-door Cavalier sedan and the Vixen.

AMC contracted Smith Inland of Ionia, Michigan to build a run of glassfibre bodies for the next batch of prototypes. One completed car fared badly in a crash test, which prompted the decision to stick with steel construction for the production version. The rumble seat was also done away with, as was the Vignale car's split-vee windscreen, while its rectangular headlights were replaced with round items for what in time became the AMX production car which went on sale in 1968.

As a coda to the story, the idea of a rumble seat – or 'dickey seat' in British parlance – refused to go away. James Jeffords, who was heavily involved in AMC's Trans-Am motorsport programme, worked closely with designer Brooks Stevens on a customised AMX which they intended offering to the public with an al fresco +2 seating arrangement. The idea was to build 500 cars, complete with super-plush cabins, but AMC's management refused to countenance the idea.

Despite the gimmicky rear seating arrangement, the AMX acted as a harbinger for AMC's entrant into the Pony Car firmament. Vignale acted as a subcontractor.

1966

AMC Cavalier

Deemed innovative in period, the AMC Cavalier's innovations had little lasting worth. Nevertheless, this four-door saloon was an interesting – and practical – concept car; one that was styled under the firm's endlessly resourceful design czar, Dick Teague. The central theme of the car was interchangeability: the wings could be swapped around – left-front to right-rear, and right-front to left-rear. The bonnet and boot lid were also transposable, while the bumpers and doors were symmetrical, too.

While not an original idea, the firm having previously exploited interchangeable parts on the prior Metropolitan under the Nash nameplate, it was thoughtfully executed. AMC claimed that should the Cavalier enter production, the number of steel pressings would be greatly reduced, while the cost of tooling and production would be cut by as much as 30 per cent. For an independent player such as AMC, which had nothing like the resources or inter-marque economies-of-scale of Detroit's 'Big Three', such a lessening of expenditure would have been seismic.

However, the Cavalier never was going to be built in series, nor was the concept car anything other than a mock-up. Nevertheless, this being AMC, nothing went to waste: such styling elements were transposed onto the Hornet production model which went on sale in 1970.

The AMC Cavalier was not the most flamboyant concept car of the period but it was an intelligently conceived one. It employed a raft of interchangeable panels front and rear.

AMC AMX II

While another member of AMC's 'Project IV' series of concept cars from 1966, the AMX II was nevertheless not styled internally. It was the work of freelancer, Vince Gardner, a highly-regarded designer whose resume included spells at Cord, Budd, and more besides, even if his contributions to many landmark motor cars weren't always recognised at the time. According to a press release from the period, the AMX II was: '...an American Motors' "Idea" car, a modified version of the fastback theme introduced earlier on the experimental AMX.'

'It features a "V" rear window with the rear deck contours,' it continued, confusingly. 'Safety taillights with green, amber, and red lenses would give five cars behind immediate indication of the driver's intentions and actions.' Like its Cavalier stablemate, this handsome, pillarless coupé featured a 2,974mm (110in)-wheelbase platform and was powered by a 343cu in V8 (although this is debatable given that no pictures exist of the car moving).

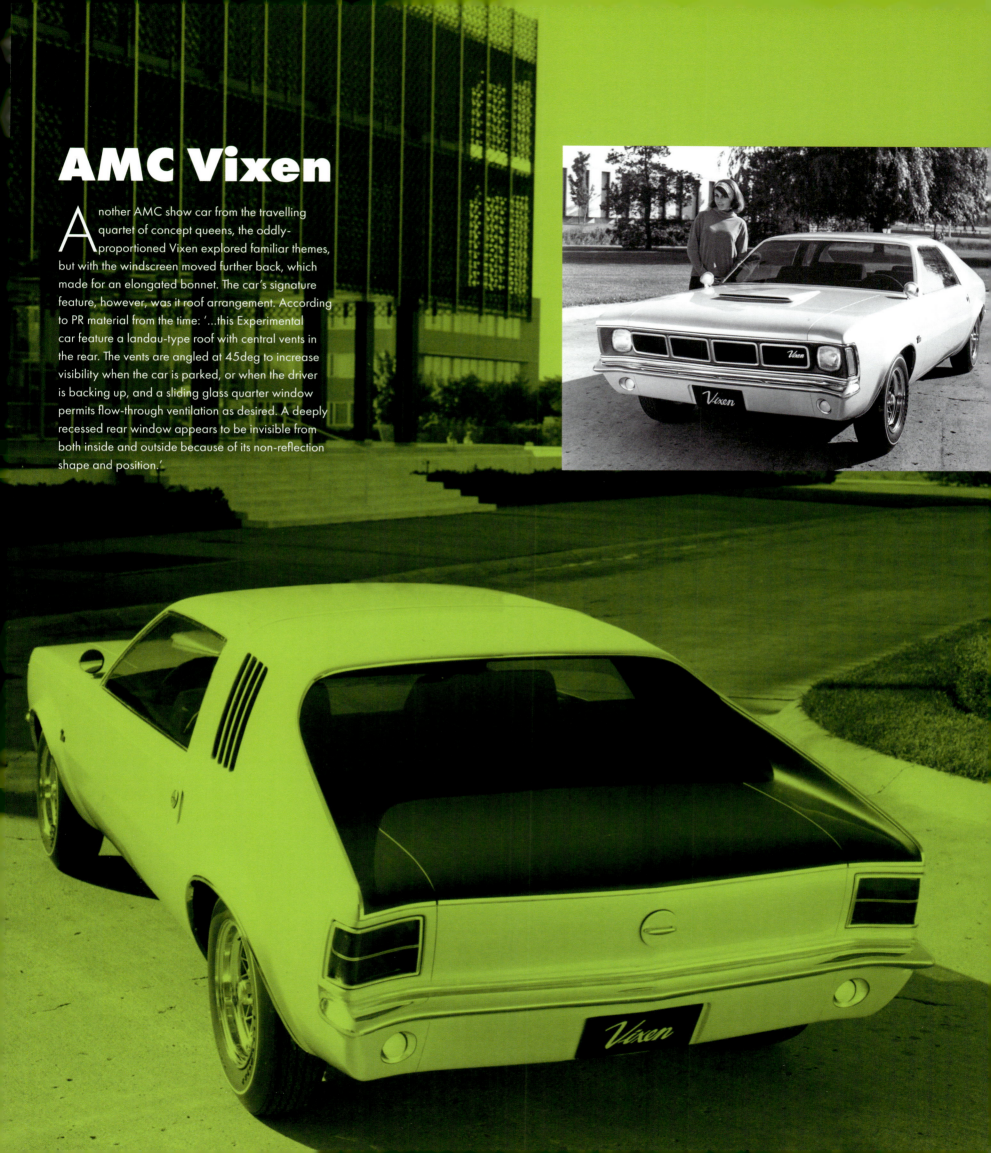

AMC Vixen

Another AMC show car from the travelling quartet of concept queens, the oddly-proportioned Vixen explored familiar themes, but with the windscreen moved further back, which made for an elongated bonnet. The car's signature feature, however, was it roof arrangement. According to PR material from the time: '...this Experimental car feature a landau-type roof with central vents in the rear. The vents are angled at 45deg to increase visibility when the car is parked, or when the driver is backing up, and a sliding glass quarter window permits flow-through ventilation as desired. A deeply recessed rear window appears to be invisible from both inside and outside because of its non-reflection shape and position.'

1966

Cycloac Research Vehicle

Originally conceived as a concept car, and unveiled at the 1966 Detroit Auto Show, the Cycloac Research Vehicle was built to demonstrate the potential of 'Thermoplastics'. This low-slung roadster's body was moulded by Marmon Chemical, a subsidiary of Borg-Warner, styled by Dann Deaver, and constructed by race-car manufacturer Centaur Engineering. Virtually all of its running gear was robbed from the Chevrolet Corvair.

Having garnered more than a few column inches in the national press, that should have been that. The CRV was, however, *too* well received. Potential customers clamoured to buy replicas, and Marmon Chemical followed through with a competition version that was campaigned extensively in SCCA events in 1965; with some success, too. A third car was built for crash-testing while a fourth prototype, with a fixed-head coupe roof and conventional lower doors with tiny gullwing upper sections, was completed in early 1966. A fifth – and final – CRV was built that same year, with prototypes four and five touring the world to promote Marmon Chemical's composite expertise. There was never any intention of putting the car into production per se, the firm instead proposing to sell the project as a turn-key car-manufacturing operation.

Remarkably, it was AMT Corporation that took the bait. It was eager to promote its plastic model kits, and reasoned that production of 50 full-scale cars would be a good fit. Customising legend and regular AMT collaborator Gene Winfield was brought in to oversee the limited run, the firm even going so far as to initiate a dragster variant along with another circuit-racing car, the definitive production version being rechristened Piranha. Winfield gave the car a minor restyle, reworking the profile of the roofline so it tapered gracefully into the cropped tail.

The Piranha was given a further promotional boost when it was picked up by NBC for use in its *The Man from U.N.C.L.E.* TV show. The small-screen variant benefited from further Winfield touches, not least a raft of Spy-Fi gadgetry. However, it was written out of the series as the unconventional door arrangement made it difficult for stars Robert Vaughn and David McCallum to get in and out of the rather cosy cockpit in a hurry. Given that the pale blue machine was often involved in chase sequences, this was rather a stumbling block.

AMT built just four cars in 1967 before pulling the plug. The $5,000 asking price was still someway short of the actual build expenditure. It didn't help that General Motors didn't offer its support, and insisted that AMT buy running gear at cost. There were several subsequent strands to the Piranha narrative, with bootleg versions being offered with VW power into the 1970s, while a variation on the theme was built with Renault running gear by Ghia's OSI offshoot in Italy. None of these added further lustre to a car whose star shone brightly only to wane almost as quickly.

Lamborghini Flying Star II

Just to prove that dying embers burn hottest, Carrozzeria Touring's appearance at the November 1966 Turin motor show witnessed the unveiling of the Flying Star II. Three months later, the doors were shuttered on this historic coachbuilder and styling house. In its final appearance at an exhibition, the Milanese concern displayed this one-off Lamborghini alongside a Fiat 124 saloon that had been turned into a two-door convertible. The two cars could not have appeared more disparate, the boxy open car appearing pedestrian compared to the 400GT's unusual coupé-cum-shooting brake outline.

The donor car's chassis was shortened by 100mm (4in), and unlike many sporting exotica of the period, there was no pretence of this being anything other than a strict two-seater. However, there was a decent amount of space for luggage, access being made that much easier thanks to the rear hatchback which mostly comprised the rear window. Touring, which had partnered the youthful Lamborghini concern from the outset, had hoped the Flying Star II might be adopted as a production model, but it wasn't to be. The one and only prototype was subsequently acquired by Jacques Quoirez, brother of the much-garlanded novelist, Françoise Sagan.

Dying embers burn hottest. The Flying Star II (right) was created by the once proud Carrozzeria Touring shortly before it was shuttered. Basis was a Lamborghini 400GT.

1966

Vauxhall XVR

General Motors' British brand, Vauxhall, exhibited at the Geneva motor show for the first time in 1966. It did so with the first concept car ever to wear the Griffin logo, the XVR (eXperimental Vauxhall Research) appearing impossibly low-slung and exotic. The firm's Director of Design, David Jones, commented following its unveiling: 'Uncompromising in its styling treatment, the XVR shows the future trend in world design.'

This was a bold statement, but the XVR was created in its entirety within Vauxhall's recently-inaugurated Design & Engineering Centre. *Autocar* reported: 'Although General Motors has for years made and exhibited "dream cars", the XVR is the first of these advanced vehicles to appear from Vauxhall at Luton. In appearance, it has obvious affinities with the Chevrolet Mako Shark II, but, of course, the whole thing is on a much smaller scale. The wheelbase is only just over 7ft, and the height 40in....'

It went on to add: 'The chassis itself is a deep backbone welded to a platform, the reclining seat-pans being an integral part of the floor structure with considerable ability to resist crushing in side impacts... Apart from a roll hoop behind the seats, the body has practically no fixed superstructure; the bonnet hinges forward for access to the engine and spare wheel, the tail hinges to uncover the boot, and the gullwing doors pivot up and out on a single centre windscreen strut.'

Henry N. Manney was less impressed, commenting in *Road & Track*: 'Elsewhere in the hall there were the usual Show Eggs, the prize in this case going to Vauxhall who cobbled up a smooth if slightly impractical coupe on the VX490 chassis [sic]. The English papers went into paroxysms over this as a prospective Le Mans world-beater, etc, but you can take it from me that this was a Show Egg to get Vauxhall's name in print.'

Fortunately, *Motor Racing* was on hand to leave readers in no doubt as to the firm's motorsport intent. 'John Aiden, Vauxhall's chief engineer, gave the answer to that one,' it stated. 'He said: "Although the XVR is clearly a high-performance model, it does not follow that Vauxhall has any plans to enter the racing or competition field."'

Three XVRs were built, of which one metal-bodied car was fully-functional and powered by a 1,975cc four-cylinder VX 4/90 unit. Two glassfibre mocks-ups were also made, one of which survives.

All three XVR 'cars' are gathered here outside the newly inaugurated Vauxhall Design & Engineering Centre. The lone runner (right) was later destroyed, although one of the mock-ups still survives.

Fiat 850 Vanessa

Created in less enlightened times, the Vanessa was aimed squarely at women motorists. Based on Fiat 850 running gear, complete with the latest Idromatic transmission (a clutchless, semi-automatic arrangement), its most prominent feature was the rear side window arrangement: they were hinged in gullwing fashion so the rear seats could be accessed from the outside. Not only that, there were integrated baby seats and swivelling front squabs (which ensured the miniskirt-wearer's dignity was maintained, according to Ghia). In addition, there were countless cubbyholes for additional storage, the cabin being awash with lilac fabric.

Other never-repeated design quirks included a fire extinguisher that could, according to the press release, also be used to inflate a flat tyre, and nothing by way of instrumentation. Instead, there were graduated lights to indicate speed, revs, etc. Attributed to Giorgetto Giugiaro, the design was well-received when first seen at the 1966 Turin motor show. However, the Vanessa was never going to enter even limited production, despite suggestions to the contrary in some period reports.

1966 Quattroruote

Scarabeo coupé sperimentale OSI

N. 12
DICEMBRE
1966
L. 300

TUTTO IL SALONE DI TORINO

OSI Alfa Romeo Scarabeo

The precise backstory behind the Scarabeo is mired in conjecture and half-truths. When OSI unveiled its latest concept car at the 1966 Paris motor show, there was no suggestion that it would inspire a competition tool, despite its racy outline. The English-language-speaking media wasn't kind about its looks, either, the styling having since been attributed to Sergio Sartorelli. *Road & Track*'s Ursula Bagel, for example, reported: 'I always knew the Kamm-style [tail design treatment] would end up this way, with the tail chopped off right behind the ears. I was disappointed to learn that the car has apparently not been tested on the road as I was curious to know how fast the Alfa engine could push a shape like this.'

However, the Scarabeo (Italian for Beetle) was something of a harbinger for Alfa Romeo's future motor racing endeavours, the prototype featuring a Giulia Sprint GTA 'Type 502/A' four-cylinder engine that was sited in-line amidships. A second open-top variant followed (although it was never finished), as did another fixed-head car, both featuring engines mounted transversely. The second coupé employed a Tipo 33 chassis.

1966

Chevrolet Electrovair II

Chevrolet engaged in all manner of experiments involving the Corvair during the 1960s including, bizarrely, the use of peroxide rockets. The Electrovair II, however, was more conventional in that it employed silver zinc battery packs in the front and rear compartments of a four-door Monza saloon. It emerged some 363kg (800lb) heavier than the standard variant, which had a corresponding knock-on effect on performance: it had a top speed of 80mph (129km/h), and range of 40–80 miles (64–129km) between charges.

An early attempt at a GM electric car, the Electrovair II was undone by its weight compared to a conventional Corvair saloon. That, and the amount of space needed to accommodate the batteries.

OSI City-Daf

The 1960s witnessed its fair share of small concept cars; the sort of machine that promised to foretell what urbanites would be driving decades down the line. The OSI City-Daf was one such creation. 1966 saw the short-lived Ghia offshoot at its most prolific, the Turin-based concern having launched its handsome Ford Taunus-based 20M TS coupé in March, while its daring Alfa Romeo Scarabeo show-stopper broke cover a few months later at the Paris motor show. Rather less flashy was the City-Daf, which emerged at November's Turin motor show where it was unveiled alongside the equally new OSI-Fiat Cross Country off-roader.

Based on an abbreviated Daf Daffodil chassis with a 1,970.5mm (77.6in) wheelbase, this boxy device retained the 746cc two-cylinder unit and 'rubber band' Variomatic transmission complete with V-belts and variable-diameter pulleys. The car's body was styled under studio chief Sergio Sartorelli, the signature feature being its unusual door arrangement. On the left-hand (driver's) side, there was a single sliding door that employed a rail-and-ball system similar to those used on commercial vehicles. The reasoning behind this was simple: at a busy roadside, you would, according to the press release, have to wait for there to be break in traffic before you could open a conventional door safely. With a sliding door, the problem was alleviated, if not removed entirely.

On the right-hand side, however, was a normal passenger door and rear 'suicide' door. This set-up was in place to improve access and ingress for passengers entering the car from the pavement. The rear hatchback, meanwhile, was hinged in the roof panel. *Style Auto* magazine reported in typically unique fashion: 'The interior echoes more or less that of the original Daf Daffodil, but the finish is more luxurious... The rear bench seat can be folded down so that the City-Daf has a noteworthy amount of room for goods. All the side glasses are sliding and various cubby holes are arranged in the doors and dashboard. The car has reversing lights and the wraparound bumpers are covered with a band of rubber which is very useful in small bumps incurred when parking... The City-Daf is 301.5cm long. In other words, [it is] halfway between the Fiat 500 and the BMC Mini. Its height is 147cm, which is most unusual for a modern car where one's hat is rarely taken into consideration.'

What happened next is open to conjecture. Following a few further show outings, the City-Daf vanished. If nothing else, it was later immortalised in 1:36th scale by Corgi Toys as part of its Whizzwheels range.

The OSI City-Daf was a practicality orientated concept car for urbanites. It featured a sliding door on the left, and a conventional hinged door on the right.

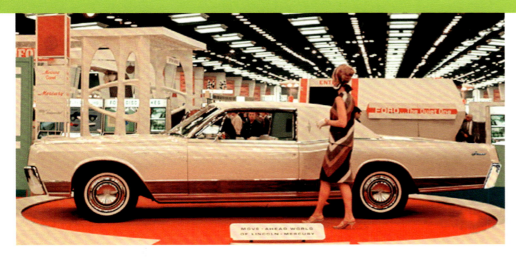

Lincoln Continental Coronation Coupe

Built at Lincoln's behest by Lehmann-Peterson, the firm that built the Continental Executive Limousines for Ford's premium brand, this one-off show car began life as a standard four-door saloon. It was transformed into a two-door coupe by the Chicago concern, the surgery stretching to a 'Levant-grained vinyl roof.' A new, bespoke grille was also installed, the most unusual aspect being a 254mm (10in)-wide band of walnut veneer inset in stainless-steel rocker-panel mouldings along each flank. A secondary version, also dubbed Coronation Coupe, was made in 1967 and featured trim updates in-line with that year's Continental production car.

Ford Mustang Mach I

One of countless Mustang styling studies produced during the 1960s, the Mach I was one of the few that saw daylight. This squat, two-seater fastback featured umpteen racer reference points, not least the twin 'Monza-style' filler-caps and fixed side glazing with sliding slats. The front-end treatment, particularly the grille, predicted the 1969 Mustang body style, while the rear hatchback would be employed on the Mustang II from 1974. Initial renderings suggested it was powered by a 427cu in big-block V8.

The aggressively-styled Mach I featured hot rod and sports-prototype design influences.

Daihatsu Sport

Daihatsu used the 1966 Tokyo motor show to introduce its new 360cc Fellow city car. Alongside it was the tiny Campagnolo-based P3 racing car and the glassfibre-bodied Sport styling study. Purportedly based on the 1000 saloon production car, albeit with a fuel-injected variant of its one-litre OHV four-cylinder unit, it bore more than a passing resemblance to the Vignale/Michelotti concepts from three years prior. Daihatsu hinted that a 1.5-litre version might be in the offing, but the Sport remained unique.

1966

Bertone Porsche 911

This one-off Porsche was conceived by Hollywood-based dealer/race entrant, Johnny von Neumann. His clientele had petitioned for a convertible model ever since the 356 was finally axed in 1965. He tasked Bertone with creating something more suited to Southern California, the result being shown at the 1965 Geneva motor show. Given that it was displayed alongside the newly-unveiled Lamborghini Miura, this Italianate take on a German product understandably received relatively little attention in the specialist press.

Motor seemed only interested in its unusual lighting arrangement. It reported it as having: '...another variation of the headlamp theme – they hide behind electronically-driven shutters which are slotted to allow reasonably effective "flashing" even when the shutters are closed, rather like wartime blackout grilles.' *Style Auto*, meanwhile, commented on its similarity in certain aspects to the prior Testudo, its sole criticism being: '...the engine compartment lid is somewhat too raised because of the engine's bulk.'

If von Neumann intended building replicas in series, he was to be disappointed. Porsche's management was not amused, not least because of the impending arrival of its Targa variant of the 911 with its lift-out roof panel. The Bertone prototype, originally resplendent in Carmine Red and riding on Campagnolo alloy wheels, was later painted black and equipped with Porsche Fuchs items, the engine also being uprated to 911S specification.

Bertone's take on the 911 didn't bare even trace elements of the car that bore it stylistically. It is seen below next to Bertone's Jaguar FT that was built at the behest of the Italian concessionaire.

The Italian concept car came of age in 1967. Some established *carrozzerie* had by now withered and died, but the likes of Bertone and Pininfarina were reaching for the stars. They were global trendsetters for whom nothing was beyond limits. Many concept cars produced by these and other Turinese concerns appeared more at home in a sci-fi opus than a show hall, but some weren't without influence over the long term. Even so, many motoring titles of the day slammed them for being little more than shiny baubles of no lasting value.

Away from gullwing doors and silver lamé seats, an increasing number of small city car concepts served to counterbalance the apparent excess, many of them battery-powered. They weren't without influence either, it's just that it took decades to realise as such.

Also in 1967
The Six Day War takes place between Israel and an Arab coalation comprising Egypt, Syria and Jordan.
Dr. Christian Barnard completes the first successful human heart transplant, in Cape Town, South Africa.
Donald Campbell is killed on Lake Coniston, while attempting to break his own World Water Speed Record.
The first scheduled colour TV broadcasts are made in the UK.

Bertone Lamborghini Marzal

Styled during what has since been referred to as Marcello Gandini's 'Hexagonal Period', the Lamborghini Marzal was the undoubted star of the 1967 Geneva motor show. Legendary motoring writer L.J.K. Setright enthused in his event report for CAR magazine: 'It is impossible to concentrate on the activities of the men swarming in and around it, so intriguing, so exciting, so utterly absorbing is the car itself... The demi-Lambo of Bertone is perhaps the most extravagant piece of virtuoso styling to have come out of Europe since the war... The Mighty Marzal has been steadily draining the rest of the hall of hangers-on... Journalists, photographers and rival stylists fought for possession of its four silvered seats.'

The idea of a Lamborghini for the family man in a hurry had first been mooted as far back as 1965, the Sant'Agata firm having by then been existence for only three years. Plans called for a production run of as many as 2,000 units per year, with a rear-sited, transversely-mounted V6 powerplant. The Marzal would be the *amuse-bouche* prior to the definitive production car coming on-line. It never did, but this one-off offered a tantalising view of what might have been, not least mechanically. The engine, for example, was created by essentially carving through the 60° vee of the 3,929cc V12 that powered the Miura and its stablemates. The five-speed gearbox-in-the-sump transmission was also carried over, along with the Miura's rack-and-pinion steering, double-wishbone suspension and disc brakes.

However, despite this being a functional concept car, the Marzal was a styling-led exercise rather than an engineering one. Gandini was given free rein when shaping the car, Bertone's styling chief creating an outline unlike any other. The slimline nose was home to a corrugated rubber bumper and a sextet of quartz-iodine Marchal lights, the rake of the windscreen and rearmost ovoid

1967

Prince Rainier III at the helm of the Marzal ahead of the May 1967 Monaco Grand Prix. His wife, Princess Grace of Monaco, accompanied him in the passenger seat.

curve of the side glazing hinting at the Miura's arrangement, while at the rear there was a riot of outlandish detailing, the hexagonal rear window louvres, and ribbed rear bumper represented pure styling trickery. Nevertheless, it was the door arrangement that prompted jaws to slacken when the car was unveiled.

Gandini and Bertone were not content with just a gullwing set-up. Here, the doors comprised mostly of glass which ensured the cabin was effectively a goldfish bowl. This was not a car for the shy and retiring, but the interior was similarly outlandish thanks to its honeycomb dashboard and silver seats (the effect was arrived at by painting them – they were still wet at the time of the car's unveiling). The irony is that marque instigator Ferruccio Lamborghini hated the Marzal, the largely transparent doors in particular being the subject of his ire. What's more, he was vocal about it in public. Even so, it garnered media attention the world over for the simple reason that there was nothing else quite like it. As *Road & Track* surmised succinctly: '[It is] a design so fresh that everything else looks old fashioned.'

Weighing in at 1,200kg (2,650lb), and with a top speed of 118mph (190km/h), the rear-engine bias reputedly made the Marzal a handful to drive. Nevertheless, the car was entrusted to Prince Rainier III ahead of the May 1967 Monaco Grand Prix, his wife Princess Grace accompanying him in the passenger seat. Ferruccio Lamborghini was dead set against the car appearing in the Principality, not least because he feared negative publicity should the car break down – or worse. Instead, all went smoothly and royal patronage, if only for a few minutes, served to generate further publicity.

However, the Marzal was then shuttered away inside Bertone's factory collection. It wasn't displayed again publicly until 1996 when it appeared at Concorso Italiano in Monterey, California. It sold for $1.52m in 2011 at RM Auctions' Ville d'Este sale, following Bertone's sale of six significant concept cars.

Pininfarina Dino 206 Berlinetta Prototipo Competizione

Pininfarina's 1967 Frankfurt motor show star was styled by Paolo Martin and based on a Dino 206 S sports-prototype platform, complete with two-litre V6 engine sited amidships. Often referred to as 'The Yellow Dino', the car featured styling themes that would appear on subsequent Dino production cars, such as conical side scoops and rear buttresses, but the overall outline was distinct to just this one-off.

Autocar reported: 'Study cars among the Pininfarina group included a new Dino-based aerodynamic coupé. Fins, scoops and air outlets are dominant features. The enclosure aft of the wide, sloping windscreen is fixed, but the doors lift up from hinges on a spine – a part of the roll-bar in gullwing style... The nose and tail ailerons can be set according to performance to suit lift conditions.' *CAR*, meanwhile wrote: 'The racing Dino chassis (making three so far) was endowed with not one but two massive spoilers – both adjustable; one aft and the other (just as well since it would certainly have taken off otherwise) elevated on miniature Chaparral stalks on the nose.'

Martin, who was 23 years old when he styled the car, loathed the spoilers. They were added at the behest of Pininfarina's general manager, Renzo Carli.

Paolo Martin's take on the Dino theme was shaped when he was just 23 years old. However, the spoilers were added at the insistence of Pininfarina's general manager, Renzo Carli.

1967

Bertone Pirana

The title of Autocar magazine's article in October 1967 said it all: 'Bertone-Jaguar: no dream car – but not for you and me.' This one-off *gran turismo* wasn't the first Bertone-bodied Jaguar, witness the Franco Scaglione-styled XK150 and Marcello Gandini-designed 'FT' that was based variously on S-type and 420 saloon foundations for Italy's marque concessionaire, Ferruccio Tarchini. However, in this instance, there was no intention of making the Pirana in even the most limited of numbers.

The car was conceived by *The Weekend Telegraph*'s editor John Anstey, the picture editor Alexander Low, art director Geoffrey Axbey and motoring correspondent, Courtenay Edwards. Following a visit to the March 1967 Geneva Motor Show, conversation back in London turned to the key constituents of the perfect GT car. What began as an office discussion soon took a turn for the serious: Anstey was keen to see their dream car made real, and stipulated that it should be built from components already in production and available to the public. 'Speed with luxury' was the mantra.

Jaguar's talismanic founder Sir William Lyons was responsive when approached by Anstey. He would supply an E-type 2+2 chassis, complete with 4.2-litre straight-six power. Nuccio Bertone then agreed to complete the coachwork in time for London's International Motor Show in October of that year. Gandini was tasked with what was essentially a rebodying exercise, the end result baring not even a passing resemblance to the donor car, despite the fastback two-seater sharing the same proportions. It was virtually the same height and length, but 63.5mm (2.5in) wider.

Other firms lent expertise, including Triplex which supplied special tinted Sundym glass in an effort to stop the sun's harmful rays from slow-baking the car's occupants. Lucas, meanwhile, supplied lights while Smith's Motor Accessory Division provided a one-off air-conditioning system. It also served up a tape recorder/player, plus a warning device that beeped should the driver exceed a pre-se speed. Connolly contributed the leather for the cabin, a special hide dubbed 'Anela' that featured a sandy tint thanks to special pigments. Britax, meanwhile, supplied special seatbelts with webbing to match the upholstery.

All told, the Pirana cost a rumoured £20,000 to construct. The Pirana's outline proved influential, too, in that it provided reference points for the Lamborghini Espada. Once its show career came to an end in 1969, it was sold for £16,000.

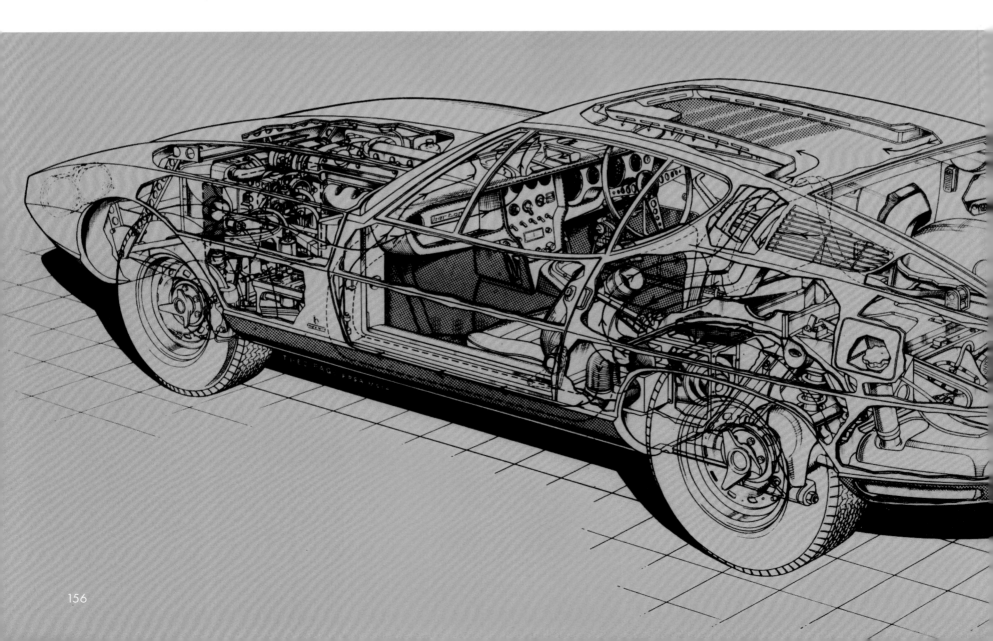

The Jaguar E-type-based Pirana was built at vast expense at the behest of *The Weekend Telegraph*. Some styling cues were transposed onto the Lamborghini Espada.

1967

Pininfarina BMC 1100/1800 Berlina Aerodinamica

One of the great missed opportunities of the British motor industry, the BMC/BLMC 1800 'Landcrab' in all in its various guises sold poorly. Much of this was due to its ungainly looks, long-time collaborator Pininfarina producing its own take on the theme in time for the November 1967 Turin motor show. Remarkably, the donor car had only been delivered to the Turin factory in August of that year, the car prototype being completed in just nine weeks.

Styled by Leonardo Fioravanti or Paolo Martin (both claim authorship), this study in streamlining was fully-functional too, proprietary parts stretching to Ferrari doorhandles and Rolls-Royce-sourced electric-window and power-seat mechanisms. However, despite rave reviews from the world's motoring media, the car was met with a degree of not-invented-here enmity from within the British automotive giant that, in 1968, morphed into British Leyland following the merger of Leyland Motors and British Motor Holdings.

According to Fioravanti, Alec Issigonis, who conceived the 1800, was particularly vocal when sharing his displeasure, while the firm's chairman Sir George Harriman reputedly claimed it looked too much like a Jaguar (something which continues to baffle the legendary designer). A second car was built subsequently using a smaller 1100 'ADO 16' platform which was similarly not received with warmth. Neither design was adopted, although Fioravanti drove the smaller car to Switzerland in 1970 and parked it near the Hotel Intercontinental in Geneva where Citroën was holding a press conference ahead of the launch of the GS. Fioravanti claims the design of the GS and the later CX were close cribs of the Aerodinamica styling studies.

The 1800 prototype was scrapped at some point during the 1970s, but the smaller car, along with the body buck, survived the chop.

Rover 2000 TCZ

First seen at the 1967 British International Motor Show at Earls Court, the TCZ echoed styling themes long established by Zagato's chief designer, Ercole Spada. Based on a 1965 Rover P6 2000S donor car, complete with an experimental 2000TC engine, it emerged 230mm (9in) shorter, the wheelbase having been abbreviated by 30mm (1.2in). It was also 20mm (0.8in) wider, and 13mm (0.5in) lower. According to *Style Auto*, it was 440lb lighter too, the bonnet-line also being appreciably lower thanks to the adoption of two sidedraught Dell'Orto carburettors on a specially-made manifold in place of the original SU HD8 items.

The conundrum for marque historians is whether or not Rover was involved in the project. Given that it was based on a development chassis, there is every reason to be believe there was a link. A report from the time in *Style Auto* suggests there was. Ivo Alessiani gushed: 'In the task under examination this technical skill has been the 'sine qua non' for Rover would not have entrusted any coachbuilder their precious shell, the fruit of many years of research and exemplary production techniques. This trust, established gradually between one journey by Ing. Gianni Zagato to Solihull, and the other by Mr David E. Bache (Rover's chief designer) to Terrazzano di Rho, is the keystone to the validity of the 2000 TCZ.'

Chevrolet Astro I
(aka Corvair Super GT Low Roof Aerodynamic Coupé)

One of the wildest-looking concept cars of the mid-to-late 1960s, the Astro I was shaped by the ever-inventive Larry Shinoda under Bill Mitchell. Incredibly, the car was just 901.7mm (35.5in) tall, with means of entry via a clamshell canopy: the body aft of the windscreen tilted up and back in one-piece. The two seats would rise simultaneously to make entry and exit that bit easier and, once strapped in, the seats and canopy would then lower again. As was typical of the period, there was nothing so prosaic as a steering wheel. Instead, it employed twin hand-grips.

Underpinned by a bespoke, semi-monocoque platform, complete with a 2,235mm (88in) wheelbase, the car was powered by a unique variant of the air-cooled, six-cylinder Corvair unit with a displacement of 2,885cc. New cylinder heads were employed that featured a belt-driven SOHC valvetrain, hemispherical combustion chambers, and inclined valves. It was fed by a brace of three-barrel carburettors that were made for this application by GM (albeit with Weber internals). This unit was reputed to produce 240bhp at 7,200rpm, and was allied to a regular Corvair Powerglide transaxle.

However, for all the hype surrounding the car following its unveiling at the 1967 New York International Auto Show, the Astro I never turned a wheel under its own power. It currently forms part of the General Motors Heritage Collection.

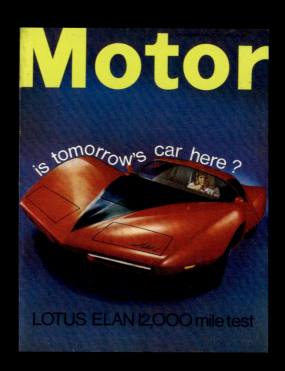

The wild Corvair-derived Astro I was a non-runner despite its unique engine set-up. Unlike many other concepts from the period, it survives to this day.

1967

Ford Mach 2

Another tantalising 'what might have been' concept car to emerge from Detroit during the 1960s, this mid-engined machine was no show queen. Created under styling vice-president Gene Bordinat, it was underpinned by a floorpan borrowed from a Mustang convertible, albeit reconfigured for this application. Power came from a small-block 302cu in V8 allied to a ZF four-speed transaxle. Front suspension and brakes were largely standard Mustang fare, other parts-bin cast-offs including rear drum brakes from a Galaxie. The use of proprietary parts also stretched to the rear bumper which was an unmodified Mustang item.

Two Mach 2 prototypes were made (just to confuse matters, Ford's press material variously dubbed it Mach 2 and Mach II). A white test mule was evaluated at Ford's Dearborn Proving Grounds, while a scarlet sister car was displayed at the 1967 Chicago Auto Show. There was no business case for the Mach 2 to move forward and become a production model, even in limited numbers. It is widely held that both prototypes were scrapped. However, that wasn't quite the end of the story. After Semon 'Bunkie' Knudsen became president of Ford in 1968, he tasked Larry Shinoda with renewing and revamping the concept. A racy-looking machine dubbed Mach 2C reached the 1:1-scale model stage but the scheme went no further.

Pininfarina Fiat Dino Bodyline Study (aka Special Line Study Coupé)

Pininfarina shaped the voluptuous Fiat Dino Spider production car, and built as many as four design studies based on the platform, three of which were variations on the existing body style with fixed roofs. This 1967 Paris motor show car, however, bore no resemblance to Fiat's range-topper stylistically. Instead, it created a pseudo shooting brake, half of the roof being glazed, while the abruptly cropped tail featured a hatchback arrangement that also largely comprised tinted glass.

A press release from the unveiling was typically self-congratulatory. 'The Pininfarina Company has built on a Fiat Dino chassis, a worldwide novelty with remarkable sport characteristics,' it gushed. 'The bodyline is based on simplicity and features an outline of very light sections. The limited use of chrome underlines the sober design of the car. The front, entirely without [a] grille, is large. The front lights fold down and represent, within the bonnet, a smooth line. The windows, extended completely down the side surface, are broken by an outlet of blued steel. The multi-curved windshield joins the roof panel, which is very slim in outline and section.'

The car wasn't shown again publicly, and it seemingly disappeared during the late 1960s. Some styling elements, however, appeared in the Aldo Brovarone-styled Ferrari Studio CR25 mock-up which appeared in 1974.

This dramatic reinterpretation of the Fiat Dino was only exhibited once in period, the shooting brake outline polarising opinion in period.

Oldsmobile Thor

It was a decade that saw General Motors become arguably the most daring of all of North American motor manufacturers. If the mechanical arrangements of its products weren't enough to raise eyebrows, the various design departments run under styling czar Bill Mitchell were full of futurists. Perhaps the bravest and most beautiful mainstream offering to emerge from its portfolio of marques was the first-generation Oldsmobile Toronado.

You could argue that it distilled the spirit of the pre-war Cord 810 in being a boldly-styled – and engineered – front-wheel drive machine. It was so radical that, on its launch in 1966, many European magazines haughtily opined that it couldn't possibly work; that front-wheel drive wasn't suitable for any car with a displacement larger than 1.6-litres. However, given the plaudits heaped upon the car's David North-penned styling, you have to wonder why GM would go to the trouble of commissioning the car pictured – the one and only Thor.

It is widely held that it was built by Carrozzeria Ghia at the behest of Mitchell. It was based on a standard-wheelbase Toronado platform and styled by the studio's recently-installed wunderkind, Giorgetto Giugiaro. While the underpinnings remained unchanged, the front overhang was reduced by 120mm (4.7in) relative to the donor car, the rear overhang by 200mm (7.8in). The beltline was also 65mm (2.6in) lower, while the bulkhead was moved forward by 75mm (2.9in) and the windscreen rake was set at 65° to the vertical (six more degrees that a regular Toronado). Overall, the car was 100mm (3.9in) lower than the production model, but it remained a proper four-seater rather than a 2+2.

Unlike other Giugiaro offerings from the period, the Thor was essentially an adaptation rather than a new design. As such, reaction was mixed. When unveiled at the 1967 Turin motor show, it was greeted with acclaim by some media, while others were less impressed (the decision to hide the rear leaf-spring shackles behind fake exhaust pipes in particular caused consternation). *Style Auto* belonged in the former camp, the design title reporting randomly: 'The roof of the "Thor" is gradually tapered with respect to the car body: its trapezoidal section makes it agile and aerodynamic and gives a sturdy appearance to the car body.'

Sports Car Graphic, meanwhile, wrote an impenetrable feature based in what *may* have been a fictional courtroom. It's hard to tell, but it did involve mention of Bill Mitchell, Abe Lincoln, and someone called 'Earth Kathy' (it *was* the 1960s). As for its coverline 'Will Detroit Build This Car?', the simple answer was 'no'. There was no desire or need to.

As for what happened to the one and only prototype following its unveiling, therein lies another story. In period, *Autocar* claimed it had been acquired off the show stand by industrialist/playboy, Gianni Agnelli. However, the car gathered dust in the storeroom at Alejandro/Allesandro de Tomaso's factory well into the 1980s, the Argentinean émigré having owned Ghia for a spell prior to selling it to Ford.

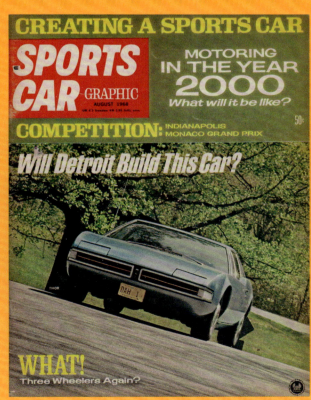

Giugiaro's reworking of the much-admired Oldsmobile Toronado was greeted with a lukewarm reception from the motoring media. The car was stored in the de Tomaso factory for decades.

1967

Gyro-X

With the possible exception of his former colleague, Syd Mead, no other American car designer was as starry-eyed as Alex Tremulis. Having envisaged the Ford Gyron in 1961, he followed through with the gyroscopically-stabilised transportation theory in the form of the Gyro-X. Created by Tremulis and gyroscope authority Thomas Summers, this 1,275cc Mini Cooper S-engined tandem two-seater was displayed for the first time in The Wonderful World of Wheels exhibition which formed part of the 1967 New York International Auto Show. Tremulis claimed it represented the future of transportation, not least because it was capable of 125mph (201km/h) despite having only 80bhp on tap. This was possible because the gyroscope stored and harnessed kinetic energy, and also because the small frontal area ensured it cleaved the air more cleanly. Not only that, two fewer tyres relative to most cars meant there was less road drag. However, period reports suggest the car was unstable at speeds above 70mph (113km/h).

Created by Alex Tremulis and gyroscope specialist Thomas Summer, the Gyro-X featured Mini Cooper A-series power. It was purportedly capable of 125mph.

Ford Bearcat

Something of a cuckoo in the nest in this company, the Ford Bearcat never saw daylight, let alone a stand in an exhibition hall. It was a one-week wonder, with only these shadowy pics emerging from Ford's design studio in Dearborn, Michigan to prove that it ever existed. What's more, it barely qualified as a 'car' given that it never ran under its own steam. It was but a mere mock-up, and its existence was seemingly lost on North America's automotive media. Oddly, it was Great Britain's *Autocar* that revealed news that Ford was considering making a junior supercar.

The motoring weekly reported: 'With all contemporary racing cars featuring mid-mounted engines, and with Ford's interest in the competition scene, it was only a matter of time before they came up with a styling exercise based on this pattern. The Bearcat is a practical shape for a road car with a seating package similar to the current Mustang 2+2 fastback. It has been built from a clay model in glassfibre... The Bearcat features flush-moulded lamp covers and retractable high-intensity driving lamps which sit under the front bumper each side of the air intake.'

It went on to add: 'The whole of the rear bodywork hinges open as one piece for access to the engine bay behind the seats, and the roof section over the cockpit is designed to lift off and fit into the front compartment between the radiator and fascia. The spare wheel is above the gearbox, behind the engine. Behind the rear window is a hydraulic spoiler, with adjustable angle, and the tail lamps are hidden behind stainless-steel panels which are perforated with millions of minute holes. The appearance is of a satin-finished opaque sheet until the lamps come on.'

Notionally powering this machine was a 289cu in small-block V8, packaged within an overall length of 4,648mm (183in) and a wheelbase of 2,641mm (104in). The Bearcat was 1,920mm (75.6in) wide and 1,209mm (47.6in) high.

Metzeler Delta 1

One of the more esoteric offerings unveiled at the 1967 Frankfurt motor show, the Delta 1 was created to promote the design consultancy of Henner Werner, Detlef Unger and Michael Conrad. Backed by Bavarian tyre company, Metzeler, the trio created a car with a body constructed of expanded foam sandwich. Based upon an NSU 1200 TTS platform, complete with a 1,085cc four-cylinder unit sited behind the rear axle, unusual features included the full-width headlight arrangement: the entire front 'bonnet' popped up when in need of illumination.

The Delta 1 also included such novelties as a flexible fuel tank that was developed by Metzeler. Weighing just 625kg (1,378lb), the prototype was purportedly capable of reaching 112mph (180km/h) outright. The outline was later adapted to suit an unmodified Volkswagen Type 3 platform and offered in kit-form. Delta Design rarely troubled the automotive world thereafter, save for the construction of an NSU-powered utility vehicle prototype, the partners instead concentrating their efforts on shaping furniture.

The Ford Bearcat (left) was a styling study that never saw daylight, let alone an exhibition hall. It was notionally powered by a mid-mounted V8.

1967

Lancia Flavia Sport Zagato

Lancia and Zagato once enjoyed a symbiotic relationship which resulted in several landmark design classics. This 1967 styling study wasn't among their number because it remained a one-off, but it wasn't without its fans. The initial Zagato-bodied Flavia Sport production car was first seen at the 1962 Geneva motor show. Styled by Ercole Spada, it went on to enjoy some success in motorsport, but its outline polarised opinion. This, his follow-up, incorporated some styling themes from the original, not least the bluff front-end and the concave rear window. However, the prototype emerged 90mm (3.5in) lower than the previous Sport Zagato, and also 90mm (3.5in) shorter.

The car was displayed at the 1967 Turin motor show alongside the Rover TCZ and a Fiat 125-based coupé that briefly threatened to enter production. Reaction to the scarlet Lancia was largely positive, with *Road & Track* commenting: 'Zagato cares not a jot for other people's trends... Quite what the Flavia resembles it is difficult to decide, unless it is a vehicle for travelling far, fast and frequently. Every element appears to have been moulded into the body. There is no waist, in the usual way, the tail neither slopes down nor breaks into two distinct parts, even the wheels (magnesium, of course) are just concave pierced discs like no other wheels. Yet the effect is pleasing and suggestive of speed, like an old-fashioned open sports car, but with the convenient characteristics of a closed coupé.'

Another Ercole Spada production, the distinctive Flavia Sport Zagato was shorter and lower than the donor car that bore it.

1967

Exemplar 1

Scroll back to the dawn of the automobile, and the use of brass in decorative form was commonplace, hence the term 'brass era'. Fast-forward to the 1960s, however, and it was a different story. The application of nickel and then chrome for brightwork had become the norm. The car pictured here, however, was meant to change that, showcasing new ornamental usages for copper and bronze to Detroit's 'Big Three' and beyond. The Exemplar 1 was commissioned by the Bridgeport Brass Company in Connecticut in partnership with the Copper Development Association, and was built in 1967 at a cost of an eye-watering $150,000.

Basis for the car was a modified Buick Gran Sport platform, complete with 430cu in V8 and automatic transmission. This was dispatched to Italy where the body was shaped by Sergio Coggiola's eponymous *carrozzeria* to a design by Count Mario Revelli di Beaumont. Nothing if not prolific, the nobleman had previously shaped everything from streamlined Maserati record-breakers to humble Simca saloons via coachbuilt Rolls-Royces. De Beaumont was also a long-time consultant to General Motors. Not only that, he also patented countless automotive innovations such as central locking.

Great attention to detail was invested in this bold coupé, with eleven distinct hues of copper alloys being applied to the Exemplar 1's brightwork. From the bumpers and grille to the specially-made Borrani wire-wheels with knock-off hubs, nothing was off limits. Exemplar 1 featured twin-tiered instruments and a fascia made of polished copper. The steering wheel column and horn were trimmed in copper, while the A-pillar and header moulding, sill covers and door cards were all equally shiny. Underneath the bonnet, the engine was similarly garnished with copper and brass, as were the disc brakes, brake lines, wiring and radiator.

Once completed, the car was shipped to the USA where it was shown at the 1968 and '69 New York International Auto Shows. It was not a huge hit with Detroit, though. Nor for that matter, was the four-door Exemplar II which followed in 1972. Not only that, Exemplar 1 didn't comply with federal safety and emission regulations so could not be legally registered for use on the road. As such, it was scheduled to be destroyed in 1970. However, it was granted a reprieve by Bridgeport Brass Company president, Herman Steinkrause, who acquired the car for an undisclosed sum.

Based on a Buick Gran Sport chassis, the brass-imbued Exemplar 1 was shaped by the brilliant Count Mario Revelli di Beaumont and constructed by Carrozzeria Coggiola.

AMC Amitron

Unveiled in a Detroit hotel conference room in December 1967, the Amitron may have been on the small side but it cast a long shadow. Designed under Dick Teague, this tiny electric car was built in conjunction with battery manufacturer Gulton Industries. Barely 2,159mm (85in) long, 1,765mm (69.5in) wide, and 1,168mm (46in) high, it boasted three-abreast seating but, according to marketing material of the time, weighed in at just 499kg (1,100lb). Despite its stubby proportions, the Amitron was relatively practical for its size, novel features including inflatable seat cushions: the passenger cushions could be deflated when driving solo so as to free up storage space. AMC claimed it had a range of 150 miles (241km) and could cruise at 50mph (80km/h). It also boasted regenerative braking which is now a standard feature of hybrids and EVs, but was then practically unheard of.

The Amitron became a media darling, and not just in the USA. There was even talk of variations on the theme entering production. However, with fuel still costing relatively little Stateside (compared to the rest of the world), AMC's management decided there would be insufficient demand on the home front. The design did, however, influence the Pacer production car, not least its three-abreast seating arrangement. In addition, following the 1973 Oil Shock, small cars took on greater relevance in North America. The Amitron was dusted down, repainted, and given a pair of exterior mirrors before being presented as the Electron in 1977.

Oldsmobile Mini-Toro

By any logical rationale, this wasn't the sort of car that manufacturers would want to promote. It was a means to an end; a works hack that was built for a singular purpose that was anything but glamorous. Nevertheless, the decidedly leftfield Oldsmobile Mini-Toro was well-publicised in period, with GM's marketing department putting out a press release and photographs to the world's media. It read: 'Lansing, Michigan: People stare when the one-of-a-kind Mini-Toro drives by on the street here…'

Built in late 1967, this stubby machine was based on a regular Toronado coupe. *Autocar* reported in February of the following year: 'Oldsmobile has built [it] to help extract employees' cars from the snow-clogged plant parking lots in these rough Michigan winters. The superior traction, with the engine over the driving wheels, is just the ticket here.' It was, too, even if the car's uncompromising looks defied belief. For starters, 889mm (35in) were removed from the overall length of the standard model, with 457mm (18in) being lifted from the wheelbase alone. This was done in order to reduce the turning radius and improve manoeuvrability in tight spaces. After all the cutting and shutting had been done, it was 4,038mm (159in) long, which rendered it three-quarters the size of a regular Toronado.

Altered proportions aside, the most obvious deviation from the script concerned the front and rear bumpers. They were made of 76mm (3in) maple wood capped in resilient black-dyed rubber. They each weighed 68kg (150lb) and were perfect for pushing cars through snow from either end, and in each direction, although the Mini-Toro was also equipped with studded tyres for extra bite. Not only that, it was conveniently equipped with a plug for jumper cables sited inside a hatch sunk into the left-hand side front wing. Other features included a Filament-heated rear window, heavy-duty radiator and fan, dual batteries and alternator, and bottles of compressed air; not the sort of thing you would expect to find on a regular Oldsmobile.

Autocar went on to add: 'You have to see this crazy car operate in snow to believe it!' before adding: 'It looked like it could go anywhere.' Having 7.5-litres of Detroit V8 firepower no doubt helped. Intriguingly, if implausibly, it also retained the donor car's chrome hubcaps… 'The Pusher', as it was also known, remained in use at the factory each winter until 1972.

As a footnote to the story, Oldsmobile also built a four-door Toronado prototype using a standard-wheelbase donor car. Intriguingly, it was also pressed into service at the Lansing factory with a snowplough attached.

Mini and maxi. The Mini-Toro, seen here with a full-size Oldsmobile Toronado, was built for a single purpose: to shovel snow. Remarkably, it still survives.

1967

OSI Bisiluro 'Silver Fox'

One of the more bizarre contraptions ever to grace a stand at a major motor show, this Sergio Sartorelli-designed mobile catamaran was named after former motorcycle star and Grand Prix winner, Piero Taruffi (aka 'The Silver Fox'). The Italian overachiever was also a prolific author, engineer and record-breaker, and had patented a design for a 'twin-boom' machine which, in turn, inspired other similar machines from the likes of Nardi. OSI's offering was similarly built with record attempts in mind, but a Le Mans bid was also mooted (not that an entry was ever made for the 24-hour endurance classic).

The OSI prototype emerged at the 1967 Turin motor show. It employed a one-litre Alpine-Renault four-cylinder unit in the left-hand pontoon, positioned transversely so that the drive ran straight to a central gearbox/final-drive unit. The driver operated the car from the other pontoon, and between the two nacelles were three individual spoilers: the front one was adjustable from outside, the middle one from the cockpit, while the rear item was fixed in place. As such, both drag and lift characteristics could be altered as required. The split bodywork reduced the frontal area to just 1.4m², while OSI claimed a drag coefficient of just 0.26Cd.

According to some sources, the car reached 155mph (249km/h) during testing. OSI was assimilated into Fiat's in-house design department in 1968.

Ostensibly made with a Le Mans 24 Hours bid in mind, the OSI-made, one-litre-engined Bisiluro 'twin-boom' reputedly recorded 155mph during testing.

Carter Coaster

One of the most obscure concept cars of the 1960s, the Coaster was conceived by Alastair Carter of Tamworth, Staffordshire. He created a small electric car with an integrated traction and braking unit that was sited inside each wheel. The design also incorporated regenerative braking. The Carter Engineering principal claimed this set-up afforded a longer range than comparable machines; as much as 25 per cent. He hoped to sell the design, and expected as many as 250,000 Coasters would be on the road by the end of the decade.

Rowan Electric

The 1967 Turin motor show was awash with battery-powered cars, ranging from oddballs such as the Urbaninia, to electric Fiat 500s from Moretti and Giannini. Ghia's take was somewhat different. Funded by the Rowan Controller Group Company of Maryland, which bankrolled Alejandro de Tomaso's various enterprises (there was a familial link via his brother-in-law Amery Haskell), it was a one-box design with minimal overhangs plus, oddly, suicide doors.

Unveiled at the 1967 Turin motor show, it was for the most part well-received by the media. *Road & Track* opined: 'In terms of appearance, the effort was worthwhile... [It is] probably the only good-looking town car yet developed... the electrical side revealed many worthwhile ideas including an ultra-lightweight sandwich-type chassis stiffened by batteries arranged in cruciform style, regenerative-type braking, which frankly would seem a better idea if the vehicle were heavy, and toothed belt drive to the rear wheels.'

Variations on the theme would be made subsequently, but none made the leap to production reality.

This Ghia-made one-box electric car was a serious project, in time spawning a series of concept cars. None made the leap to production-car reality.

Ford Commuta

Despite its dinky appearance, the Commuta represented something of a mission statement on the part of Ford of Britain. In the spring of 1966, designers and engineers were tasked with creating a car specifically for use in urban environments that employed electric propulsion. The Commuta was designed and built at the Dunton Technical Centre, near Laindon, Essex, which was also the site of the car's media launch on 8 June 1967. However, it was styled at Ford's design studio in Cologne.

The Commuta's footprint was tiny: it had an overall length of 2,030mm (79.9in), width of 1,260mm (49.6in), and height of 1,420mm (55.9in). Nevertheless, it boasted a 2+2 seating layout with four batteries sited below the front seats. The car weighed 544kg (1,199lb) and had a top speed of around 25mph (40kph) plus a range of 40 miles (64km).

Ford's marketing material from the launch stated: 'We regard this as a step in our programme to develop a commercially practical electric car.' However, despite plenty of coverage in both print and broadcast media, only two prototypes were ever built. One survives and is on display in London's Science Museum.

Ford's stubby Commuta was intended to act as a city car with battery power and a 2+2 seating arrangement. It arrived half a century too soon.

1967

Mazda RX-87

The Japanese motor industry made massive strides during the 1960s, some manufacturers making the leap from building imported cars from CKC (Completely Knocked Down) 'kits', to making their own standalone products. Several brands employed Italian design houses, too, Mazda among them. Bertone was employed to shape the Luce saloon (badged as the 1800 in the UK), which entered production in 1966. Its stylist, Giorgetto Giugiaro, followed through with the RX-87 concept car which emerged at the following year's Tokyo Auto Salon. However, he had departed for Ghia by the time it was unveiled.

The car's pillarless outline was supremely elegant, and was subsequently adopted for production with only minor changes. The Luce Rotary Coupé (aka R130) boasted a slightly more conventional grille, and did away with the quarterlights, going on sale in October 1969. However, only 976 were made to October 1972.

AMC AMX III Sports Wagon

First seen at the February 1967 Chicago Auto Show, this practical concept car married the forthcoming frontal bodywork of the AMC Javelin/AMX with an estate car outline aft of the A-pillars. However, despite appearances to the contrary, it shared the same 4,800mm (189in) wheelbase with a regular Javelin coupé. According to its manufacturer, it represented: 'American Motors Styling's evolution of today's station wagon. A high-performance sports wagon vehicle designed especially for the young married man with a family who needs full four-passenger seating, safety and comfort, but still wants sports-car performance, appearance and handling characteristics.'

Jensen Nova

Alfredo Vignale's eponymous *carrozzeria* bodied the initial batch of Jensen Interceptors to a design by Touring of Milan. He unveiled his own take on the theme at the 1967 Geneva motor show. The Nova featured an unmodified Interceptor chassis, complete with a 383cu in Chrysler V8 engine, and a fastback body made of aluminium and glassfibre. The car was initially painted dark green, with an interior clad in beige and black hides. However, after its unveiling, the car received detail revisions, primarily to the rear bumper treatment. It was repainted in a shade of off-white, the interior being retrimmed in red leather, ahead of its appearance at the April 1967 Turin motor show. It was sold via Jensen's French concessionaire, Monsieur Ladouch of Société France Moteurs, in November of that year. As to the identity of the stylist, some sources insist it was rooted in a design by Giovanni Michelotti, others that it was penned by Vignale himself.

Alfredo Vignale's Jensen Nova was attractive in its own right, but perhaps failed to improve on the Touring-shaped Interceptor that bore it.

Italian design studies continued to be in the ascendent, 1968 seeing the release of ever more outré supercar proposals where form mostly trumped function. It was the year in which wedge-shaped outlines took centre stage; where lairy colours, elaborate means of entry and egress became commonplace, and racing car foundations became the norm. Nothing, it seems, was too out there. However, as with the previous year, many motoring pundits were aghast. The public, by contrast, was enthralled.

1968 also saw 20-something Giorgetto Giugiaro make the leap from employee to employer on cofounding Studi Italiani Realizzazione Prototipi S.p.A (soon to be renamed Italdesign) with Aldo Mantovani. 'Il Maestro' would go on to create many landmark classics, but then the same was true of his arch rival, Bertone's Marcello Gandini.

Also in 1968
Martin Luther King is assassinated in Memphis, Tennessee. **Britain's last scheduled steam train service runs, on a route from Liverpool to Carlisle.** The UK's M1 motorway is completed when the final stretch between Rotherham and Leeds is opened. **Double F1 World Champion Jim Clark is killed in a Formula 2 race at Hockenheim.**

1968

The Carabo married Alfa Romeo Tipo 33 sports-prototype running gear with cutting-edge styling from Bertone's resident genius, Marcello Gandini. It ushered in the soon to be prevalent 'origami' design trend.

Bertone Alfa Romeo Carabo

The Alfa Romeo Carabo is often cited as being among the most significant concept cars ever made, and with good reason. The brainchild of studio head Nuccio Bertone and his stylist Marcello Gandini, the car was created in just ten weeks and it didn't so much cross boundaries as establish them. It represented an act of provocation; landmark styling icons such as the Lancia Stratos Zero and the original, unsullied Lamborghini Countach were built on the revolution the Carabo ignited.

Three decades after the car was unveiled at the 1968 Paris motor show, Bertone recalled: 'I wanted to produce a car that would be best-suited for the high-speed super highways of Europe, and I think the car represents the best compromise yet developed between interior space and comfort, aerodynamics, aesthetics and marketability. The Carabo was never intended to be a competition car, despite the fact that it was based on the extremely fast Alfa Romeo Tipo 33 chassis.'

Gandini was keen to avoid the front-end lift that hounded the Lamborghini Miura, the original template-setting supercar that he co-authored with Giorgetto Giugiaro. Forecasting – or perhaps channelling – aerodynamic principles that would soon be in vogue in Formula 1, he created a wedge; one with a taut, largely uninterrupted profile and a small frontal area. Just 990mm (38.9in) high, but 1,785mm (70in) wide and 4,175mm (164.3in) long, the car's squat profile was further emphasised by the choice of colour. In an era when dream cars tended to be saturated in fluorescent hues, the Carabo's lime-green coat with semi-reflective delineations for the nose and tail appeared almost subdued.

The car's party trick was its means of access. The doors opened vertically like a beetle's

1968

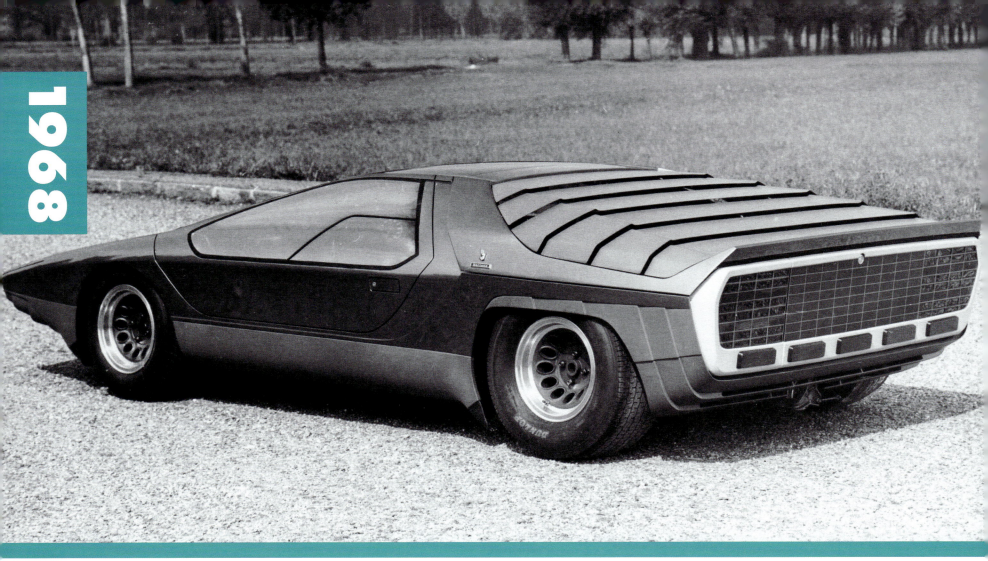

The Carabo was a fully-functional prototype, if perhaps not one that was user-friendly. The car still survives, but minus its original quad-cam V8 engine.

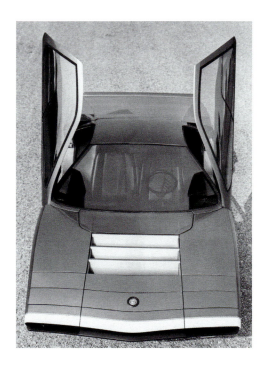

wings via a hydropneumatic strut arrangement, hence the name Carabo (a species of green/gold coleopteron). Bertone boasted that this arrangement allowed the car to be parked within 200mm (8in) of a wall. What's more, the Carabo was fully functional. Motoring writer Gianni Rogliatti reported in period: 'Driving the Carabo on Italian roads was immensely enjoyable. Pedestrians and other motorists were dumfounded, not so much at the car itself, which has been well publicised in Italy, but by the fact that it really works.'

Predictably, Bertone was inundated with calls for replicas. Among the more persistent of would-be customers was King Faisal of Jordan. Bertone refused to sell the prototype but did agree to loan the car to His Royal Highness during a visit to London. With an air of predictability, the Carabo's racy running gear wasn't best suited to the cut and thrust of the British capital and it expired with a broken clutch. It remained in an inoperative state for a further 20 years, the one-off windscreen made in Belgium by Glaverbel being broken during its time in storage.

In 1989, the Carabo was disinterred and renovated. However the titivation was only

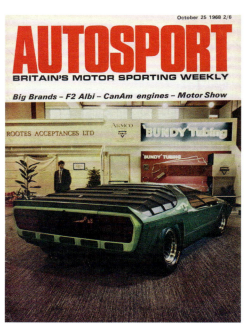

skin deep, for its 1,995cc V8 remained silent. The car made its comeback in Paris, the city where it first found fame, at an exhibition entitled Les Maîtres de la Carrosserie Italienne (The Masters of Italian Coachbuilding) which took place at the equally left-field Pompidou Centre. It is currently exhibited in the Museo Storico Alfa Romeo, minus its quad-cam engine.

Bertone Panther
(aka Sbarro Tiger)

Straddling the line between would-be competition tool and concept car, the Bertone-built Panther was commissioned by Scuderia Brescia Corse. According to financier Alfredo Belponer, and driver Umberto Maglioli, the plan was to compete in the top-flight Group 6 category of the International Championship of Makes. French magazine *L'Auto Journal* reported: '[It has] a monocoque chassis type light alloy and plastic bodywork. Titanium alloy has been widely used, this which explains the relatively low weight of the whole: 650kg.'

According to *Style Auto*, the full-scale mock-up began testing in the wind tunnel at the Politecnico di Torino in December 1967. The intention was to employ BRM V12 power ahead of the car's competition programme. However, the scheme unravelled amid recrimination between the various partners, with Bertone presenting the unraced prototype at the 1968 Turin motor show. That, however, wasn't the end of the story.

Maglioli purportedly received the unraced car as compensation. In 1972, he sold the prototype to Franco Sbarro who displayed the car at the 1973 Geneva motor show. The Sbarro Tiger, as it was now dubbed, was allegedly powered by a 6.3-litre Mercedes-Benz V8, a brochure trumpeting a small run of replicas with the choice of eight-cylinder Chevrolet and Ford engines. However, the Panther/Tiger remained unique.

Conceived with a Group 6 motor racing bid in mind, the Panther was exhibited by Bertone in 1968. The car reappeared five years later minus its massive wing as the Sbarro Tiger (above).

1968

Italdesign Bizzarrini Manta

The first car styled by Giorgetto Giugiaro as an independent designer, the Manta acted as a calling card for the Studi Italiani Realizzazione Prototipi (aka Italdesign) concern he formed with Aldo Mantovani. Based on a Bizzarrini P538 sports-racer chassis, and powered by a mid-mounted Chevrolet V8 engine, it broke cover at the 1968 Turin motor show and became a media star in an instant. Finished in a striking shade of turquoise, it was a radical-looking device with an equally outré interior. Like the Ferrari 365P, the Manta was a three-seater: the driver sat in the middle, flanked by the passengers.

The wild Manta acted as a calling card for the newly freelance Giorgetto Giugiaro. This centre-seat supercar was based on a Bizzarrini sports-prototype platform.

Giugiaro told *Style Auto*: 'Firstly, let me say it wasn't my intention to carry out any stylistic virtuosity. In fact, for such exhibitions it is better to choose much more conventional themes... Instead, I restricted myself to a well-defined aim and tried to stick to it with the greatest coherence possible. Starting from a very simple idea, I have – I think – reached an interesting result. Usually, the stylist who has to design the bodywork of a rear-engined sports car tries, with a variety of devices, to develop the bonnet and entire front end, and lighten the rear in order to rebalance the masses. Instead of following this traditional criterion, I asked myself was it not possible to load the rear, in order to leave the engine all the room it deserves, and to reduce – if not exactly do away with completely – the front end.'

Motor Trend raved of the newcomer, stating: '...one of the major stars of the exhibit [was] the "Manta". The car was built on the chassis of Bizzarrini's racing prototype, which took part in the 24 Hours at Le Mans in 1967. An extremely compact car, the Manta is only 13.6 feet long and its maximum height does not exceed 41.5 inches... The unusual width of the car (six feet, one inch) increases the impression of compactness. Lateral visibility is exceptional. Once again, Giugiaro, Turin's 28-year old boy genius, showed new ways in car design.'

The car subsequently went on a world tour, and had undergone a change of hue in time for its appearance at the following year's 1969 Los Angeles Auto Expo. *Road & Track's* Henry N. Manney went against the herd. He dismissed it as being: '...yet another 200mph suppository in bright orange. A big Chevy (engine) inhabited the back along with a sort of baking tin for luggage, while the lucky driver sat between his two passengers (birds, I should think) terribly close to the accident in front. [Bernd] Rosemeyer himself would think twice about driving that one fast in the wet, what with the weight distribution, venetian blinds on the nose and chrome bushbars on the rear. I'm afraid it wasn't my cup of tea.'

The Manta was soon resprayed again, this time in a rather more sober shade of metallic silver, before being sold on. The car has since been restored to the same specification as when it was first seen in 1968.

Pininfarina Ferrari 250 P5 Berlinetta Speciale

Widely touted in retrospect as being among the all-time great concept cars, the P5 was nevertheless conceived with motor racing in mind. According to its designer, Leonardo Fioravanti, it was to be a replacement for the P4 sports-prototype. In July 1967, he presented his ideas to Enzo Ferrari and *Il Commendatore* reputedly gave his blessing. However, by the time the P5 was unveiled at the Geneva motor show in March 1968, all thoughts of competition had been consigned to history. This was a styling study, and a remarkable one at that, even if Mr Ferrari apparently likened it to a suppository.

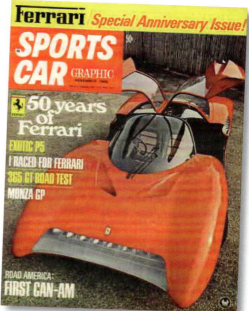

The P5 went on a tour of motor shows into 1969, but a degree of mystery surrounds what happened next. Some sources insist the donor chassis came from a V12-engined P4 sports-prototype. Either that, or a Dino 206 S, another constant rumour suggesting the P5 body was removed from the Dino which served as a basis for the 212E Montagna hillclimber. However, the 206 S had a V6 engine. There are also suggestions that the P5 body was remodelled to form the basis for the Alfa Romeo Tipo 33/2 Coupé Prototipo Speciale which emerged at the 1969 Paris motor show. Leonardo Fioravanti states in *Il Cavallino Nel Coure* that he '... adapted the lines of the P5 to the famous 33 chassis.'

1968
Pininfarina Ferrari P6

Unveiled alongside the Alfa Romeo P33 Roadster GS at the 1968 Turin motor show, this Leonardo Fioravanti-penned machine was perhaps less out there than many other concept cars of the period. However, the 'visuals' told only part of the story. Pininfarina was keen to espouse the 'developments' taking place beneath the skin, *Road & Track* devoting several paragraphs to the newcomer in its event report. It stated: '...the Ferrari P6 prototype actually had no engine fitted, there being some doubt whether Ferrari wants his V12 installed traditionally lengthwise, or sideways, which would mean doing the same as Lamborghini [did with the Miura].

'Either way, it will live amidships in a backbone-type chassis, and the cooling arrangements are very intriguing; air is ducted aft of the nose intake through the backbone member itself, and there are two radiators, one each side above the rear wheel-arches, the lot exhausting through Miura-style slats in the top rear panel. The entire engine compartment is designed to act as a chimney, drawing in cold air and expelling heat, and then standing still will cool itself by convection. The car's interior is carefully insulated from heat and fumes, while Pf claims a useful drag reduction since the air can gallop unrestricted through the nose to the engine. The wedge motif doesn't click very well on a coupé, and this isn't a very nice looking Ferrari...'

This was perhaps a little unkind, but the P6 did establish styling themes that Fioravanti explored subsequently on the 365 GT4 BB production car that emerged three years later. The sole P6 prototype remained engineless and resides in the Pininfarina factory collection.

Leonardo Fioravanti's outline for the Ferrari P6 established styling themes later explored on the 365 GT4 BB production supercar.

Pininfarina Alfa Romeo Roadster GS

One of the more uncompromising Alfa Romeo Tipo 33 Stradale-based concept cars, the Roadster GS was styled by Pininfarina's Paolo Martin. Unveiled at the 1968 Turin motor show, it represented an intriguing amalgam of curves and angular surfaces, its most prominent feature being a roll-bar-cum-aerofoil sited behind the cockpit. According to Pininfarina, this was angled automatically by suspension movement and braking, and also incorporated a finned aluminium surface oil cooler.

Cyril Posthumus claimed in Road & Track that: '[It was] apparently built in about three weeks, and finished half an hour before Turin opening day.' He went on to describe it as being: '...a two-place spider with a straight upward taper from low, rubber-capped nose to high, chopped-off square tail, interrupted only by the wraparound screen and an anti-lift air-foil mounted behind the seats.'

The Roadster GS was subsequently reconfigured as the Spider Cuneo which was unveiled at the 1971 Brussels motor show.

One of several concept queens based on Alfa Romeo Tipo 33 foundations, the Roadster GS enjoyed only the briefest of show careers before it was reconfigured into the Spider Cuneo.

1968

Autobianchi Coupé

Despite falling short of production status, the Autobianchi Coupé nevertheless cast a long shadow. The idea of a small, mass-manufactured sports car was first mooted within parent company Fiat as early as 1964. Engineering legend Dante Giacosa initiated the G31 programme ('G' for Giacosa, '31' for the project number), the project subsequently falling under the auspices of the Autobianchi sub-brand.

This was understandable given that Autobianchi was associated with innovation. In 1964, the firm introduced the Primula, the first-ever product from within the Fiat combine to employ a transversely-mounted engine and front-wheel drive. The Primula provided its engine (itself derived from a Fiat 124 unit) for the G31, construction of the prototype being farmed out to OSI. Austrian-born stylist Werner Hölbl created a pretty fastback silhouette during 1967, working under the direction of Sergio Sartorelli.

However, OSI was assimilated into Fiat in May of the following year and, accordingly, the G31 project returned in-house. The design was subsequently reworked by Pio Manzù who had been recently installed at Fiat Centro Stile, the renamed Autobianchi Coupé (aka Sports Coupé) emerging at the 1968 Turin motor show. The fully-functional, glassfibre-bodied prototype was resplendent in 'Geranium Red,' the dashboard, inner doors and pillars being swathed in polyurethane foam panelling by way of a safety measure.

However, despite entreaties from the motoring media for the car to be put into production, this was strictly a concept car. Unbeknown to them, Giacosa had already decided that a new mid-engined sports car should be created using componentry from the soon-to-be-announced Fiat 128, the following year's Autobianchi Runabout foretelling the Fiat X1/9 production car which went on sale in 1972.

Tragically, Manzù didn't live to see the X1/9 or even his 127 reach production. He died in May 1969 after his car collided with a bridge near Turin. As to the fate of the Autobianchi Coupé, it is widely held that it was scrapped.

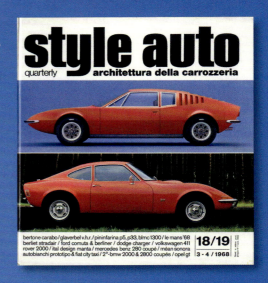

The strikingly-attractive Autobianchi Coupé was fully functional and, in a roundabout way, it foretold the Fiat X1/9. Sadly, the lone prototype was probably scrapped.

1968

Pininfarina Fiat Dino Ginevra

The Ginevra bore more than a passing resemblance to the previous year's Fiat Dino 'Line Study.' They were likely the same car with only minor detail revisions.

Bearing more than a passing resemblance to the Dino 'Line Study' displayed in Paris a year earlier, this 1968 Geneva motor show car was perhaps more conventional in terms of detailing. The front end featured semi-enclosed headlights, while the cropped tail was home to four circular lamps, the general consensus among the contemporary media being that it was the 1967 car that had been lightly reworked. *Road & Track* seemed to think so, its show report stating: 'Pininfarina's Fiat Dino design study reappeared with minor changes.'

Ivo Alessiani critiqued the Ginevra for *Style Auto*. He reported: 'Aesthetically, as Ing. Sergio Pininfarina admits it amounts to a tamed version of the Parisian Dino which thrilled many but left some puzzled... This is an attractive car – from the aesthetic point of view – but one which, just because of a certain conventionalism due to the bodywork itself, does not set a new trend nor give rise to particular criticisms.'

Ghia Checker Centurion

For the first four decades following World War II, Checker was the de facto marque of American taxi operators. The Kalamazoo concern did make cars for public consumption but overwhelmingly it sold them for use as taxis or hotel/airport shuttles. What they lacked in style, they more than made up for in durability. There simply was no need to perform endless makeovers. Checkers never went out of style because they were never *in* style, but that did not stop Ghia from building the Centurion.

According to Italian sources, the car was built at the behest of Checker directly. However, historians from the Checker Car Club of America say otherwise, and claim they have been unable to find any evidence to suggest the prototype was commissioned by Checker. Whatever the truth, it was created during a period of upheaval for Ghia. Recent incumbent Leonidas Ramades Trujillo had little interest in coachbuilding. After finding himself in legal jeopardy, he hurriedly offloaded the business in 1967 to Argentinian émigré Alessandro (né Alejandro) de Tomaso.

It was against this backdrop that de Tomaso purportedly did a deal with Checker to build a prototype based on an A-12-E chassis, the extended version of the usual taxi chassis with a 3,227mm (129in) wheelbase. Giorgetto Giugiaro was tasked with shaping it, but 'Il Maestro' fell out with de Tomaso and the design was subcontracted to Tom Tjaarda, instead. The American-born designer claimed in later years that the car took five months to build and he was given nothing by way of a brief or instructions, nor did he have any contact with anyone from Checker.

The Centurion broke cover at the 1968 Paris motor show, and generated plenty of interest in the media, although bewilderment might be more apposite. *Road & Track* reported: 'Very unexpected from an Italian coachbuilder was Ghia's Checker... A great slab of real "Big Mutha".' The 327cu in Chevrolet V8-engined prototype wasn't on the basic side, either. In the back there was a drinks cabinet with crystal decanter and glasses, along with a telephone, 305mm (12in) television and other luxury items that suggested a limousine rather than a taxi cab. Construction of the Checker Centurion reputedly cost $125,000, and, following its appearance at the 1969 New York International Auto Show, the car was used by one of Rowan Industries' board members.

The Checker Centurion was styled by Tom Tjaarda who was subbing for Giorgetto Giugiaro. A degree of uncertainty surrounds who commissioned its construction.

Fiat City Taxi

Unveiled to great acclaim at the 1968 Turin motor show, the City Taxi was conceived by Dante Giacosa, and realised by Pio Manzù. Based upon a Fiat 850 Super platform, the car boasted a tiny footprint but was a masterwork in packaging. While the driver 'made do' with a conventional door, passengers entered and exited the car via a sliding door on the right-hand side (the kerb-side in Italy). It was operated pneumatically by a lever near the driver. Despite being barely 3,200mm (125.9in) long, it could accommodate three rear-ferried passengers, with their luggage carried up front in the compartment next to the driver.

Road & Track's Cyril Posthumus was uncharacteristically gushing about the design, stating in his show report: 'This vehicle maybe came as a cold shower after the coachwork exotics, but it is plain common sense right through... With the 850 engine lost somewhere in the rear, the front hood is very short and sloping; that is, indeed, sheer transport without elegance, though no uglier than the average British taxi and lot more advanced with its all-independent suspension and Idroconvert automatic transmission.'

Despite rave reviews in this and other publications, Fiat's latter-day Multipla was destined to become a museum exhibit rather than transporting the masses in urban cityscapes.

Conceived by Dante Giacosa, and realised by Pio Manzù, the City Taxi was masterfully packaged and could have been a latter day Fiat Multipla had fate been kinder.

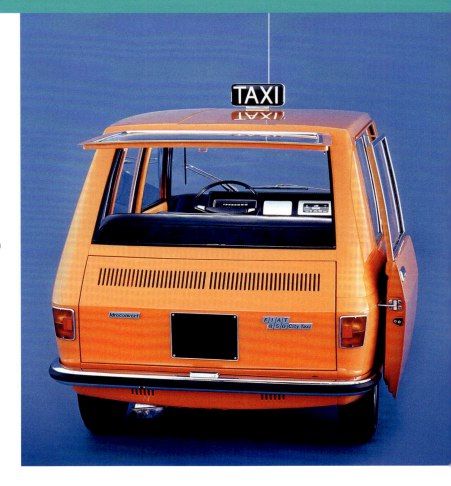

Serenissima Ghia Coupé

Count Giovanni Volpi di Misurata's Serenissima racing team in its various guises enjoyed success as an entrant but conspicuously less so as a constructor. The nobleman also dabbled in road cars. The Jungla appeared in the paddock at the 1966 Le Mans 24 Hours, but never entered series manufacture. The same was true of the 3.5-litre Agena which similarly remained unique. The Ghia Coupé, by contrast, was something of a halfway house between a concept car and a would-be production model.

Powered by an Alf Francis-designed, 3,470cc 'M-167' V8 engine, and equipped with a backbone chassis that closely mirrored that of the de Tomaso Mangusta, it was styled by Tom Tjaarda shortly after he rejoined Carrozzeria Ghia in 1967. According to Tjaarda, the Count and Ghia principal de Tomaso were friends [Serenissima had fielded an OSCA-powered de Tomaso in the 1961 French GP where it was shared by Nino Vaccarella and Giorgio Scarlatti], but the nobleman displayed little interest in the scheme.

The Ghia Coupé was displayed at the 1968 Turin motor show, Cyril Posthumus' event report in *Road & Track* gushing: 'Grace, not gimmickry, is Ghia's strong point, and the mid-engined Serenissima on a backbone chassis is a fine exercise in elegant simplicity, not without a touch of [Chevrolet] Astro II about its shape; it is finished in an apple green shade contending strongly with that eggy yellow as the "in" colour at Turin.' He also credited the design to Giorgetto Giugiaro.

Tjaarda, for his part, stated decades down the line that he wasn't happy with the car's outline, and that the prototype had been fashioned in a hurry and suffered for it. The Ghia Coupé subsequently went into storage in the grounds of Count Volpi's castle while the marque had all but petered out by 1970.

1968

Maserati Simun

Displayed at the 1968 Turin motor show by Ghia, the Simun was styled by the recently-departed Giorgetto Giugiaro and mooted as a replacement for the Maserati Sebring production car. It was a functional prototype, and powered by a 4.2-litre V8. *Road & Track* wrote: 'The Ghia Simun (that's another of those Continental winds so handy to name after) is a sort of 2+2 Maserati Ghibli, its sleekness mildly marred by acres of window glass.' However, the design was not adopted, Maserati opting instead for the Vignale-shaped Indy, although the sole prototype still exists.

Ford Berliner

Ford's flirtation with battery-powered city cars during the 1960s culminated with this one-box design. The Hans Muth-styled car was as tall as it was wide – 1,370mm (53.9in) – and a four-seater despite its stubby 2,130mm (83.8in) length. The front seats were designed for adults, while the rear items were intended for children. What's more, they were mounted back-to-front so junior ferried passengers viewed the world through the rear window. The one-piece, side-hinged rear door afforded them access, and the seats could be folded or reconfigured in a variety of ways. Conventional doors were used for adults to gain entry, although the original intention had been for much of the front end to tilt upwards in one piece. However, this design feature was dropped early on because it was deemed impractical.

The Berliner was equipped with a bank of batteries sited below the passenger seat. All in, the car weighed 590kg (1,300lb) and at least one test hack ran under its own steam. The car was unveiled in 1968 at the Ford of Europe headquarters in Cologne, and it is widely held that more than one glassfibre-bodied prototype was constructed.

AMC AMX GT

Styled under the direction of Dick Teague, this unusual variant of the AMC AMX production car employed existing panelwork fore of the A-pillars. However, the rest of its distinctive glassfibre bodywork was all new. When first seen at the 1968 New York International Auto Show, it was resplendent in red and white, and also boasted a ram-air bonnet scoop, and a roof-mounted spoiler. The car was later resprayed in red and blue, the dummy side exhausts being among the casualties of the makeover. Strictly a mock-up, it is widely held that the AMX GT was destroyed. However, some styling features, not least the cropped tail, were later employed on the AMC Gremlin.

Oldsmobile Toronado XP-866

This oddity was ostensibly created as a one-off for the use of General Motors' styling chief, Bill Mitchell. Based on a first-generation Toronado, it was reworked by ex-Ford stylist Roy Lonberger, the most obvious deviation from the production car being the shortened wheelbase, elongated front wings, and mild 'roof chop.' The strangest part, however, was the use of a body-coloured rear window. The XP-866 was never displayed publicly, but it did appear in specialist titles in period.

1968

Chevrolet Astro II (XP-880)

Unlike the previous year's Astro, the second-generation 'XP-880' variant looked like it could be production-ready when it was unveiled at the April 1968 New York International Auto Show. Inevitably, this led to speculation that it was to form the basis for a mid-engined Corvette. The fact that much of the running gear employed here was available from the General Motors parts bin served only to heighten conjecture: beneath the swoopy, and comparatively conventional outline (which featured regular doors unlike Astro I), sat a 427cu in V8 mounted amidships that, initially at least, was mated to a two-speed transaxle from a Pontiac Tempest. Overall, it was 4,597mm (181in) long, 1,880mm (74in) wide, and 1,100mm (43.3in) wide. It even had reasonable headroom and something approaching space for your luggage up front.

Road & Track made this raciest of Chevrolets its cover star in July 1968, its show report stating: 'Chevrolet, using a magician as a lure, got the crowd so involved in figuring out how to untangle steel hoops that they may have missed the attractive Astro II and the rather lumpy Astro Vette... [The] car is very bulky, and lacks rearward vision, but the mechanical layout, chassis design and clean styling make it an impressive package.' It was not, however, a harbinger of an imminent mid-engined Corvette production car, but rather another stepping stone to one that would eventually arrive in 2020.

The super-sleek Astro II was a mid-engined Chevrolet Corvette in all but name. Sadly, this big-block V8-equipped supercar didn't inspire a production run.

1968

Ford Techna

The 1960s witnessed a seismic shift in the way the American motor industry viewed passenger safety. The publication of Ralph Nader's *Unsafe at any Speed* in 1965 in particular did much to focus the attention in the corridors of power in Detroit, albeit belatedly. The car pictured here was Ford's response. Designed in 1965, but not seen publicly until the 1968 New York International Auto Show, according to the press release, this brave new world was: '...a test bed for more than 50 innovations which might become Ford better ideas for the future.'

It was clearly referring to the very near-future. 'Ford's Car of the Seventies has a honeycomb-construction steel platform and bonded body panels first seen on the Ford MkIV sports-prototype', it continued. 'The basic theme of [the] Techna is more-effective utilisation of space within the car's streamlined, 51-inch profile. With a wheelbase of 120-inches, the Techna is between Thunderbird and Mercury in size. A major contribution to greater spaciousness in Techna is made by the powertrain configuration. The engine and transmission are nine inches forward of their usual position and canted downward and to one side so to connect with an off-centre, triple-jointed driveline.'

Tellingly, whoever wrote this PR copy neglected to mention what engine and transmission were being employed or what they meant by 'forward of their usual position'. The press release went on to add: 'Occupants have unobstructed front visibility through a structural windshield that literally wraps around. It completely eliminates the front corner pillars. The low-profile hood is designed to reduce reflections into the driver's eyes... The Techna's electric shift control mechanism uses a rotated ring control instead of a gear-shift lever. An electronic speedometer senses speed with an infrared light beam.'

That wasn't all. 'The entire front end sheet metal tilts forward for complete access to the engine compartment and front chassis', it stated. 'For routine inspection of service items such as oil level and carburettor setting, there is a convenient hatch which opens in the middle of the hood.' Other features included, 'plastic bumpers with load-supporting steel structures', 'supplementary indicators mounted on the C-pillars', and an 'odour detector'.

Following its unveiling, the Techna spent the next two years spreading the gospel about safety before it was put out to pasture.

Chevrolet Astro-Vette Concept

This super-smooth one-off was recognisably a Corvette, but with extended nose and tail sections, rear wheel spats and partial under-car belly pans. The lack of a bonnet-sited 'power bulge' suggested it was equipped with a small-block V8. In reality, it was powered by a 427cu in big-block unit. The design also incorporated pressure-actuated flaps sited in the front wings. These would open to alleviate under-bonnet pressure. However, in reality they were non-functional. The car still exists.

1968

VIC BERRIS

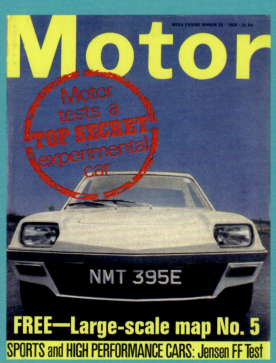

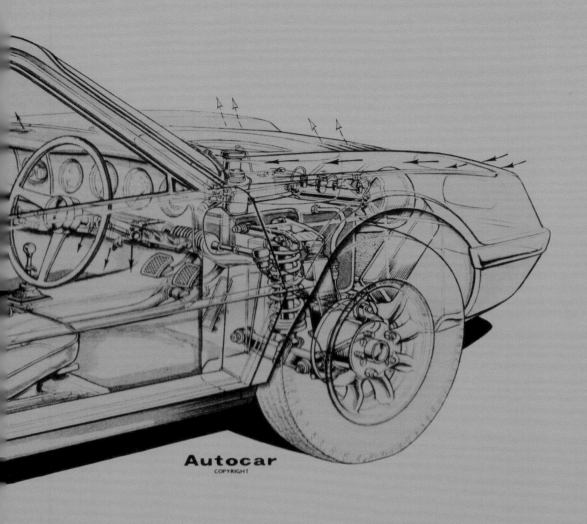

This mid-engined machine was allegedly killed off out of fear that it would provide unwelcome competition for its BLMC stablemate, the Jaguar E-type.

Rover BS (aka Leyland Eight)

Very much a prototype rather than a concept car in the accepted sense, this angular machine was nevertheless a media magnet in period. However, a certain number of mistruths and a degree of conjecture have trailed the car since its creation. Think back to the mid-1960s and Rover was one of the most innovative car manufacturers in the world, having largely thrown off the shackles of its staid image thanks to the likes of the P6 saloon and its gas-turbine programme. The BS, as it would become known, was born of a group of engineers working under Spen King kicking around ideas for a mid-engined sports car.

There was no intention on their part for it to become a production car, or even for it to be seen in public. Nor, it must be said, was much thought given to aesthetics: no stylists were consulted. Nonetheless, the resultant prototype exuded a certain charm, the intention being to make as much use of P6 components as possible. What really ignited the project, however, was Rover's acquisition of the rights to the General Motors Buick/Oldsmobile 3.5-litre V8 engine. This all-alloy unit would be developed extensively and became a marque mainstay. Here, the engine was sited amidships, and a Buick unit may have been used rather than an actual Rover variant (BS was engineer-speak for Buick Sports, or Buick Special).

Remarkably, Rover was happy to loan the car to *Motor* in early 1968, and it was displayed at that year's New York International Auto Show. Confusingly, it was given a new name too, *Road & Track* commenting: 'A car that grabbed us was Rover's experimental Leyland Eight. This stubby coupé has the 215cu in Buick V8 aluminium engine mounted amidships with its two carbs in a raised plastic bubble behind the rear window. There's a purposeful anti-dream car air about this 150mph grand tourer.'

The project had been annulled by the time it resurfaced at the January 1969 Brussels motor show, with some sources claiming the car was killed off by Sir William Lyons who feared competition for the Jaguar E-type (Jaguar and Rover by now co-existed under the British Leyland umbrella). Despite scale models suggesting a restyled variant of the BS might have reached production, King and his team were fully engaged elsewhere, primarily in creating and developing the Range Rover.

1968

GKN Lotus 47D

Built in 1968, this one-off supercar was based on the Lotus Europa's racing cousin, the 47, albeit with a specially-widened bodyshell and lengthened chassis. 'The differences start with the chassis frame which, although of the Europa large box-section backbone type, is some 10in longer than standard', *Autocar* reported in 1969. 'Rear suspension is pure Formula One with reversed lower wishbones and adjustable single-tube top links; long double trailing arms, picking up with the extremities of the backbone, provide longitudinal location... '

It went on to add: 'Front suspension is reminiscent of the type used on the Lotus 23 and 33, with welded tube wishbones. Armstrong co-axial coil spring and damper units are used front and rear. Vandervell Products' racing department, which built the Vanwall racers, made the front and rear roll bars.' Powered by a 184bhp Rover V8 that was allied to a five-speed ZF 'box, the 47D was intended to act as a mobile testbed while also showcasing GKN's various automotive wares to the motor industry and wider public.

Formula 3 star Mike Walker demonstrated the car at various race meetings in 1969–70, and in 1972 it received a displacement hike to 4.4 litres. That, and a quartet of twin-choke Weber 45DCOE carbs. In September 1975, *Autocar* tested the car and recorded a 0–100mph time of just 11.1sec. The car was later sold to the USA.

There is a sidebar to the story, however. In the late 1980s, GKN announced plans to revive the Vanwall marque as a supercar brand. What's more, the 47D was to serve as a template, albeit with a new body styled by Simon Saunders (later of Ariel Atom fame). Despite renderings appearing in the specialist press in period, the scheme soon unravelled.

The GKN Lotus 47D was somewhat larger than the sports-racing car that lent its basic architecture. Power came from a Rover V8 unit that became incrementally more powerful into the 1970s.

1968

Mercury LeGrand Marquis

This one-off show car employed an unusual feature that has yet to be incorporated on a mainstream production car: a combined boot lid and right-rear wing that swung upwards to afford access to the boot. The benefit of this 'innovation' was, according to its maker, heightened ease of access at curb level, but also greater protection from oncoming traffic. The car also boasted two lift-out roof panels and stacked headlights.

Cock Cockpit II

Shown at a variety of major car shows in 1968–69, the Cockpit II followed a prior city-car prototype that did not break cover publicly. Devised by Cock, an electro-mechanical engineering giant from the Netherlands, the car was, predictably, battery-powered. It was designed to accommodate two adults and as many children, all within a tiny footprint. The car purportedly had a maximum speed of 31mph (50km/h) and a range of around 31 miles (50km).

The name may have raised titters among native English speakers, but the Cock wasn't without ability. It offered another take on the electric city car theme.

Ford Thunderbird Saturn

Conceived in the Ford Design Centre in Dearborn, Michigan, the Saturn was essentially a 1968 Thunderbird Tudor Hardtop with a fastback roofline that was 50.8mm (2in) lower than the standard item. The front wings and bonnet were also extended by 101.6mm (4in), other changes including – bafflingly – 'European-look' headlight covers. There were no externally-visible doorhandles either. The car was unveiled at that year's Southern California Automobile Show, the silhouette when seen in profile foretelling the 1970 Thunderbird production car.

Citycar

Very much a homebrewed concept car, the Citycar was nevertheless well-publicised in period. It was conceived and built by former RAF pilot Mike Forrest and comprised Mini subframes and a 750cc flat-twin engine of indeterminate origin. The front end of the car was hinged on the right-hand side and opened as one piece, much like on an Isetta microcar. Another unusual feature was the back-to-back seating arrangement. Forrest claimed it could accommodate the driver plus four passengers, and he hoped to attract a mainstream manufacturer to acquire the design.

1969

The 1960s drew to a close with car design having been transformed from sculptured forms with lashings of chrome to geometric shapes. Nevertheless, some of the more celebrated concept cars of the period weren't lacking for whimsy. Stateside, custom-car influences continued to permeate throughout Detroit's output, this being the era where the muscle car held sway. Even so, General Motors and Ford in particular continued to produce small city concepts at a time when fuel costs were minimal, if only when compared to those in Europe.

The 1960s had seen the concept car come of age, the praises of many being sung that much higher in the here and now. They pushed boundaries, uprooted goalposts and inspired many. That, in itself, was rather the point.

Also in 1969
NASA astronaut Neil Armstrong becomes the first human to set foot on the Moon, during the Apollo 11 mission.
The Woodstock festival takes place in New York State, reportedly with a crowd of 500,000.
The prototype Anglo-French Concorde supersonic airliner makes its maiden flight.
The Kray twins are found guilty of murder and sentenced to life imprisonment.

Mercedes-Benz C111

Mercedes-Benz withdrew from top-flight motorsport following the infamous 1955 Le Mans disaster. However, by the mid-1960s, former competition chief Rudolf Uhlenhaut had become head of passenger car development, but he craved something more; something he could get his teeth into. The firm's output had reached a plateau technically and a radical new supercar would be just the ticket to keep his engineers happy while potentially providing a dazzling halo product, he reasoned. With his former accomplice from the disbanded competition department, Hans Scherenberg, becoming Daimler-Benz's managing director in 1965, Uhlenhaut's scheme was greeted with enthusiasm.

Under Scherenberg and old-hand Uhlenhaut, a new, more youthful engineering generation would assume control at the development branch in Untertürkheim. Nothing was too daring, Uhlenhaut in particular being keen to explore the potential of a mid-engined sports car, if only for possible motorsport applications. A design study had first been mooted in 1964, but it wasn't until 1968 that the proposal, initially codenamed C101, gained traction. This new breed of Benz would be powered by a Wankel 'rotary' engine, the firm having acquired a patent for the design back in 1961. It would also act as a test bed that foretold advances in composite construction, ABS braking and suspension arrangements, many of which would be applied to more mainstream products. Volume manufacture wasn't on the agenda but this engineering hack was about to become a show-stopper.

Uhlenhaut's team had evaluated established marques, acquiring a Lotus 47 (competition variant of the Europa) among others, but typically went its own way with a semi-spaceframe chassis with deep sills to provide torsional stiffness. Suspension was via unequal-length wishbones and an anti-roll bar up front, unequal-length transverse links, upper and lower trailing arms and an anti-roll bar out back, with coil springs all-round. Power came via an extremely compact three-chamber rotary combustion engine, which displaced 600cc per chamber – the equivalent of a 3.6-litre piston unit.

The first test mule – dubbed 'Tin Box' - took to the road on 16 April, Hans Liebold flogging it around the Nürburgring and Hockenheim circuits barely a month later. Meanwhile, the body-engineering department under Werner Breitschwedt and Karl Wilfert set about transforming Bruno Sacco's rendering into three-dimensional reality. In July 1969, the definitive glassfibre bodyshell was glued, riveted and screwed into place and then tested in a wind tunnel where it recorded a drag coefficient of 0.335Cd. Such was the reception to the car internally, the already exhausted test team was told to have the renamed C111 ready for a series of press demonstrations to coincide with September's Frankfurt Motor Show.

The fabulous Mercedes-Benz C111 proved a media sensation, with many titles opining that it would become a latter day 300SL 'Gullwing'. Sadly, they were soon proved wrong.

205

1969

Predictably, reaction among the media was one of jaw-slackened disbelief, even if insiders remained mum over whether it would ever reach even limited production. After its debut, *Road & Track* wrote: 'Unlike GM or Ford, Daimler-Benz doesn't make a habit of building dream cars, and we can't recall any previous experimental Merc that didn't eventually go into production. Maybe they'll race it and maybe they won't, but it would be unlike D-B to waste it.'

It didn't, even if the board that had once been so smitten with the project effectively nixed it. In 1970, a restyled quad-rotor-powered variant – the CIII-II – broke cover at the Geneva Motor Show, and it seemed ever more likely that the car would be offered for public consumption. The big draw for the management was making use of the Wankel engine to which the firm had devoted vast resources. The C111 was the ideal platform with which to usher in this brave new world before it found a home in a range of more conformist products.

Unfortunately, there remained serious doubts that the rotary motor could ever provide the sort of reliability and longevity expected of a Mercedes-Benz. Its hellacious thirst also counted against it, as did the USA's proposed emissions regulations under the Clean Air Act. The other alternative was a regular piston engine, and one of the original prototypes was fitted with a 4.5-litre V8 which Fritz Naumann, one of Uhlenhaut's lieutenants, used as a company car for two years. Sadly, though, the board vetoed each scheme. However, it allowed a further batch of cars to be built, explicitly for research purposes.

Of the first two series of C111s, seven were of the C111-11 configuration. Just to confuse matters, one of them was also known as the C111-11D. It was the first example of the second batch of prototypes, which was relegated to a life of dusty stasis in the experimental department's backroom until 1976 when it formed the centrepiece of Daimler-Benz's campaign to modernise the image of its diesel engines. It was making a big push on the global stage with its new five-cylinder oil burner and what better way of showcasing its durability, economy and performance capabilities than with a record-breaking attempt?

Out came the rotary and in went a humble diesel unit taken from the 240D saloon, one with the standard 3,005cc displacement reduced ever so slightly by a cylinder bore 1mm smaller. With the addition of a Garrett AiResearch turbocharger, a slightly smoothed out body and experimental Michelin rubber, the 'D' collected all international records in the three-litre diesel class. Averaging 157.161mph (253km/h) on the 7.8-mile (13km) Nardo circuit, and requiring only five changes of rear tyres during the round-the-clock record run, the C111 had more than proved its worth; even more so when you consider it also averaged 11.9mpg.

Several variations on the C111 theme were made, all of them drivable. In later years, a diesel variant broke several world records at the Nardo circuit in Italy.

1969

Bertone Spicup

Bertone's awkwardly-named Spicup prototype improbably ended up recording a six-figure mileage. The lone prototype still exists and is a concours regular.

It was a cryptic title for a brilliantly left-field concept car, 'Spe-e-coop' being a contraction of 'Spider' and 'Coupé'. Unveiled at the 1969 Geneva motor show, the 'Spider + Coupé', as Stile Bertone put it, was conceived in 1968, in part to promote an idea developed by Bertone engineer Enzo Cingolani for a retractable roof; one where stainless-steel panels would withdraw into an oversized roll bar at the touch of a button. The Spicup was built to showcase the 'umbrella roof', with BMW deemed the perfect partner for an ambitious dream car. The two firms had previously collaborated on the Giorgetto Giugiaro-styled 3200 CS coupé which had been bodied at Bertone's Grugliasco plant.

While the Spicup was dreamed up in Italy, BMW undoubtedly played its part, as the donor for the project was a pre-production E3-generation 2500 saloon, chassis V*0010* (V standing for Versuchswagen, or 'experimental car') which came complete with the latest 2.8-litre straight-six. That said, it was clearly hedging its bets, as according to BMW's historical archives, chassis V*0011* was dispatched concurrently to Pietro Frua.

Nuccio Bertone also played more than a supervisory role in the Spicup's creation. While not a stylist per se, this was a collaborative exercise with chief designer Marcello Gandini, insiders from the period claiming that 'Project 1010.0' was very close to his heart. The end result was perhaps not conventionally attractive, Road & Track reporting: 'Bertone's latest effort, BMW-based and bearing the ugly name of Spicup, is short, heavy-hipped, faintly wedgy and not so nice looking as a normal Teutonic BMW costing much less.'

Subsequently displayed at the June 1969 Concorso d'Eleganza in Alassio, and finally at the Frankfurt motor show two months later, the car was sold in that same year. What followed next is highly speculative, but several sources say the Spicup passed between several German dealers including Auto Becker of Düsseldorf, which in period was well known for selling exotica. What is known for sure is that a Dutch motor trader acquired it in the mid-1970s, the vivid green body colour being changed for a nasty shade of orange while the elaborate cabin trim was *painted* black. Improbably for a concept car, it went on to record a mileage that stretched into six figures.

Pininfarina 512S Berlinetta Speciale

One of the less ornately decorated Ferrari styling studies of the late 1960s, the 512S Berlinetta Speciale was nonetheless spectacularly proportioned and not lacking for exotic underpinnings. Beneath the dart-like outline was a Ferrari 512S semi-monocoque platform with a 4,993cc V12 sited amidships. The chassis once formed part of a 312P sports-prototype that had been returned to the Ferrari factory following a fiery accident at Monza. It was subsequently used as a basis for developing the 512S racer, with an engine block from a 612 Can-Am car, before it was handed over to Pininfarina once Scuderia Ferrari had no further use for it.

Stylist Filippo Sapino didn't hold back. The wedge-shape profile was a lesson in boundary-pushing. The front-end, unencumbered by a radiator, ensured a low frontal area; the huge one-piece plastic windscreen swept almost horizontally to the rear engine deck, replete with three rows of lateral cooling louvres, much like on Bertone's Alfa Romeo Carabo. To either side of the glasshouse were long rectangular slots to carry cooling air to the radiators, although onlookers with a technical bent doubted this set-up would ever work. Below the upswept rear skirt, the gearbox and four exhaust pipes poked out menacingly, Pininfarina emphasising the car's competition ancestry. Just 980mm (38.5in) from top to bottom, and almost twice as wide, this show-stopper feature the *de rigeur* one-piece flip-up canopy but, despite talk to the contrary, it was a non-runner.

Filippo Sapino's bold outline for the Pininfarina Ferrari 512S Berlinetta Speciale was brilliantly realised even if form clearly trumped function.

1969

Autobianchi A112 Runabout
(aka Bertone Runabout)

While lauded in retrospect, this Marcello Gandini-styled roadster was not warmly received by the specialist press in period. What they didn't know, however, was that it foretold a production car – the Fiat X1/9, much of the basic layout having already been established. What's more, it wasn't going to be displayed at the 1969 Turin motor show until the eleventh hour. It was the same event that witnessed the introduction of the new Bertone-styled Autobianchi A112 hatchback, and much of its running gear was adopted for the Runabout according to PR material from the period.

Road & Track reported: 'Bertone's other *Novità* was just silly. After all the trouble Autobianchi engineers took to envelope an east-west-engined, front-wheel drive [car], Bertone turns the lot back to front, locking the original steering, and produces a wedge-shaped two-seat Runabout of decidedly limited use! The whole thing was exquisitely made, but, as [Nuccio] Bertone said, it was: "Just a *leedle* piece of fun."'

Autocar reported: 'Again, the wedge-shape is used for this red, white and silver two-seats, boat-influenced creation with its chopped-off tail and strong roll-over bar on which, above the driver's and passenger's outside shoulders, are mounted the square headlamps. The lower part of the body is formed of large stainless steel scales – the armadillo influence again, which is so much in evidence for ventilating mid-engined cars – and a red band around the waist

accentuates the arrow-like appearance. As its manufacturer told it, it is for the young, designed for no specific purpose save to give pleasure.'

According to some sources, the car's body was only completed two days before the show. What's more, it also had a 1,290cc four-cylinder engine from the innovative Fiat 128. The car was subsequently made driveable, albeit not at speeds above walking pace. It was later left to fester but has since been restored.

The striking Runabout was another Marcello Gandini production, one of its more outré features being the 'headlights' sited in the roll-over bar. It established styling themes explored on the Fiat X1/9.

Pininfarina Sigma

The editors of Switzerland's *Automobil Revue* initiated the Sigma project as a means of showcasing ideas of how to build a safer racing car. Having attracted a cadre of respected experts such as Professor Ernst Fiala (later engineering chief of Volkswagen) and Dr Michael Henderson (an Australian structural-design authority), their biggest coup was tapping Enzo Ferrari for the supply of a 1967 312 Grand Prix car to use as a donor vehicle: Pininfarina would build the Sigma with Paolo Martin interpreting the ideas into an attractive whole. Respected journalist and former Le Mans 24 Hours winner Paul Frère was on board to offer a driver's perspective.

Designing a car with the principal parameter that having an accident is highly probable, a rigid safety cell was created with crumple zones front and rear to absorb forces on impact. Pontoons were added to the car's flanks to dissipate some energy in the event of being struck side-on, a quick-release mechanism between the crash helmet and headrest being in place to reduce the risk of neck injuries. Many of the ideas promoted on the Sigma were never applied in motorsport in period, but others arrived in altered form over ensuing decades. Ultimately, though, it was a safety crusade led by Jackie Stewart that brought about the painfully slow realisation among the powers that be that racing drivers weren't expendable.

Chevrolet XP-882

General Motors chief engineer Zora Arkus-Duntov was a racer to the core and, inspired by the likes of CERV I and CERV II, he constantly pushed for a mid-engined Chevrolet Corvette production car. XP-882 was powered by a 400cu in V8 that was sited transversely amidships and allied to a front-wheel drive Oldsmobile Turbo-Hydramatic transmission with its driveshaft running through the oil pan to the differential. Two test mules had been completed by early 1969. However, the scheme was then shelved, in part due to the influence of Chevrolet's newly-anointed general manager, John DeLorean. However, on learning that the Ford-backed De Tomaso Pantera and AMC AMX/3 supercars were to be displayed at the April 1970 New York International Auto Show, he ordered that one of the mules be painted silver and displayed at the event. Variations on the theme would be a constant source of media attention throughout the ensuing decade.

Pininfarina Fiat-Abarth 2000 Scorpione
(aka Fiat-Abarth 2000 Pininfarina, aka Fiat-Abarth 2000 Coupé Speciale)

One of the most striking concept cars of the late 1960s, this rebodied Fiat Abarth 2000 Sport Spider SE racing car nevertheless enjoyed a short shelf life as a concept queen. It was unveiled at the January 1969 Brussels motor show and later exhibited in Canada before disappearing from view. The donor car was carried over unmodified, the rear-sited 220bhp, 1,946cc four-cylinder engine being left exposed. The car's signature feature, however, was the line that began with the stubby bonnet and flowed in one continuous line to the rear deck with its multiple lateral louvres. The 'prismatic shape' roof tipped forward in one piece to facilitate entry, the vestigial doors being all but redundant.

Style Auto commented in typically leftfield manner: 'The Abarth 2000... has been dressed by Carrozzeria Pininfarina without making any modifications to the original chassis. This pragmatic task was complicated, in this particular case, both by certain characteristic constraints – the divided water radiators in the front overhang, the twin oil radiations in the sides, and the high beltline of the tubular frame governing cockpit entry – and by various other details typical of a competition car...'

'The restrains, as often happens in Pininfarina designs, are evidentiated [sic] in the formal and stylistic solutions which are unusual even for a special coupé,' it continued. 'Pininfarina's Abarth 2000, which can be associated with the zoological family of Loricata, is noted for the lively movement of its surfaces, underlined by angular unions, and for the convincing taste of graphic decoration, reduced to the essential.' *Motor*, by contrast, described it as being the 'crustacean car,' although it went on to say: '...for the back of the car is simply a hole which exposes all the Abarth works. Which could make the rear view quite exciting: imagine looking at the car after being overtaken on the road, watching the suspension work, hearing the engine's angry scream, and seeing the oil-pump toothed belt busily whirring away as the coupé receded into the distance...'

Pininfarina's striking 'crustacean car' was based on an Abarth sports-racer with its competition roots being highlighted rather than concealed as on some of its contemporises.

Pininfarina Alfa Romeo 33/2 Prototipo Speciale

Perhaps the least controversial of the many concept cars based on the Alfa Romeo Tipo 33 platform, this voluptuous one-off was unveiled at the 1969 Paris motor show. The design was influenced by the previous year's Ferrari 250 P5, both cars being the work of Leonardo Fioravanti. With its concealed headlights, butterfly doors, and large greenhouse, it appeared every inch the exotic supercar, but one that was less compromising than Bertone's wedge-shaped Carabo.

For many years, a degree of confusion surrounded this car, not least the origins of the body. In some period reports, the inference was that the car's glassfibre body was simply that of the 250 P5, but reworked for this application. Fioravanti wrote in *Il Cavallino nel Cuore* that it was: '...clearly a "clone" of the P5.' However, the Prototipo Speciale was restored during the early 2000s and it was established that the bodyshell was unique to this car rather simply a rehashed variant of the earlier show-stopper.

1969

De Tomaso Mustella

Unveiled at the 1969 Turin motor show, the Mustella represented yet another collaborative project involving Ghia, the Ford Motor Company, and Alesandro (né Alejandro) de Tomaso. As with so many other schemes involving the Argentinian émigré, it proved a one-week wonder. Styled by Tom Tjaarda during his second stint at Ghia, this Ford V6-engined 2+2 coupé was one of seven cars designed concurrently by the Michigan-born artist, and the first to wear a de Tomaso badge (he would go on to style production models such as the Pantera, Deauville and Longchamp).

Shorter, wider, and lower than a comparable Ford Capri, the Mustella was also considerably more powerful. If the press release was to be believed, the car's 'Cologne' V6 was equipped with aluminium cylinder heads and Lucas mechanical fuel-injection among other tweaks, which resulted in a quoted power output of 230bhp at 6,500rpm. This high-compression unit was allied to a four-speed manual transmission with overdrive. Inside, the wooden dashboard was near-symmetrical with slabs of polished timber either side of a central instrument binnacle.

Tjaarda was unhappy with the end product, as was his paymaster. Nevertheless, the concept was clearly deemed sound because an updated variant – Mustella II – was displayed extensively in 1973.

The handsome if utterly orthodox Mustella was another de Tomaso-instigated mayfly. Nevertheless, this V6-engined coupé later spawned a sequel.

Chevrolet Astro III

Reputedly the brainchild of John DeLorean, the final Astro in the concept car trilogy was radically different to its predecessors. Unveiled at the 1969 Chicago Auto Show, Astro III employed an Allison 'Type 250-C18' gas turbine that purportedly produced 317bhp and was intended for use in helicopters (Allison was a subsidiary of GM). Power was transmitted to the rear wheels via a Hydra-Matic transmission.

Apparently inspired by contemporary business jets, the phallic silhouette incorporated a lift-up canopy for means of access. This design element was almost obligatory for concept cars in period, as was the use of joystick controls. With the powered canopy raised, the pilot and co-pilot were then obliged to get their posteriors into the 'elevator seats' which then lowered them into position with the touch of a button. The angle of the seats could be described as 'semi-repose' in true fighter-aircraft-style. Rear visibility was at a premium given the lack of a rear screen, but fortunately Astro III came equipped with a rear camera and a TV monitor. The rectangular headlights, meanwhile, were concealed in the flanks and popped out when required.

Weighing in at 892kg (1,966lb), and standing barely 900mm (35.4in) at its highest point, this was a radical-looking device for sure, but performance figures were conspicuously absent from promotional material. Also, contrary to contemporary reports, Astro III wasn't a three-wheeler in the strictest sense: the front wheels were mounted close together so as to be almost touching. Astro III made few show appearances in period, but didn't suffer the fate of many concept cars in that it wasn't scrapped.

1969

Ghia Lancia Fulvia HP 1600 Competizione

A degree of confusion surrounds the reasoning behind this car's construction, and its intended purpose. According to its designer, Tom Tjaarda, it was built at the behest of Ghia's latest principal, Alejandro de Tomaso, who was looking to acquire Lancia, and hoped to do so using Ford's money. The Competizione and the concurrent Marica were made to show exciting possibilities for future models. Tjaarda also claimed that the car was built with an attempt at the Le Mans 24 Hours in mind.

Serious effort was invested in the Competizione's construction, too; much more so than your typical rebodying exercise. This wasn't just a reclothed Lancia Fulvia. First of all, the donor car's V4 engine was sited far forward in the platform which was a bit of an issue considering the dramatic low-line bonnet Tjaarda had in mind. Writing in *Style Auto*, he stated: '...the biggest problem was solved by rotating the powerplant around the axle shafts and by lowering the subframe by 30mm...' The changes didn't end there, the solid rear axle being substituted for an independent double-wishbone arrangement devised by Giampaolo Dallara.

The ultra-thin aluminium body panels were draped over a self-supporting steel skeleton, the doors alone weighing less than 6kg (13lb) each. The bespoke windscreen, meanwhile, was barely 3mm (0.11in) thick. Tjaarda's Competizione outline was typically crisp, the only jarring aspect being its signature feature – a movable rear spoiler. The centre rear deck lid could be raised on hydraulic arms to become an aerofoil-like rear wing that could then be adjusted for rake. When retracted it would, in theory, fit flush with the rear window and C-pillars.

Making its debut at the 1969 Geneva motor show, the car was generally well received. Writing for *Road & Track*, Cyril Posthumus levelled some particularly tart comments at rival offerings before stating:

'Ghia's latest effort on a Lancia Fulvia is a clean cut, so-called competition coupé with a chopped-off rear, concealed headlights, Glaverbel screen and a slim roofline a la De Tomaso Mangusta and drilled door pillars a la Serenissima. Only the spoiler spoiled it – a retractable device set over the tail on two telescoping tubes, seemingly cut from circular stock and not even faired in. Rush job, maybe?'

As for the possibility of the car helping to catch Ford's eye, this was academic if true given that Fiat acquired the ailing marque that same year. There is every reason to believe Tjaarda's insistence that the Competizione was built with circuit use in mind, because the car was tested at the Circuit de la Sarthe, the outing getting the briefest of mentions in *Auto Italiano* magazine. By this time, the car had gained rear-arch extensions, an unsightly bonnet scoop and the black highlights over the original yellow hue. These modification had a nick-of-time look about them, which is in keeping with a show car being handed over to a bunch of racers.

As for the reason behind the pop-riveted bonnet bulge... The car was running a full-house 'Esperienze Meccaniche' Group 4 1,584cc Lancia Corse V4 engine, complete with monstrous Solex carburettors. The flip-forward bonnet wouldn't close without this ugly box-like addenda.

AMC AMX/2

The mid-to-late 1960s witnessed the emergence of the American mid-engined supercar, or at least concepts that suggested they were in the offing. In 1967, AMC initiated its AMX/K programme, the plan being to build a supercar in series as an image-building exercise. It came tantalisingly close to realising its objective via the AMX/3 which emerged in early 1970, only for the scheme to be axed later that same year. However, before that came the AMX/2 in 1969.

Road & Track reported in period: 'It isn't an operational car yet, but is planned as a mid-engined road or racing car using an American Motors V8 engine and independent suspension of a "unique design". Its wheelbase is 105in, overall length 171.5in, height 43in; the tyres are obviously racing ones and mounted on 15in wheels of different widths for front and rear. Nice – we hope they're serious about it.'

AMC was clearly serious, but this Chicago Auto Show attention-getter was an engine-less mock-up; a teaser outlined by Dick Teague and completed by Fred Hudson and Bob Nixon. It foretold styling themes that would be explored – exaggerated even – on the AMX/3 that was to follow.

AMC attempted to take on the exotica elite with the AMX/2, if only in theory. The prototype was a non-runner but the AMX/3 that followed came tantalisingly close to entering production.

1969

Austin Zanda

Styled by Harris Mann, and breaking cover at the 1969 British International Motor Show at Earls Court, the Zanda was exhibited by Pressed Steel Fisher (the body-building subsidiary of Austin-Morris). According to Road & Track: 'It has the usual rather silly shape prophetic vehicles seem to take, but the object of the exercise, assisted by films, diagrams and well-informed stand attendants, was to show how quickly a specific body form could be evolved using modern computer methods, wherein dimensional requirements and restrictions are fed into the machine and design disgorged with immense saving in man hours. Only a big group with big resources could employ computers to this degree, but the Zanda exhibit certainly provided a fascinating look at modern design ways and means.'

While strictly a mock-up, the Zanda was notionally powered by a mid-mounted 1.5-litre four-cylinder engine from the recently-introduced Austin Maxi. This styling study still exists and is on display at the British Motor Museum in Gaydon, Warwickshire.

Ghia Lancia Marica

Despite its relative obscurity, the Ghia-crafted Marica wasn't without influence. It was also the second one-off based on a Lancia Flaminia shaped by Tom Tjaarda following the Pininfarina 3C 2.8 Coupé Speciale 2 Posti. Based on a short-wheelbase platform, the Marica (which was named after a Roman nymph) was a crisply-styled GT that was well-received in period following its unveiling at the 1969 Turin motor show. Road & Track labelled it; '...an extremely elegancy coupé... Its lines were unmatched for good taste.' Autocar, meanwhile, labelled it : '...a very fresh, crisp-looking car.'

While only displayed publicly once in period, the Marica went on to provide inspiration for the sadly ill-starred Momo Mirage. Tjaarda also reported that it acted as the springboard for the de Tomaso Longchamp (which, it has to be said, was also inspired by the Mercedes-Benz R107-series SL at its maker's insistence). The one and only Marica still exists.

Suzuki Punch Buggy

Suzuki's stand at the 1969 Tokyo Motor Show was awash with oddities. These included a Group 6 sports-prototype, a 'long-distance rally car' proposal, a single-seater powered by a transversely-mounted three-cylinder two-stroke engine, and the Punch Buggy. This Lotus Seven meets dune buggy was created in-conjunction with a weekly boys' magazine. It featured a spaceframe chassis and a glassfibre body designed by Motoki Hama, who also created the Honda S800-based Hama Coniglio sports car.

Zagato Volvo GTZ

Blurring the line between concept car and would-be local market-only offering, the GTZ was conceived by Volvo concessionaire, Motauto. Italian design houses have collaborated with the Swedish car maker as far back as 1953, when Vignale and Michelotti teamed up to create a small run of coachbuilt offerings. Frua, or rather his protégé Pelle Petterson, enjoyed rather more success with the P1800 production car. However, by the mid-to-late 1960s, the Italian agent thought it was becoming a bit old hat stylistically. It went so far as to commission Fissore to produce a fastback variant in 1965, but it remained unique. The GTZ, by contrast, was an attempt at an all new design rather than a remodel.

Zagato's soon-to-depart styling chief Ercole Spada created an outline for the Volvo 142S-based coupé which, not unsurprisingly, borrowed elements from his earlier Lancia Fulvia Zagato and Alfa Romeo Junior Zagato outlines. Resplendent in dark blue with orange accents, the prototype was unveiled at the 1969 Turin motor show where it found a buyer. Volvo's management in Gothenburg, by contrast, was not interested in assisting Motauto with the supply of running gear. However, a further prototype, this time based on a Volvo 164 and with pop-up headlights, was revealed at the 1970 running of the event, the GTV 3000 similarly failing to find favour.

Striking if perhaps not conventionally beautiful, the Zagato Volvo GTZ could have been a worthy successor to the P1800 production car, but the management in Sweden wasn't interested.

1969

Opel CD

General Motors' Opel division outshone all of its rivals at the 44th Internationale Automobil-Ausstellung (International Motor Show Germany) thanks to this simply-named concept. Displayed alongside an experimental version of Opel GT with a Targa-style roof (the Aero GT), this styling study was styled under the aegis of American Chuck Jordan, and based on the marque's range-topper, the 5.4-litre Chevrolet V8-engined Diplomat saloon. The chassis was shortened for this application, although a mock-up of a dedicated platform (rather than an adapted one) was displayed nearby.

As was almost mandatory in the late 1960s, the CD (Coupé Diplomat) boasted a one-piece, tilt-forward canopy rather than doors. What's more, the steering wheel and instrument binnacle moved with it. The two seats were fixed, although the pedals and steering column were adjustable. Unlike many of its contemporaries, this concept car was almost practical to the point that it had a luggage compartment and even a spare wheel. While the rushed nature of the build was commented on in several publications, not least the small matter of the wraparound windscreen being held in place with black tape, it caused a furore. Opel was inundated with requests that it be put into series production, but that was clearly unviable.

However, Opel did rework the outline for a second-series variation on the theme with conventional doors. This Frua-built car would, in a roundabout way, spawn the Bitter marque.

The Opel CD featured the obligatory flip-up, one-piece canopy and represented quite the daring leap for the conservative General Motors brand.

Italdesign Alfa Romeo Iguana

Of all the various concept cars based on Alfa Romeo Tipo 33 foundations, perhaps the least fanciful was the Giorgetto Giugiaro-styled Iguana. By contrast with flamboyant offerings from Pininfarina and Bertone, here the outline bordered on the conventional. That said, it was undeniably exotic-looking, the nose in particular foretelling future Giugiaro offerings such as the Maserati Bora and Porsche Tapiro show car. The rising window line was also redolent of many other cars penned by the Italdesign co-founder, the Iguana nomenclature being coined to denote the rear side air intakes: according to its creator, they evoked the scales found on herbivorous lizards.

First seen at the 1969 Turin motor show, the car was partially bodied in glassfibre, and painted in a Metalflake grey. However, the skeletal roof structure plus the A- and B-pillars were finished in brushed metal (this treatment was later applied to the Giugiaro-penned DeLorean). *Autocar* reported: 'Though the basic shape is beautiful and striking, it has become subservient to a mass of applied detail, so that a feeling off aggressiveness has been achieved instead of flowing sleekness.'

The Iguana was initially powered by a SPICA fuel-injected two-litre V8 allied to six-speed Colotti gearbox. At some point, the original unit was replaced with a 2.5-litre V8 from the Alfa Romeo Montreal coupé. The lone prototype resides in the Museo Storico Alfa Romeo collection.

Giugiaro's Iguana was more soberly styled than the many Alfa Tipo 33-based show cars created by rival Italian carrozzerie. Nevertheless, it was not lacking unusual touches.

1969

Holden Hurricane

Wizardry from Aus. The incredible Hurricane was unlike anything ever to have emerged from Holden, General Motors' Australian brand. It was 39.2in (996mm) high. The prototype still survives.

Revealed to the local media on the eve of the March 1969 Melbourne Motor Show, the Holden Hurricane caught everyone off-guard. Much like Vauxhall, the British manufacturing arm of General Motors, the resolutely Australian Holden marque was not known for its daring. The arrival of this incredibly low flight of fantasy changed all that. The brainchild of American chief engineer Bill Steinhagen, who had established the firm's research and development department with the backing of Holden's marketing and engineering wings, the 'RD-001' project was given the go-ahead in 1968.

Steinhagen's successor, Bern Ambor, acted as midwife to the scheme, but the identity of those who actually shaped the car remains a source of much debate. Legend suggests that the Hurricane was penned in Detroit, and a scale model was transported to Australia which acted as the jumping-off point for the finished article. However, some historians are convinced it was styled closer to home. Regardless of who penned it, the Hurricane appeared every bit as daring as any styling study to emerge from Europe at the time. The compact design was just 161.8in (4,110mm) long, 71in (1,803mm) wide, and 39.2in (996mm) high, access being by a one-piece canopy which raised upwards and forwards, the seats moving upwards in synch for that added dose of theatre.

The Holden was also a driver: some components were borrowed from the C2-series Chevrolet Corvette, while the early-1960s Pontiac Tempest provided the four-speed transaxle. Power came from a 4.2-litre ohv V8 mounted longitudinally ahead of the rear-axle line. Once its brief publicity-generating career was over, the Hurricane was saved from being scrapped by a senior engineer who deliberately hid it. The car has since been restored to its period splendour.

1969

Buick Century Cruiser

Almost a relic from the previous decade in terms of looking to the distant future, the Century Cruiser was derived from the 1964 Pontiac Firebird IV. Some of its design features appear improbable decades later, while others are rather more commonplace. The Century Cruiser was intended to be guided along electronic highways on a route pre-programmed using a punch-card. It could be driver-operated using pistol-grip controls, or alternatively the car could drive itself while the occupants enjoyed the home comforts of a television set, a fridge, and so on. Means of entry and exit was via the obligatory one-piece canopy that slid forwards and up.

The Bellett MX1600 was one of Tom Tjaarda's less celebrated design studies. The car was later reworked and shown again, but the American emigre wasn't responsible for the makeover.

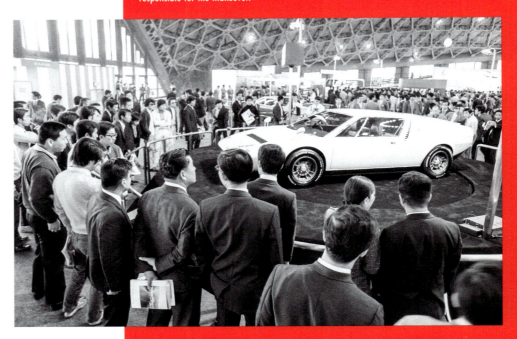

Isuzu Bellett MX1600

This striking mid-engined sports car concept was styled by the prolific Tom Tjaarda. Unveiled at the 1969 Tokyo motor show, it employed a 1.6-litre DOHC four-cylinder engine from the Bellett GT-R production car, tuned to produce 120bhp. This was allied to a Hewland FT200 transaxle. *Road & Track*'s Jack Yamaguchi reported: 'The steel body had a unitary box-section frame and suspension inherited from the Isuzu R6 racing coupé... An interesting feature was a forward wing which could be raised about two inches from its normal flush position in the wedge nose by an electric servo motor controlled from the cockpit.'

Tjaarda subsequently reworked and amplified some aspects of the styling for the de Tomaso Pantera. The MX1600 morphed into the MX1600-II in time for the following year's Tokyo motor show, the pop-up headlights of the original car making way for circular fixed items, although Tjaarda had nothing to do with the makeover.

Lincoln Continental Town Sedan

Echoing pre-war chauffeur-driven limousines, the Continental Town Sedan featured a driver's compartment that was left open to the elements, and a rear compartment that incorporated a colour TV, a 'multiplex' stereo system, and an intercom system via which rear-ferried passengers could instruct the chauffeur without having to lower the glass divider. Painted in pearlescent 'Antique Moss', the cabin was trimmed in green leather with gold accents.

Lincoln was Ford's premium brand and few Lincolns were ever more premium than the Continental Town Sedan with its open chauffeur compartment. It is seen here at the 1969 Chicago Auto Show.

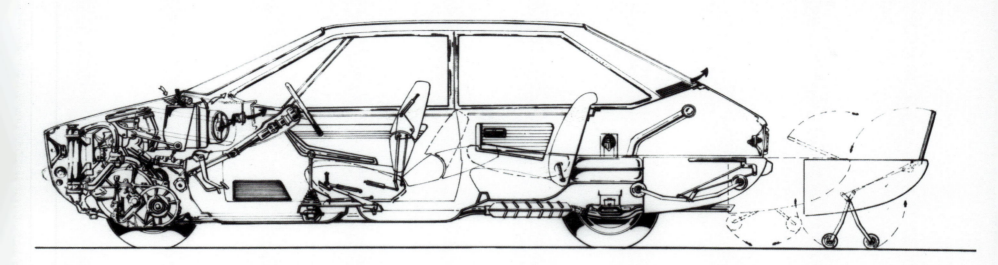

128 coupé 4 posti

bertone
ottobre 1969

Bertone Fiat 128

Styled by Marcello Gandini, Bertone's take on the newly-introduced Fiat 128 was unveiled at the 1969 Turin motor show. Resplendent in Metalflake brown, complete with a roof covered in mock Hessian, the car was, according to its creators, aimed at women motorists, hence the car's signature feature: a roll-in, roll-out shopping trolley with retractable wheels. This wasn't a new idea, having first been seen on the 1964 GM Runabout, the difference being that this was a functional prototype rather than a mere mock-up.

Sessano Mongho 650

Designed by Aldo Sessano, and constructed by Carrozzeria Fissore, the Mongho 650 was a miniscule city car based on a Fiat 500 Nuova platform. Power came from a highly-tuned 650cc Fiat two-cylinder unit that produced 29.5bhp. In something of a change of normal practice, the car was seen at the October/November 1969 Turin motor show in two forms: as a wooden 1:1-scale model, and as a finished prototype.

Cyril Posthumus wasn't shy of sharing his opinions following its unveiling. He opined in *Road & Track*: 'One of the smaller [styling] houses, Fissore naturally made the most of their designs for Monteverdi of Switzerland, but also showed a wooden mock-up for an all-plastic town car called the Mongho 650 produced for the Glazurit glass people. The finished job on the Glazurit stand was needlessly ugly, with its curveless wedge sedan body, although so small a vehicle with a Nardi-doctored 650 Fiat engine should be quick.' The one and only functional prototype still exists.

1969

Abarth 1600GT

First seen on the Abarth stand at the 1969 Turin motor show, the Abarth 1600 was styled by Giorgetto Giugiaro of Italdesign. Based on a Fiat 850 platform, but powered by a rear-sited 1,592cc twin-cam four-cylinder unit fed by two twin-choke Weber 45DCOE9 carburettors, it produced an alleged 145bhp at 7,200rpm. Nevertheless, despite the engine's competition-rooted origins, this was promoted as being a practical 2+2 sports car, and one that bore many of Giugiaro's hallmark styling flourishes, not least the upswept window line. It weighed 674kg (1,486lb) and had a top speed of 150mph (241km/h).

Giannini 650 Caterinetta (aka Sirio)

Produced by Giannini Automobili, this doorless device was based on a Fiat 500 and emerged at the 1969 Turin motor show. *Road & Track* reported in period: 'Giannini, a long-established Fiat tweaker, has diversified this year with an astonishing little fibreglass projectile called the Caterinetta. This has the usual 650 Fiat *elaborato* engine at the wedge end, which also embodies an airfoil, with a low, curved front like a miniature Chaparral 2H.'

Ford Thunderbird Saturn II

Bearing a striking resemblance to the previous year's Thunderbird Saturn, albeit with an even longer snout, the second car in the series was purported to be a: '...personal luxury car of the future.' The car's striking 'Colorado Topaz reflective paint' was complimented by a similarly gilded interior, special features including a radar screen, on-board computer, two-way radio, a tape recorder, and so on. The car was unveiled at the 1969 Chicago Auto Show.

Ford Super Cobra

Styled by Larry Shinoda, and based on a regular Fairlane fastback production car, the Super Cobra was a muscle-car concept that emerged at the 1969 Chicago Auto Show. Finished in a retina-bothering Candy Apple Red, and equipped with a two-tone 'Candy Murano and Hot Red' interior, it was powered by a 428cu in big-block V8. It featured several signature Shinoda features, such as the full-width rear-light arrangement and louvred rear window. Some sources claim it was constructed by Carrozzeria Vignale but that is debatable.

1969

Toyota EX-I

Distinct from other Japanese concept cars of the period, the EX-1 was designed in its entirety in Japan. A logical follow-up to the small-series Toyota 2000GT production car, this striking coupé was a front-engined grand tourer with a low roofline and a distinctive slatted front end. Riding on small 13in wheels, complete with petal-like detail, it purportedly had independent suspension at both ends, but had no engine when revealed at the 1969 Tokyo motor show. It was rumoured, but never confirmed, that the intention was to equip the car with the firm's 540bhp V8, as fitted to the Toyota 7 sports-racer.

Toyota EX-II

In marked contrast to its sportier concept-car stablemates at the 1969 Tokyo motor show, the EX-II barely qualified as an automobile. Ironically, the design was conceived by the firm's competition chief, Jiro Kawano. This tiny two-seater city runabout was powered by a two-cylinder, two-stroke (of Yamaha origin) installed at the rear of the vehicle. The rear wheels were inset, much as on an Isetta microcar.

A car for extrovert urbanites? Possibly. The EX-II was powered by a tiny two-cylinder engine, other variants following in its wake.

Other variants included the EX-II-B which boasted a one-piece transparent canopy, and the EX-II-C which was more akin to a golf cart.

Mitsubishi Commuter

Mitsubishi used the 1969 Tokyo Motor Show to announce a joint venture with the Chrysler Corporation: a joint company would market the new Colt Gallant in the USA, while Chrysler products would be sold in Japan. The firm also announced its intention to reach every market segment, the Commuter being a three-door small car that purportedly possessed '...international charm'. A one-box, wedge-shaped machine, the rear-end comprised almost entirely of glass but, in reality, it was just a mock-up.

One of the more obscure concept cars of the period, the Mitsubishi Commuter was a one-show wonder that was little more than a full-size mock-up.

Toyota EX-III

This amorphous device represented Toyota's take on what mid-engined GT cars would like in the 1980s. Improbably low, sleek, and equipped with a smooth undertray save for louvres behind the rear wheels to expel heat from the engine bay, it was designed in-house in its entirety. However, *CAR* suggested that outside influences may have come into play: 'The EX-III had definite overtones of recent Pininfarina styling exercises on Ferrari and Alfa Romeo [platforms], which we think is no great recommendation.' Sadly, it was an engineless mock-up.

1969
General Motors XP-511 Commuter

This rather phallic-looking trike was styled by Larry Shinoda and employed a one-piece, slide-forward canopy and a rear-sited 1.1-litre Opel four-cylinder engine. This 66bhp unit was allied to a three-speed transmission. 149in (3,785mm) long, 63in (1,600mm) wide, and just 40in (1,015mm) high, it weighed 590kg (1,300lb) and its makers claimed it could reach 80mph (129km/h). It also reckoned it was good for 0–60mph in 16sec and could return 30–35mpg during city use.

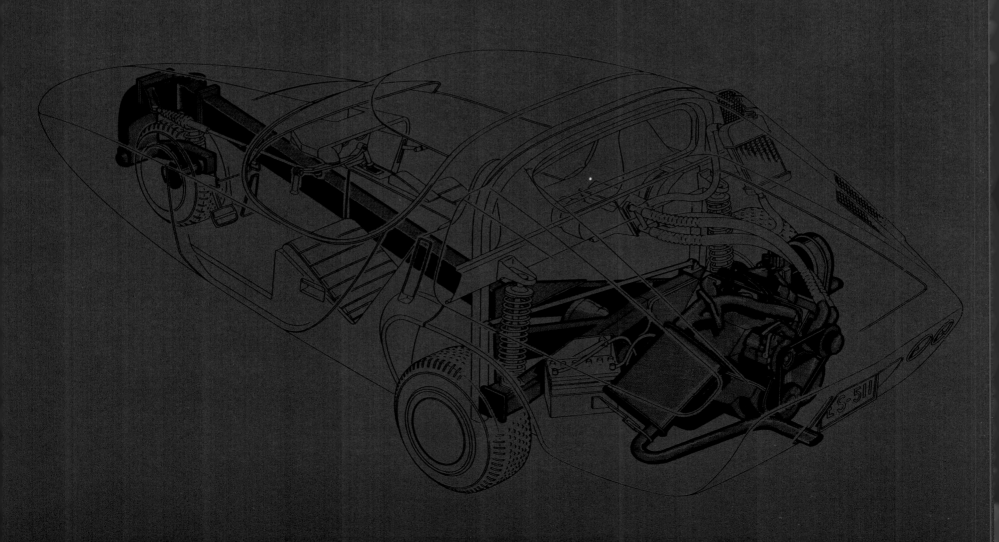

General Motors XP-512

General Motors created a raft of different iterations of the 512, with variously battery and internal-combustion power, and also a pioneering hybrid version that employed a 200cc engine and a DC electric motor with a 72-volt lead-acid battery. Its estimated range using battery power only was 5.2 miles (8.4km) at a sustained speed of 30mph (48.2km/h), while it was reputedly capable of 150mpg, with a fuel-tank capacity of 13.9 litres (3 gallons). Top speed was 35mph (56km/h). Several iterations were made, some in open form, each with a 1,321mm (52in) wheelbase, overall length of 2,192mm (86.3in), and width of 1,422mm (56in).

General Motors XP-833

Another in General Motor's bevvy of concept cars aimed at urban dwellers, the XP-883 was an experimental plug-in hybrid vehicle, one that was powered by a combination of a 570cc two-cylinder petrol engine and a DC electric motor. A bank of six 12-volt batteries was housed between the rear wheels. The car's glassfibre body was conventionally-styled, some design cues foretelling the Vega production model. The electric motor powered the car up to 10mph (16km/h), after which the petrol engine kicked in and it ran in hybrid mode. It had a top speed of 60mph (97km/h). GM's Pontiac division also made a variation on the theme – the X-4 – that employed a two-stroke radial engine.

The XP-833 (below) foretold the plug-in hybrid. It was powered by a 570cc 'twin' and an electric motor. Further variations on the theme followed.

Index

Designers

Arkus-Duntov, Zora 29, 35, 44, 103, 213
Bailey, L. Scott 109
Bertone, Nuccio 58, 71, 109, 156, 177, 178, 208, 210
Bordinat, Eugene 'Gene' 49, 73, 98, 117, 160
Brovarone, Aldo 43, 51, 112, 132, 160
Busch, Fritz B. 121, 123
Carli, Renzo 43, 154, 155
Conrad, Michale 55, 121, 123, 163
Deesen, Paul 57
Di Dia, Andrew 20
Earl, Harley 11, 38
Engel, Elwood 72, 79, 105, 116
Exner, Virgil 12, 21, 27, 37, 90, 96, 97, 109
Farina, Battista 'Pinin' 16, 38, 67, 116
Fioravanti, Leonardo 132, 158, 181, 182, 215
Francoise, Edward V. 20
Frua, Pietro 26, 208, 223, 224
Gandini, Marcello 153, 154, 156, 175, 176, 177, 208, 210, 211, 231
Giacosa, Dante 184, 187
Giugiaro, Giorgetto 39, 58, 71, 89, 109, 111, 112, 141, 161, 172, 175, 177, 181, 187, 189, 190, 208, 224, 232
Jordan, Chuck 24, 224
Kelly, Gordon 36
Lapine, Anatole 57, 71, 103
Loewy, Raymond 19, 83
Maguire, Bob 49, 73
Mantovani, Aldo 175, 180
Manzù, Pio 55, 68, 121, 123, 184, 187
Martin, Paolo 155, 158, 183, 213
Mead, Syd 39, 42, 162
Michelotti, Giovanni 12, 54, 76, 83, 90, 147, 173
Mitchell, Bill 30, 35, 44, 45, 60, 75, 115, 117, 159, 161, 191
Morelli, Alberto 16
Najjar, John 39, 49, 50
Ogle, David 118
Rocha, Ari de 127
Sapino, Fillipo 90, 111, 209
Sartorelli, Sergio 77, 143, 145, 184
Scaglione, Franco 12, 72, 128, 156
Segre, Luigi 12, 31, 83, 90, 109, 121
Sessano, Aldo 231
Shinoda, Larry 44, 57, 60, 69, 103, 159, 160, 233, 236
Snyder, George 11
Spada, Ercole 128, 158, 165, 223
Stephenson, C.N. 31
Stevens, Brooks 36, 55, 83, 103, 135
Teague, Dick 166, 191, 219
Thompson, McKinley 39
Tjaarda, Tom 24, 27, 31, 51, 67, 68, 82, 91, 94, 112, 187, 189, 216, 219, 220, 228
Tremulis, Alex 39, 41, 162
Vignale, Alfredo 12, 54, 81, 83, 98, 135, 147, 173, 190, 223
Werner, Henner 55, 163
Zanzellato, Alfredo 83

Design companies

Autonova 121, 123
Bertone 12, 39, 43, 57, 58, 71, 72, 89, 109, 112, 129, 148, 151, 15, 154, 156, 172, 175, 177, 178, 179, 208, 209, 210, 215, 224, 231
Ghia 12, 21, 27, 31, 37, 42, 43, 67, 77, 79, 87, 90, 96, 109, 111, 116, 121, 139, 141, 145, 161, 169, 172, 187, 189, 190, 216, 219, 220
Italdesign 175, 180, 224, 232
Officine Stampaggi Industriali (OSI) 87, 121, 122, 139, 143, 145, 168, 184
Ogle Design 118
Pininfarina 12, 16, 24, 38, 43, 51, 52, 55, 65, 67, 68, 82, 91, 94, 95, 112, 113, 116, 132, 133, 151, 155, 158, 160, 181, 182, 183, 186, 209, 213, 214, 215, 220, 224, 235
Pinin Farina 12, 16, 18, 24, 38, 39, 53, 58
Sibano & Basano 36, 83, 97, 98, 123
Studi Italiani Realizzazione Prototipi S.p.A 175, 180
Vignale 36, 54, 81, 83, 135, 233
Zagato 89, 122, 128, 158, 165, 223

Picture credits

Richard Heseltine
Cover (top right)6, 13, 16-17, 18 (middle), 19-22, 24-27, 31, 34-36, 38, 39 (bottom), 42 (top), 43, 48-52, 54, 57, 60, 61 (left pair), 67, 70 (bottom), 71 (inset), 73, 75, 76 (bottom right), 77 (top and middle), 80-82, 86-87, 89 (top), 90-91, 94, 95 (top), 96 (bottom), 98, 100-101, 103 (bottom), 108-109, 112-114, 116 (bottom left), 117-120, 121 (middle), 122, 123 (top), 126-129, 132-134, 135 (bottom), 138-143, 152-157, 158 (top), 160 (right), 161-163, 165-167, 168 (bottom), 169-170, 173 (top), 176 (top), 177-183, 186, 187 (top), 188, 190, 191 (bottom), 194, 196 (bottom left), 198-200, 201 (top), 204, 206-210, 212-219, 221-223, 225, 230, 231 (top), 232 (bottom), 234 (top), 236

Alessandro Sannia
53, 68, 70 (top), 71 (main), 89 (bottom), 164, 187 (bottom), 231 (bottom), 232 (top)

Chicago Auto Show
41 (top), 55 (right-hand pair), 76 (left pair), 135 (top), 145, 229, 233

Chris Rees
72 (bottom), 83 (right pair), 121 (top), 147 (bottom), 173 (bottom), 220 (right), 235, 237 (bottom)

Getty Images
45 (top right), 201 (middle), 228 (top)

Magic Car Pics
Cover (top left and bottom), 9, 10, 18 (top), 28-29, 30, 39 (top), 40, 41 (middle and bottom), 42 (lower), 44-45 (lower and top left), 59, 61 (right), 62-63, 69, 74, 78-79, 83 (left), 92-93, 97, 99, 102, 103 (top), 104, 105, 116 (top pair), 123 (left pair and bottom right pair), 124-125, 136-137, 144, 146, 147 (top), 158 (bottom), 159 (main), 168 (top and middle), 172, 184 (main), 185, 191 (top pair), 192-193, 195, 201 (bottom), 211, 220 (left), 226-227, 228 (bottom), 234 (bottom), 237 (top)

Motorsport Images
37, 55 (left), 58, 66, 76 (top right), 77 (bottom), 95 (bottom), 96 (top), 110-111, 148-149, 196-197 (main), 224 (top and bottom left)

Pininfarina
18 (bottom)